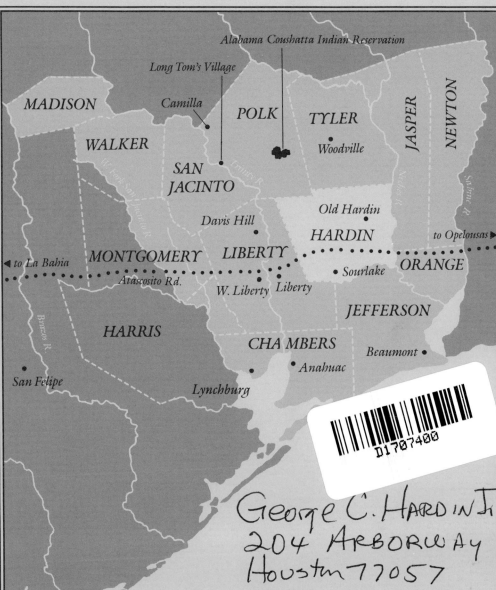

Alabama Coushatta Indian Reservation

Long Tom's Village

Camilla

MADISON

WALKER

POLK

TYLER

JASPER

NEWTON

Woodville

SAN
JACINTO

Davis Hill

Old Hardin

HARDIN

to Opelousas

to La Bahia

MONTGOMERY

LIBERTY

ORANGE

Atascosito Rd.

W. Liberty

Liberty

Sourlake

JEFFERSON

HARRIS

CHAMBERS

Beaumont

Anahuac

San Felipe

Lynchburg

George C. Hardin Jr
204 Arborway
Houston 77057

Atascosito District
of Coahuila y Tejas

(showing present counties
which were carved out of it)

SEVEN PINES

ITS OCCUPANTS AND
THEIR LETTERS, 1825–1872

SEVEN PINES

ITS OCCUPANTS AND
THEIR LETTERS, 1825–1872

CAMILLA
DAVIS TRAMMELL

HOUSTON

1986

Copyright © 1986 by Camilla Davis Trammell
Distributed by the Southern Methodist University Press
SMU Box 415, Dallas, Texas 75275; (214) 739-5959
Printed in the United States of America
All rights reserved

ISBN 0-87074-218-3

The paper in this book meets the standards for permanence and durability established by the Committee on Production Guidelines for Book Longevity of the Council on Library Resources.

Design by Barbara Jezek
Whitehead & Whitehead
Austin, Texas

PHOTOGRAPHS

FOREWORD

*H*ISTORIANS, ALWAYS FASCINATED WITH OTHER PEOPLE'S MAIL, have used family letters as the essence of social, economic, political, and military history, as background to gossip and romance, and as chords of chronology. Usually family collections are fragmented and disconnected—they offer just enough to whet curiosity and answer scattered questions. Now and then such collections are buttressed by diaries which fill in gaps and bridge times—and historians sigh with relief!

In some rare instances family letters run through years and generations and weave rich pageants for history. Fairly recently Robert Manson Myers' *Children of Pride* gave letters of the Charles Colrock Jones family of Georgia. These letters traced the Joneses so well through the 1850s and into the late 1860s that readers were part of the family, knew their thoughts, shared their hopes and crises, kept their councils and faiths. Few books have so comprehensively captured a clan and captivated an audience.

Camilla D. Trammell's *Seven Pines* is likely to captivate a considerable audience because it also captures a clan and an era. Her book provides the Hardin family letters from 1825 to 1872—a rich, virtually unique collection which addresses Texas, Louisiana, the Texas Revolution, and the Civil War, people famous and infamous, intrigues and battles and alarms and business. These pages reveal a close family with especially winning members, some of whom readers will wish to know better. I'd like to know more about Shattee, for instance, whose spirit shines from her letters, and of Cynthia, Frank Hardin's stalwart bride, and about some of the family slaves who shared so much of the heart of history.

Details abound about life in pre-revolutionary Texas, about Indians, such Texas heroes as Sam Houston and the defenders of San Antonio, the Alamo, about the drabness of life in the republic and about its charms and chances, too, of the importance of such sciences as surveying in a nation which granted land for military service (something George Washington would have understood!), about love and life on a frontier and over in Louisiana's sugar country.

Here is a sweep of history seen and endured with love, insight, and fortitude by a family. How does that make these letters different? Most families could certainly claim similar qualities. Events make the difference for the Hardins—to quote the ancient Chinese curse, they "lived in interesting times!" Not only are the letters from Texas before and during the republic's years informative and historically valuable, the ones covering Texas in the Confederacy are rich in family and war history.

Some family members went from Texas to such fearsome war places as Gaines' Mill (where Texas troops won honors the hardest way), Vicksburg, Holly Springs, fields strewn across the South; some of them were wounded, some died. Back home the ladies worked to sustain their men and their cause. Across the South, even in relatively unscathed Texas, a brutal physical change marked the land—there were maimed and halt everywhere. Scarcely a man who had fought seemed to return entirely whole. Women had to redefine their views on male beauty. They had to hold households together and prop Texas on hope and faith and tenacity—and the Hardin women did just that. When it all ended they were relieved and heartsick. After the war the letters show the scars of defeat and the persistence of deep-struck family ties.

This, then, is an unusual collection. These are letters that speak beyond their time because they are voices of honesty, passion and essential goodness. They will inform, beguile and ensnare all readers.

Camilla Trammell is one of the Hardin women and she has held this collection together, put it in shape, and kept pushing until at last, it is published. The service is in keeping with her family tradition and she deserves the thanks of all who love history.

Frank E. Vandiver
Texas A&M University

PREFACE

I N 1975 I WAS ASKED OVER FROM HOUSTON TO CUT THE RIBBONS AT
the dedication of the Sam Houston Regional Library and Research
Center in Liberty, Texas. After the ceremony a woman came up to me
and said that she was my cousin, Martha Mahavier, and that if I would
come by her house she had a present for me. When I was seated in her
parlor she brought out a box of nineteenth century family letters. Some
were from my grandmother, Camilla G. Hardin Davis; seeing her signature brought back to mind her stories of the hurricane, the bear hunt,
the Indian trading stump. I said I wished I knew what the other letter
writers looked like, and with that Martha brought out a box of daguer-
reotypes for me. Each picture was sparklingly clear in its little gold
frame, protected by a red velvet lining and enclosed in an embossed
leather box. With each writer's likeness looking on, I read the letters in
the quiet of my home.

Surely since these fascinating letters had survived, some as long as a
hundred and fifty years, these strong-minded early Texans deserved to
be heard. There were some two hundred more letters which my Aunt
Geraldine Humphreys had given to the Sam Houston Regional Library
and which had been transcribed by Joyce Calhoon. I later gave most of
my letters to the same repository. As I worked with all the letters they
turned into a personal history of our state. The result would never be
entirely cohesive because such different writers were the authors, but
it would be the unvarnished, unromanticized documentary of these
pioneers.

I traveled to Berwick, Louisiana, where Cousin Clegg Caffery secured photos of some O'Brien portraits for me and introduced me to

another cousin who shocked me by announcing, "I have your great-grandfather's legs in the attic." Then she explained, "His table legs. The Union soldiers hacked up the dining table top so badly it had to be discarded." My Houston cousins Virginia O'Bryan and Felide Robertson fired my imagination. I amassed a lot of documents from courthouses, archives, and newspapers. Miriam Partlow's fine book, *Liberty, Liberty County*, was extremely helpful. A book over which I had little control was writing itself as characters with strong emotions and complex personalities began to emerge. They spoke for themselves, with me supplying only the introductions to the letters and historical filler where gaps occurred. For some of the earliest strands of the story, other sources had to be relied upon and are documented accordingly.

Some mysteries have never been completely resolved. I feel sure there was more than the Nicaraguan fiasco to account for the "cup of bitterness which humbled the life" of John Isaac Davis, but I have found no letters by him, not even a will. His mother-in-law's letters I have omitted because their entire content is confined to how much she missed her daughter after he took her from the gentle civilized ambiance of Augusta, Georgia, and neighboring South Carolina to Fort-Davis, Alabama, and on to Texas. Many of the letters have been shortened, and superfluous names and commonplaces omitted. Minor changes in spelling and punctuation have been made when necessary for clarity. Otherwise, the letters appear as they were written.

Because many of the letters were addressed to, and most of them stored in, the family house called Seven Pines for a hundred years, that seemed an appropriate name for the book. Dr. Robert L. Schaadt at the Sam Houston Library in Liberty was most helpful to me. I have learned a lot about early Texas while working with the letters. I hope the reader will enjoy the feel of Liberty and of the Louisiana coast as well as get an intimate look at the Texas Revolution and some of the lesser participants in the Civil War.

C.D.T.

Christopher O'Brien (1779–1853), son of Christopher O'Bryan, born in Virginia. Came to Berwick in 1800 with siblings Luke, Catherine, George, Nancy.

Ann Dawson Berwick Brien (1796 – 1864), youngest child of Thomas and Eleanor Berwick; married Christie O'Brien (1779 – 1853).

CHAPTER ONE

Casa de Piedras

IN THE LATE FALL OF 1825, TWO tired young horsemen trotted up to the old stone fort in Nacogdoches that was called Casa de Piedras in honor of the Mexican commissioner. The men were Augustine Blackburn Hardin and a black slave named Rankin. The last leg of their trip had brought them along the Camino Real (Ap. 2a) through Louisiana. Somewhere along the way they had crossed the unmarked border between Louisiana and Mexico. When Rankin was sure he was in the new country, he felt a great exhilaration because he knew that here they would make a new life. Blackburn felt a great relief because he had gone beyond the clutches of United States law enforcement.

The town of Nacogdoches was small and very foreign-looking, with the startling sight of serapes and rebozos and padres in their cassocks and sandals and everyone speaking a strange language. Rankin looked in vain for other blacks, and seeing none, he clung closer to his master.

Blackburn soon met up with a colonel in the Mexican militia, an Anglo named Ellis P. Bean,[1] and asked him how to go about locating some good land which he could clear. His new friend arranged for him to meet José de las Piedras and the political chief, Ramón Musquiz, who happened to be in town. These men welcomed Blackburn as an immigrant, and, although they asked no personal questions, he could feel them sizing him up as belonging to the "genteels."

An Indian trader offered to let Blackburn and Rankin travel with him, and helped them gather the supplies they would need for a stay of several months in the woods. They set out on a southward course along an Indian trace through forest so thick they could not see the country on either side. They came to a Coushatta Indian village, where they were warmly received by Chief Long King, whose tribe had moved to Texas from Alabama in 1807. They were peaceful and sedentary Indians, unlike the Karankawas further south, who scalped settlers. Here the Indian trader taught them sign language, a skill they would need later.

The three men continued on down the trace until they came to a beautiful river called *La Santisima Trinidad*, or The Most Holy Trinity, and indeed it did seem to be a holy river. In those days, the water was clear, not muddy brown with silt as it became many years later when the forests had been cut down to make way for cotton plantations.

Blackburn and Rankin continued south on their own, and after a couple of days' travel, found the farm of a man named Hugh Johnston. He showed them land just south of his that was available for the claiming. Blackburn explored the land on horseback, and marked some of the trees, thus asserting first claim by a Tennessee Hardin to land in Texas.

Winter began to catch up with Blackburn and Rankin, who realized they would soon need shelter. Johnston, who turned out to be a first-rate carpenter, offered to help them build a cabin. In return for Johnston's help, the two men worked on his farm and made him a corral.

Blackburn and Rankin had grown up together on the Georgia plantation of Blackburn's grandfather, Colonel William Hardin. In 1807, Blackburn's father, Swan Hardin, took his wife, Jerusha, and his sons west to carve a new plantation out of the Tennessee wilderness. Rankin had stayed on in Georgia until, after the Colonel's death, the widow Sarah Hardin divided the old place among the older sons (Ap. 9) and moved with a number of her slaves, including Rankin, to College Hill, Mississippi; she went to the house of a daughter, Sukie, who was Mrs. Alexander Shaw. It was here that Blackburn had recently come and was reunited with his boyhood friend.

Blackburn liked to reminisce with Rankin about the military exploits of his forebears (his father, Swan Hardin, had fought in the War of 1812) and about the old days in Georgia. Both recounted the tales they had heard of the Revolutionary adventures of Blackburn's grandfather and great-grandfather, both of whom had fought under the "Old Swamp Fox" Marion (Ap. 8). The younger William Hardin and some of his sons had moved to Franklin County, Georgia, after the Revolution, and there his grandsons, including Blackburn, were born.

On one of the long winter evenings in their cabin, Blackburn told Rankin the story of why he was running from the law. The Swan Hardins had been living north of Columbia, Tennessee, in Maury County, in a red brick house set back from the turnpike near Spring Hill. The family had become well respected in the community. Swan Hardin was a justice of the peace; Blackburn was a deputy sheriff. His brother William was editor of *The Columbia Reporter* and a lawyer. A younger brother, Frank, worked as a surveyor, and the eldest brother, Benjamin Watson Hardin, managed the farm. The youngest child, Milton, was thirteen years old in 1825. The only daughter, Elizabeth, was married to a man named Tom Rhoads.

One wintry day early in 1825, Blackburn's brother William informed Swan that the local Lothario, named Isaac Newton Porter, was bragging that he had had his way with Blackburn's wife, Mary Elizabeth. Swan called the family together. They decided that Blackburn must avenge the family's honor by calling Porter out. The four older boys and their father armed themselves with pistols and rode into town.

Porter was expecting them and had his brother-in-law, William Williamson, acting as his bodyguard. Blackburn called out to Porter to draw his gun. Out of the corner of his eye, Frank saw Williamson raise his pistol to kill Blackburn. Frank fired before Williamson could get off a shot, killing him. Meanwhile, as Porter turned to pull his gun, Blackburn put a fatal bullet through the man's left side (Ap. 10).

Although according to the old code the matter had been handled properly, Tennessee now had a new law which outlawed settling private grievances with a gun. The Hardin men had broken that law. To make matters worse, Isaac Porter had been a member of the most influential family thereabouts. For a time, Swan, Frank, William, and Watson avoided arrest because a neighbor would forewarn them of the sheriff's approach by a blast on his cowhorn,[2] but Blackburn had decided he must flee.

Believing that he would not get a fair trial in Maury County with Isaac Porter's cousin its sheriff, Blackburn quickly left town, taking with him his six-year-old son, Blackie, and Mary Elizabeth, who he had decided had indeed been unfaithful to him. He took his wife and son back to her family, telling Blackie that he was leaving to prepare a place for him in a new land where he hoped his son would join him as soon as he was big and strong enough.

Blackburn then headed south to his Aunt Sukie Shaw's home in College Hill, Mississippi. Although his grandmother, Sarah Hardin, was over eighty years old, she was the matriarch of the family and held her place as "Old Miss" in Sukie's household. Sarah approved of what Blackburn had done and wanted to help him flee to Coahuila y Tejas. The young slave Rankin, whom she was keeping for Swan, was strong, intelligent, and loyal, just the type of man Blackburn would need with him for travel to Mexico, whose Imperial Colonization Act of 1823 offered liberal land grants. (Until 1824, Anglos had not been warmly welcomed there.) Intrigued by the adventure, Rankin was eager to accompany Blackburn in starting a new life.

After they were settled on the bluff overlooking the Trinity River, Rankin was content clearing the land and living in the cabin. Blackburn, however, was concerned about the Hardins' legal troubles and was anxious to communicate with his family. Hugh Johnston suggested that a man named George Orr, who lived ten miles to the south, would be able to help. Blackburn journeyed down the Trinity to the Atascosito Road (Ap. 2b), which connected south Texas to Opelousas, Louisiana. Here Orr's inn and smithy were located.

To Blackburn, the inn looked like a great luxury after his two months in the woods. George and his wife, Tilpah, welcomed him warmly. Tilpah, twenty years George's junior, was a tall, slender, swarthy young woman who laid a fine table.[3] She told Blackburn that she had been baptized Priscilla Berwick, but that she was now called Tilpah, and that she had eloped from her family's sugar plantation in Berwick, Louisiana. Her dark looks led Blackburn to believe she was part Indian.[†]

George was a helpful host. He was a skillful gunsmith and repaired Blackburn's flintlock rifle, also providing him with shot and powder. During their time together, Blackburn eagerly listened to news about the States and to George's account of several hundred colonists who had just settled across the river, led by an empresario named Stephen F. Austin. George also entertained him with tales of Jean Lafitte, the smuggler who had worked out of Galveston until about five years before. One day Tilpah and Blackburn rode a few miles south to view the ruins of the

[†]The Berwicks of Louisiana become increasingly important in our story, but Tilpah remains something of a mystery.

site where four hundred of Napoleon's followers had settled eight years earlier in a community called Champ d'Asile.[4]

Blackburn wrote to his brother Frank Hardin, urging him to start immediately for Texas and instructing him to travel along the Atascosito Road and meet Orr at the inn. By the time Blackburn's letter reached Tennessee,[†] all the local families had taken sides in the Hardin-Porter feud. The trial was set in Rutherford County, Tennessee (Ap. 10b), where it had been transferred because Maury County was controlled by the Porters. Most people felt that Williamson had got what he deserved. The politically powerful Porter family, nevertheless, wanted vengeance for the death of Isaac Porter. Isaac had been the county clerk like his father, Joseph, before him, and Isaac's cousin, Nimrod, was the high sheriff. The Porters vowed to punish all the Hardins. Joseph Porter ran ads in the Columbia newspapers and had handbills passed out in four counties, giving his version of the shootout. Frank Hardin soon decided to take his chances in Texas.

The two brothers were settled deep in the woods along the Trinity River when the first census taker came in 1826 to make his list of the population of the Atascosito District. This region sprawled over approximately 8,500 square miles and eventually comprised ten Texas counties (see map, inside front cover). Although this official recorded a population of 331 whites and 76 blacks for the district, the names of Frank, Blackburn, Rankin, and sixty other whites known to be living in the area did not appear.[5]

Frank was pleased with the land he patented, which was just south of Blackburn's and on the banks of the Trinity. The Hardin brothers liked their neighbors, the Devers and the Johnstons. The old and new settlers split rails for one another and joined forces to clear land and build barns. The Hardins put in their first crop with hand spikes. To Frank's surprise, wild cows lived in the brush, descendants of those brought in by the Spaniards. These long-horned "mossbacks" thrived remarkably on the prairie grass.

George Orr had taken charge of submitting the land grant applications for the settlers along the Trinity. On February 4, 1825, Stephen F. Austin had written the governor of Coahuila y Tejas on the importance of granting land to these people east of his colony:

These families being farmers and of most industrious habits, have no

---

[†]The letter has not survived.

leisure to encourage vice but dedicate their whole time to the maintenance of themselves, the accumulation of wealth and the observance of
the laws. But they are without any municipal regulation. The deep
interest I take in the prosperity of the state, seeing that the families
above mentioned are wealthy and possess adequate means and that
lands have not been apportioned to them . . . [If not] they will be
under the necessity of returning to Louisiana, in which event we shall
lose these valuable members of society. . . .[6]

The Sovereign Congress of Coahuila y Texas replied to him that it desired "by every possible means to augment the population of his territory and to promote the cultivation of land and raising of stock and
arts and commerce."[7]

A married man was eligible for a headright of one league (4,428 acres
of pasture) and one labor (177 acres of cropland). An unmarried man
was entitled to one-third of this amount.[8] Since Frank was unmarried,
he received only 59 acres of cropland and 1,475 acres of pasture. Frank
did the surveying for his and Blackburn's pieces of land, and then they
paid the commissioner's fee (Ap. 26). As required by Mexican law, they
joined the Catholic Church and agreed to support the Mexican Constitution, to stay in the state, and to improve the land within six years.

The following year they were joined by Watson and William Hardin,
who brought a wagonful of tools and more news of the criminal proceedings. Sheriff Nimrod Porter had hired Congressman James K. Polk
of Columbia as his lawyer and insisted he contact President John Q.
Adams through the Secretary of State, Henry Clay, who was related by
marriage to the Porters. The president was to petition the Mexican
president through the U.S. ambassador, Joel Poinsett, to extradite the
miscreants (Ap. 10c).

Swan asked for a separate trial and was found guilty as accessory to
manslaughter. He appealed this verdict and the court temporarily freed
him, but required him to post a bond of four thousand dollars' worth of
goods and slaves until the Supreme Court of Tennessee could meet. His
cousin Martin Toney and friends Dr. Allen Brown and William Brady
put up part of the money to help him (Ap. 10b).

Although the four Hardin brothers resembled each other, having
similar light hair, blue eyes, short necks, and medium stature, each had
his own distinct personality and interests. William, the most entrepreneurial of the group, managed to acquire several headrights (Ap. 16).

He also liked being in the political action at Anahuac, the new port settlement on the coast. Frank, on the other hand, was particularly interested in raising stock and in maintaining good relationships with the Indians. In these early days, the Indians were still a strong presence in the area, a power to be reckoned with. A young Coushatta chief called Kalita was particularly admired by Frank because he was able to control his braves. From these Indian neighbors, Frank bought baskets and fur rugs and bowls for his cabin. He even tried to learn their language.

Whatever their special interests, all the Hardins envisioned a great future for their Texas plantations. They decided to send Rankin back to Tennessee to fetch the remaining family members: Swan and Jerusha, young Milton, and Elizabeth and Tom Rhoads. Upon arrival, Rankin gave glowing reports to Swan, who made secret plans to leave. When Swan told Jerusha, who was short of stature, that they were going, she replied, "I have counted up husband, sons, and son-in-law, and it makes seven. I will be happy as long as I am surrounded by my seven pines."

It was a dark night in the fall of 1828 when they set out along the western road in two covered wagons drawn by oxen. They numbered fifteen in all, including nine black slaves. The prettiest of these, recently purchased from Dr. Allen Brown, was a young, light-skinned girl named Emily, who caught Rankin's eye. The youngest slave was six-year-old Harriet, who more than seventy years later remembered the trip this way:

> When Rankin arrived to guide us, we set out before light for fear of being attached. Marse Swan and Mistress Jerusha took with them Rebecca and Jim Evans and their daughters, Betsy and me . . . also Mary, mother of Delphi, George and Sam. We went first to Uncle Page Watson's [Jerusha's family] and spent the winter there, put in a crop in his fields. I recall threading needles for "Granny Mistis" Blackburn [Jerusha's mother, who lived on Page's plantation]. Rankin and Emily jumped the broomstick before they left on this trip, and Emily produced a baby, also named Emily, the night before we all boarded a boat headed down the Mississippi to New Orleans.[9]

The city looked very different to Swan from when he had fought there in the great battle under Andrew Jackson. From New Orleans the travelers chartered a schooner to the port of Anahuac, where they were reunited with Watson and Blackburn, both newly married. The two sons hired the sloop *Ohio* to take all of them thirty miles up the Trinity to their neighbor Spinks' landing.

Jerusha asked about her other sons, Frank and William. Blackburn told her that both men were in Mexican jails, one at the Alamo and the other at La Bajía (Ap. 10d). She guessed immediately that the Porters' machinations had led to her sons' confinement. Blackburn confirmed that William knew he risked being arrested if he traveled to the seat of government. Land fever had seized him, however, when he heard that Juan Martín de Beramendi,[†] the commandant in Bexar, had given as much as ten leagues to one person. He rushed off to Bexar, where he was arrested and incarcerated in a strong room next to the soldiers' barracks at the Alamo (Ap. 10d). Then Frank set out for La Bajía (Goliad), where he hoped a Mexican contact could help William. Instead of helping, the man had Frank jailed also. In that jail, Frank improved his Spanish and sized up the weaknesses of the Mexican soldiers.

Hearing all this, Jerusha was frantic, but Blackburn merely laughed and told her about his own confinement in 1827. After he had been arrested, he was sent to Nacogdoches to await the arrival of Joseph Porter's agent, who was to conduct him back to Tennessee. As soon as Blackburn's friend Piedras found out, the guard was removed, allowing the prisoner to escape. Blackburn reassured his mother that Frank and William would soon get out. He also told her that the preceding August, Ramón Musquiz had mulled over what to do about two of their number, Watson and himself, who were the ones then "at large." Not wishing his soldiers to look ridiculous in their inability to apprehend them, Musquiz had taken Vice Governor Beramendi's advice and ordered Stephen F. Austin to round them up. If the U.S. wanted these men, Beramendi opined, then let the American empresario go get them.

Austin knew the Hardins because Frank and Blackburn had marched with him to subdue Haden Edwards in the Fredonian Rebellion in Nacogdoches in 1826–27. The more Austin knew about the Hardins, the better he liked them. Complying with Musquiz' order, but with a plan in the back of his mind, he called up eight militiamen and headed for the Hardin lands on the Trinity.[10] But along the way, he crossed the river to George Orr's place and suggested that he and his men camp there overnight and enjoy the hospitality of the inn. Of course when Austin and his men arrived at the Hardin cabins next day, they found no sign of Watson or Blackburn. Then Austin delegated further searches to Orr, who turned the job over to Hugh Johnston. In time word went

[†]Some current sources render this spelling *Veramendi*. See Ap. 10d.

back along the Mexican chain of command that everything possible had been done and no arrests could be made. Besides, there was no extradition treaty between Mexico and the U.S.

No new orders ever came from Mexico City, and William and Frank were released as Blackburn had predicted. Before the year was out and with his parents' blessing, William married Sarah Looney, who had just arrived from Kentucky. Blackburn had already wed Maria Dever, the daughter of his neighbor, and Watson had married Adelia Coleman, another local girl. All three marriage ceremonies were performed by Father Michael Muldoon, the priest who had baptized the brothers into the Catholic faith.

Swan settled on land to the west of the Trinity, not far from his sons (Ap. 16). Thus Jerusha finally realized her dearest wish; the "seven pines" were reunited in Texas. But her dream was not to last for long, for Swan died the following year.[†]

Two decades later, a house called Seven Pines would be built in Liberty in remembrance of Jerusha's wish. But before that event occurred, another family arrived in Texas whose history became closely intertwined with that of the Hardins. Their story began in Ireland with young Christopher O'Bryan, who had been caught poaching and decided to head for America, shipping out of Dublin as a cabin boy (Ap. 1b). Christopher had red hair and blue eyes, and by the time he joined Colonel Grayson's regiment of Continental troops in Virginia, he had attained the imposing stature of six-foot-four. Christopher served at Camp Paramis, White Plains, Robinson's Farm, and Middlebrook.[11] During this period, he married a young woman named Katherine Kimberland (Ap. 1c). After the war he took up surveying.[12]

By the year 1784, Christopher and Katherine had six children: Luke, Christopher Jr. (called "Christie"), Daniel, Mary Catherine, Andrew, and Nancy. The youngest child, George, was born in 1789, and by that time the O'Bryans had made the arduous trek out to Bryant's Station on the Ohio River. There was a lot of talk among his kinsmen there about a town Colonel Morgan was developing down the river.[13] It was to be called New Madrid as it was just inside Spanish Territory, near the present St. Louis, Missouri. Christopher moved to New Madrid, expecting it to become a booming trade center because of Mississippi River traffic, but his wife died there, and Christopher felt that the cli-

[†]Since Rankin is never again mentioned in family records, it is presumed he achieved his freedom when Swan died.

mate was unhealthy. He decided to relocate again. His imagination was fired by talk of fortunes to be made in the growing of sugar cane, now that a way to refine sugar had been developed.

Christopher received a passport from Commandant Manuel de Salcedo at Baton Rouge which said that he was moving south to start up a tavern. By 1800 he had persuaded two kinsmen from Bryant's Station to join him. Rafts and a flat-bottomed boat were built, and three families of Bryans[†] got on board with their goods and cattle and started down the Mississippi River to New Orleans.

It was a leisurely trip. They stopped for a while at Natchez, Mississippi, long enough for Mary Catherine to fall in love with a young man named John Choate. She wanted to marry him and remain there, but her father insisted that she stay with him to look after the younger children. Catherine obeyed, but she did not forget John. A little farther on, the O'Bryans left the Mississippi and floated across to the Atchafalaya River, because Christopher heard of great markets open to men willing to cut the giant cypress trees and get them to the dock at the village of Berwick (Ap. 2d).

Just before the Christopher O'Bryan family arrived at Berwick, France reacquired Louisiana from Spain in the secret Treaty of San Ildefonso, but Christopher was issued a Spanish title to his land. He applied to the Spanish authorities and received patents for land on Tiger Island, called "The Big Woods," because of its great number of large trees. (The name Tiger Island, as it is still called today, came from the panthers which roamed its swampy land.) The U.S. soon purchased the territory from France, and from then on, of course, the O'Bryans were subject to U.S. law.

Christopher soon built a dock to enable him to market the cypress to passing sea captains, and he planted indigo and corn—his first crops. He named his plantation Wyandotte after the Midwestern Indian tribe.

At Berwick the O'Bryans met Eleanor, widow of old Thomas Berwick, the first Anglo to live across the Mississippi (Ap. 2d). Old Thomas had been born in Philadelphia in about 1740. He sailed to Charles Town, South Carolina, where he met and married Eleanor Wallace of Scotland via Ireland (Ap. 1e). They proceeded to Pensacola, Florida, in 1760. Thomas was negotiating for land near Natchez (Ap. 2d) when the newly arrived Spanish governor, Bernardo de Galvez, offered him a

[†]Sometime after arriving in Louisiana, the younger Christopher adopted the spelling *O'Brien*. Many times a family member would drop the *O'* prefix (meaning "son of"), so that the primary variations in spelling were: *O'Brien, Brien, O'Bryan*, and *Bryan. Bryant* was another early variation. (See also Ap.1b)

position as royal surveyor. Accepting it, Thomas moved his wife and two babies to Louisiana, where he laid out the towns of Opelousas and New Iberia. He believed that one day the Mississippi River would spill more water into the Atchafalaya, and he was fascinated with the possibility of a big port at the wilderness mouth of the Atchafalaya. For this reason he staked a grant at its mouth.

Eleanor Wallace Berwick had become attached to the place where she had been living on the Bayou Teche, which she called Ellerslie, after the Wallaces' Scottish home. Nevertheless, she accompanied her husband to the west bank of the Atchafalaya, which grew into the town of Berwick, and she raised her six children there, retiring to Ellerslie for a few years after Thomas's death in 1789.

Joseph Berwick, Thomas's youngest son, was sixteen years old when Christopher O'Bryan and his family arrived at Berwick. Joseph was born and had grown up in this frontier Attakapas District. He had lost his father when he was only nine. Environment and experience shaped him into a man made to give orders, and he was remembered in this way:

> He was a strong, picturesque character. Denied in youth the benefits of education, nature gave him a strong mind and will power. Right or wrong, few had more emphatic opinions, and they were all his own. If he had any religious preference, he kept it to himself—his word was his bond and so received at par by all who knew him.[14]

On June 24, 1804, Luke and Christie O'Brien, joined by a notary named le Cournand, accompanied their sister Catherine to St. Martinsville Church, sixty miles by boat up the Bayou Teche, where she was married to John Choate. He had come southwest from Natchez by boat to the wedding, accompanied by his mother. Because Louisiana was now U.S. territory, it was possible to marry according to the Anglican rite, but an old Catholic priest performed the service (Ap.3). The Frenchman, le Cournand, swore that the bride's father had given his permission for the marriage, but it seems likely Catherine eloped.

Within the next few years, four more weddings took place, uniting four Berwick children with four of Christopher O'Bryan's, making for many double first cousins. Little Ann Dawson Berwick, the youngest Berwick girl, was only sixteen years old when she married Christie O'Brien.

The Berwicks and O'Bryans prospered. In 1811, Governor William Claiborne appointed Luke O'Bryan sheriff of St. Mary's Parish. Luke was developing a 640-acre plantation on the west side of the lower Atchafalaya. His brother Christie had the same number of acres on Lake Verret, at the mouth of the canal on Bayou Lafourche. By 1813 both men were successful enough to own field hands. Christie had three, and Luke, two.[15]

To clear the title on their holdings, the boys brought a lawsuit against the U.S. government for the original 1500 acres of cypress granted to Christopher, their father, by the Spanish representative. The U.S. Court of Appeals ruled against them in 1816, however, because the original document failed to list the names of all of Christopher's children.[16] This loss rankled long in O'Bryan breasts, but they continued to encourage colonization and joined in the exuberant optimism of an ad that the young entrepreneurial Joe Berwick ran in the St. Louis *Gazette* on August 12 that same year:

> The planter has nothing to do but build his house, inclose his fields, and commence plowing. Once the crop is sown, with moderate industry, the excellent quality of the land will furnish abundant crops of size including indigo, cotton, corn, potatoes, oats, etc. all of which are made in Attakapas in great abundance. The lands of Attakapas are far superior to those upon the banks of the Mississippi and immediately in the neighborhood of New Orleans. On the Mississippi an hogshead of sugar per acre is considered a fine crop. But in Attakapas a hogshead and a half are common. Our sugar lands can be purchased at present for one-third of the price they are selling for on the Mississippi, and the Wells [Fargo] carriage to market to New Orleans is at the door of the plantation.

In 1819, the President of the United States, James Monroe, received the report of James Leander Cathcart, who had been sent to reconnoitre the Louisiana Purchase. Cathcart's journal included accounts of his meeting and examining the plantations of Christie O'Brien and Joe Berwick. Cathcart was impressed by the appearance of Luke O'Bryan's house and the blondness of his children (Ap. 4). He spent two days at Joseph Berwick's and was intrigued with the high Indian mound near the house. He noted that Joseph's mother had been buried near the

mound's thirty-foot-high summit, from which she continued to domi-
nate the scene. Cathcart's journal records:

> . . . We [stopped] at Bryants where we landed to look at the tim-
> ber . . . [Christopher raised] red maize, cabbage, garlic, beans,
> and sweet potatoes—They have some poultry, and what I thought
> a curiosity, their dog which was very tame, eat corn with them in
> perfect harmony, picking the grain from the cob with his teeth
> and generously permitting an old hen to pick up all that fell on the
> ground. . . .
>
> We landed on Bryants plantation . . . some of the timber is ex-
> cellent, the largest piece contains about 40 cubic feet or one Ton;
> in the woods are much larger trees, [made] impervious at present,
> by a thick growth of cane from 30 to 40 feet high and 2 inches in
> diameter, all the trees in sight are of a middling size and are girded
> round and dead, which renders the wood hard to work. . . .
>
> In a conversation with Mr. Christie Bryant at Franklin some
> time afterwards, he informed me that a part of Tiger Island on
> which grow live oak, was the property of the United States and
> that for a small consideration he would dispose of all the live oak
> on his part of the island to government provided they would take
> it away as fast as they could cut and mold it. . . .
>
> Southwest from Bryants, just at the entrance of Berwick bay . . .
> which is a bend of the Atchafalaya river, where the confluence of
> the Teche bears NW . . . [Joseph] Berwick's house bears WNW
> distance 1/2 mile. Here we landed. Mr. Berwick is the son of the
> man who gave name to the bay. He has five children who look
> healthy, he was born on this spot, is unlettered but civil and intel-
> ligent; he presented us with some good oranges fresh from his trees
> which are the first we have had since we left New Orleans. . . .
>
> On Mr. Berwick's place are four Indian Mounds. . . . They are
> situated at right angles, pointing to the four Cardinal points, in-
> cluding a square of about an acre in which about 30 years ago,
> there were several strata of ashes very visible, supposed to have ac-
> cumulated from the council fires of the aborigines, who were of
> the Chetimachaux tribe at that period. . . .
>
> It is worthy of remark that many human bones have been dug
> up on Mr. Berwick's plantation in the vicinity of the mounds
> while they have remained undisturbed. Mr. Berwick seems to have

more genius to cultivate cotton—having raised last year 150,000 lbs. on his own plantation with three negroes besides his family and household domestics—than to pry into the curiosities of antiquity, although they have been in his view for more than 30 years. We propose remaining here tomorrow to refresh ourselves and crew and to procure provisions for our next cruise . . . [Ap. 4].

The big shift from timber and crops to growing sugar was under way, and when they had a good year, Louisiana planters had lots of money to spend. The O'Bryans and the Berwicks could afford clothes and furniture sent from New Orleans. They all had their portraits done. Doctors, teachers, and dancing masters were brought to live with the families and teach the children. A well-trained doctor was offered as much as two thousand dollars a year to go there.

When Henry Wise Farley finished at Harvard Medical School in 1814,[17] he practiced in his home town of Ipswich, Massachusetts. Then came "the year without sun" followed by two crop failures, and Henry decided to leave that land of hunger. Farley's two brothers had previously gone to the West Indies, but they both lost their lives there. He decided to go to New Orleans instead. However, behind New Orleans' outward glitter and *joie de vivre*, he discovered shocking slavery and sanitation problems. As one observer wrote, "New Orleans is a dreadful place in the eyes of a New England man. They keep Sunday as we in Boston keep the Fourth of July."[18] Yellow fever was often followed by cholera. Debauchery and bribery were as rampant as he had heard they were in the West Indies.

Dr. Farley decided to move westward. He found employment on the Berwick plantation, where he treated slaves and owners alike. There were also French refugees in the area from the destruction of Champ d'Asile, across the Sabine River in Texas,[19] and he treated them. They spoke highly of that land to the west in Texas. In 1824, the gentle young doctor courted and married Catherine, the eldest daughter of Ann and Christopher O'Brien Jr.

It was several years after their marriage that the Farleys, with their two sons, Henry and Brien, left Berwick and moved west to the land of the doctor's dreams. Their new home soon became a village called Atascosito because it was located north of the road of that name, on the east bank of the Trinity River. In Spanish, *atascosito* means "a small barrier." In the early days the river was a barrier to the advance of the French and their Indian allies. The Spanish hoped that the village's location on a high bluff would continue to provide such protection. Now, however, the barrier was broken by the liberal immigration law, and the colonists flooded in (Ap. 5), including many of Christopher O'Bryan's progeny.

In the case of the Hardins, brother followed brother to Texas, but the first Berwicks to come were two women: Tilpah, teamed with the swash-buckling George Orr, and Catherine, wife of the intellectual Dr. Farley. And the 1831 closing of the Texas border by the Mexicans did not keep young Luke Bryan and six of his seven sons and their families from moving to Texas to join them.

The O'Bryans moved on west from the coast of Louisiana because they had already exhausted the available cypress along the water's edge, and the sugar cane crops had not lived up to their expectations. The great attraction of Texas was that the plentiful land was free, its grass the best ever found for horses and cattle, and many of its fields just right for cotton. The early pioneers had already formed the nucleus of a commu-nity at the Trinity River crossing and were getting along well with the Mexican officials. A relative like George Orr or Henry Farley gave the newcomers confidence that the local leaders would punish or run off thieves or cutthroats who had slipped into the area. It was a dream land.

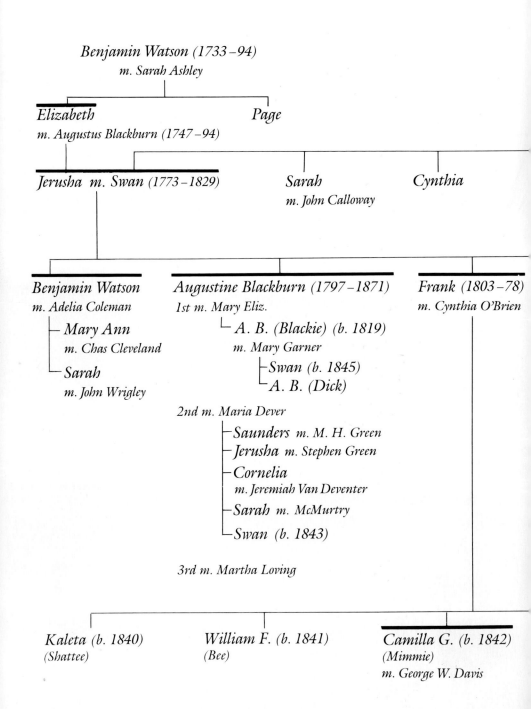

Benjamin Watson (1733–94)
m. Sarah Ashley

Elizabeth
m. Augustus Blackburn (1747–94)

Page

Jerusha m. Swan (1773–1829)

Sarah
m. John Calloway

Cynthia

Benjamin Watson
m. Adelia Coleman

— Mary Ann
m. Chas Cleveland

— Sarah
m. John Wrigley

Augustine Blackburn (1797–1871)
1st m. Mary Eliz.

└ A. B. (Blackie) (b. 1819)
m. Mary Garner

├ Swan (b. 1845)
└ A. B. (Dick)

2nd m. Maria Dever

├ Saunders m. M. H. Green
├ Jerusha m. Stephen Green
├ Cornelia
m. Jeremiah Van Deventer
├ Sarah m. McMurtry
└ Swan (b. 1843)

3rd m. Martha Loving

Frank (1803–78)
m. Cynthia O'Brien

Kaleta (b. 1840)
(Shattee)

William F. (b. 1841)
(Bee)

Camilla G. (b. 1842)
(Mimmie)
m. George W. Davis

THE HARDINS

Col. William Harden (1720–1782)
m. Cynthia of Edgefield Dist. S.C.

Col. William Hardin (1741–1810)
m. Sarah Bledsoe (1743–1845)

Sukie (1786–1842)
m. Alex Shaw

Henry
Wake Co. N.C.

Richard
Beaver Crk N.C.

Mark
m. Nancy Toney

Elizabeth
m. Tom Rhoads

Milton Ashley
m. Mary Isbell

William (1801–39)
m. Sarah Looney

Toney

Cynthia
m. Sam Cade

William Joseph   **Ophelia** *m.* **Jim**

William
m. Betty Day

Sam C.

Jane Jerusha (b. 1837)
m. L. E. Edmondson

Wm. Bledsoe (b. 1841)

Christy O'Brien (b. 1846)
(Tah)

Cynthia A. (b. 1848)
(Nan) m. John Skinner

Helen Berwick (b. 1853)
(Pep)

THE BERWICK–O'BRIENS

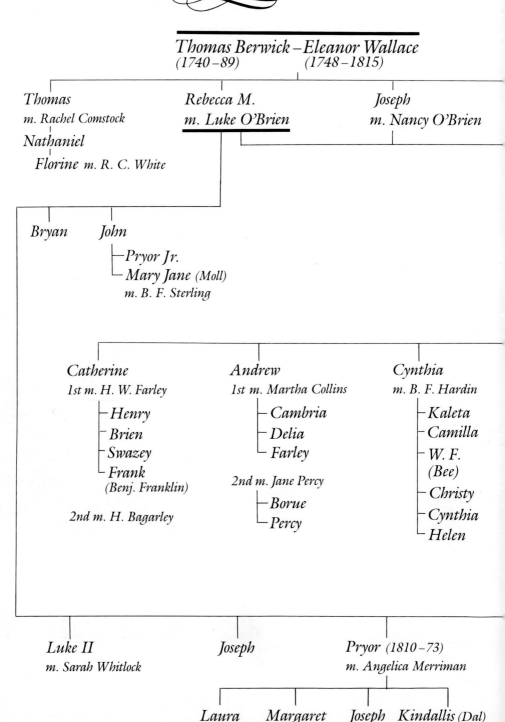

Thomas Berwick – Eleanor Wallace
(1740–89)   (1748–1815)

Thomas
m. Rachel Comstock
Nathaniel
  Florine m. R. C. White

Rebecca M.
m. Luke O'Brien

Joseph
m. Nancy O'Brien

Bryan   John
  ┌ Pryor Jr.
  └ Mary Jane (Moll)
     m. B. F. Sterling

Catherine
1st m. H. W. Farley
  ┌ Henry
  ├ Brien
  ├ Swazey
  └ Frank
     (Benj. Franklin)

2nd m. H. Bagarley

Andrew
1st m. Martha Collins
  ┌ Cambria
  ├ Delia
  └ Farley

2nd m. Jane Percy
  ┌ Borue
  └ Percy

Cynthia
m. B. F. Hardin
  ┌ Kaleta
  ├ Camilla
  ├ W. F.
  │ (Bee)
  ├ Christy
  ├ Cynthia
  └ Helen

Luke II
m. Sarah Whitlock

Joseph

Pryor (1810–73)
m. Angelica Merriman

Laura   Margaret   Joseph   Kindallis (Dal)

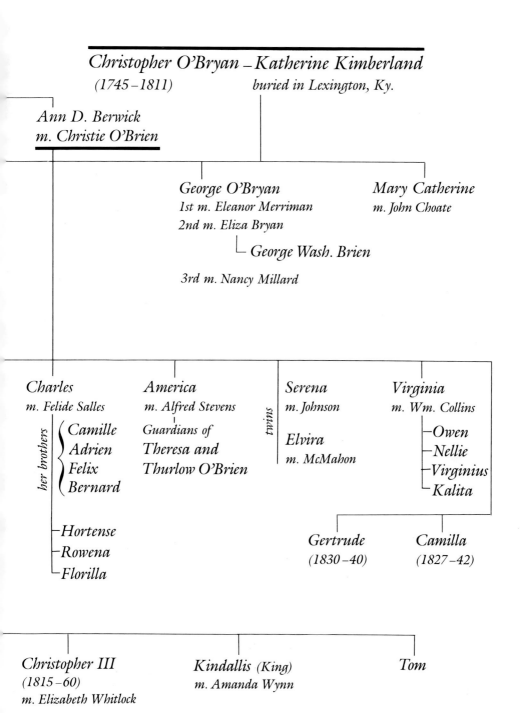

Christopher O'Bryan – Katherine Kimberland
(1745–1811)   buried in Lexington, Ky.

Ann D. Berwick
m. Christie O'Brien

George O'Bryan   Mary Catherine
1st m. Eleanor Merriman   m. John Choate
2nd m. Eliza Bryan
   └ George Wash. Brien
3rd m. Nancy Millard

Charles   America   Serena   Virginia
m. Felide Salles   m. Alfred Stevens   m. Johnson   m. Wm. Collins

  ⎧ Camille   Guardians of   twins   Elvira   ⎡ Owen
her ⎪ Adrien   Theresa and   m. McMahon   ⎢ Nellie
brothers ⎨ Felix   Thurlow O'Brien   ⎢ Virginius
  ⎩ Bernard   ⎣ Kalita

  ⎡ Hortense
  ⎢ Rowena   Gertrude   Camilla
  ⎣ Florilla   (1830–40)   (1827–42)

Christopher III   Kindallis (King)   Tom
(1815–60)   m. Amanda Wynn
m. Elizabeth Whitlock

*Augustine Blackburn Hardin
(1797–1871), second of five
brothers, delegate to the Convention and signer of the Declaration
of Independence of Texas.**

*Milton Ashley Hardin (1813–
1894), youngest son of Swan and
Jerusha Hardin. Married 1839
to Mary Isbell, resided at Old
Hardin till the war.**

CHAPTER TWO

Martín Perfecto de Cós

ATASCOSITO VILLAGE IN 1830 MET THE Mexican requirements to become a town. The law specified that a new town comprise four square leagues, with building lots to be given free to contractors and to artists of every class, but the rest sold to other settlers at public auction. The money from sales of these lots would be used to build a church. Families like the Hardins and their friends who founded towns would be exempted from taxes for ten years and would also eventually make up the regional government council, called an *ayuntamiento*.

Frank Hardin helped lay out the new town and drew the original map (Ap. 17b). The lots for private homes surrounded a three-block central plaza, with the block on the east, located between the courthouse and the jail square, belonging to Watson and Blackburn Hardin. Since Watson was sheriff it was convenient to have his house located across the street from the jail. Frank's block was on the south side of town. William had no town house because his farm was situated just to the east of town.

The plans were duly conveyed to the land commissioner, Francisco Madero, who declared that the little village, now blooming into a full-fledged town, was to be called "Villa de La Santisima Trinidad de la Libertad."[1] As secretary of the council, Frank wrote a letter to the governor, asking his permission to build a church. Only nominally a Catholic and awkward in Spanish protocol, Frank turned out a letter that was profusely polite:

Sept. 22, 1831

Most excellent sir:

One of the first considerations of this Council has been to promote the construction of the temple in which the faithful reflect upon the active worship of God but as for this the superior permission of your Excellency is needed, one pleads that you may grant this to us, and that you entreat the venerable Chapter of the Cathedral his permission to proceed immediately on the construction of the proposed temple. In Texas it is in keeping with your accustomed zeal that you advance that there may be sent to this Villa an ecclesiastic who may administer the Holy Sacraments. For a long time these inhabitants have lacked these spiritual aids, and for this reason one beseeched your Excellency that you deign to grant them this so great a good. . . .

> Hugh B. Johnston
> Amos Green
> Jno. W. Allen
> Franklin Hardin, Sec.[2]

It would be a long time before anything concrete would be done about the church. In general, however, things were moving smoothly for the town of Liberty. In the Mexican capital, on the contrary, all was turmoil and revolution. In 1830 President Anastacio Bustamante, worried about the increasing Anglo influence in Texas, had signed a law to Mexicanize Texas before it was too late. Americans already in Texas could stay, but no more could enter. Poor Mexican families and convicts would be planted among the Americans at public expense. Customs officers would be sent to collect newly imposed taxes.

A Hungarian opportunist named George Fisher was designated customs officer at Anahuac, and to the intense annoyance of the colonists, an obnoxious, half-crazy Kentuckian, Juan Davis Bradburn, was named military commander. He closed all the ports except Anahuac to centralize customs collections. To control smuggling, Bradburn put all land within ten leagues of the coast under martial law. He also encouraged the colonists' slaves to seek freedom, since Mexico had abolished slavery in 1829.

In spite of Bustamante's prohibition, more settlers arrived in Anahuac, bringing more slaves with them, and Bradburn harassed them for not calling slaves indentured servants. The settlers found out that Brad-burn had been indicted in Kentucky for what was to them the "basest of crimes . . . kidnapping colored persons and attempting to sell them to other than their original owners."[3] Since Bradburn would not help them get back their runaway or stolen slaves, the Anahuac citizens took the law into their own hands. Lynch law became the practical solution. One judge sanctioned it and clinked glasses to "Justice modified by cir-cumstances."[4] Scorn replaced loyalty to the Mexican government.

Early in 1831, Bradburn left Anahuac in a desperate attempt to per-suade a high Mexican official to make Anahuac instead of Liberty the site of the new ayuntamiento. But in early May word reached Anahuac from Liberty that Hugh B. Johnston was about to be elected alcalde of the new council, that William Hardin would be the new commissioner of police, and Frank, secretary of the council. Father Michael Muldoon, who was trying to keep the peace and feared Bradburn's vengeful rage, wrote immediately to William Hardin:

Anahuac, 5/8/31

Mr. Wm. Hardin,
    Being credibly informed that Hugh Johnson intends to disturb the peace of this country by holding an election for Alcalde and other officers on Monday next at the town of Liberty and being a minister thereof, I call on you in the name of the Nation and our absent head, Colonel Bradburn, to detain said Johnson in your house until after next Monday, or the return of our colonel— You will be answerable for the fulfillment of this request.
                                        The Vicar General of Liberty and Anahuac
                                        Michael Muldoon[5]

But Muldoon's letter was ignored. Hardin and Johnston had already held the election and outmaneuvered Bradburn by transmitting the re-sults of the election to the governor via their friend Madero, the land commissioner. Bradburn arrested Madero in retaliation, thereby anger-ing more of the Libertians.

Bradburn continued to make trouble. When Colonel William B. Travis and Patrick Jack complained about the new taxes, Bradburn locked them up. Soon Judge "Three Legged Willie" (Robert McAlpin) Williamson got them released, and they fled north and "found their way to the neighborhood of the Hardins," who "hospitably received them, as they did all strangers."[6] Next, Bradburn took William Logan's three slaves, who "had asked the protection of the Mexican flag,"[7] and he refused to give them back to Logan.

All of this so alarmed Stephen F. Austin that he agreed with William Hardin to confront Bradburn. Forty men from Liberty, including Frank Hardin, joined ninety from Austin's colony in June of 1832, and they marched to Anahuac. They captured nineteen of Bradburn's cavalry and demanded that he give them Travis and Jack, who, on their return to Anahuac, had been reincarcerated. A meeting of the two opposing factions was held at William Hardin's house.

Both groups promised to uphold the peace and decided to swap prisoners, but Bradburn broke his agreement by vowing to pillage the homes of all who sided against him. This so angered the opposition that they wrote out their grievances at the village of Turtle Bayou, thereby changing their actions from rebellion to "legal revolutionary activity" such as was convulsing all of Mexico. In the documents they drew up, which have become known as the Turtle Bayou Resolutions, the Texans, including William Hardin, made clear what they disliked about President Bustamante and threw their support to Santa Anna, the presidential contender against Bustamante, because Santa Anna favored the liberal constitution of 1824. Bradburn began to hunt down all the signers to put them in jail.

William Hardin, who, according to Dr. N.D. Labadie "was foremost among us in resistance to Bradburn,"[8] had his closest shave one night when he stopped at the home of Captain John Dorsett and his family in Anahuac. Here is Labadie's account of what happened:

> Learning of the arrival of Hardin at Anahuac, [the pro-Bradburn forces] declared they would have him, dead or alive. . . . At about ten o'clock at night, this Tory company arrived, but as they were seen coming, [Hugh] Johnson made his escape through a back door. Hardin, not having time, hid under two beds—Dorsatt's daughters lying on them, one on each side. A cry is heard: "We want Bill Hardin; let him come out!" They searched all through the house. "Here are his shoes," said one. "Here is his hat," says another. "Get him out, he is in the house." They looked everywhere, under the bed, the tables, and in every corner. Finally they pulled down the mosquito bar. A cry is heard: "Oh, shame, do not disturb the girls." Dorsatt became enraged and was preparing for a fight to defend his house when an exclamation is heard:

"Here he is, here he is!" His head protruded a little at one end of the bed, and he was recognized by his sandy hair. "Well," says he, "boys, you have found me, but give me time to get out." "Make room for him," they said, and all prepared to secure him. A moment more, a crash is heard. Hardin, gathering all his strength, and with great presence of mind, broke through the weatherboarding with a desperate effort, and instantly disappeared through the side of the house. He made his way toward Liberty, and having caught a horse on the prairie, he arrived . . . at Liberty by seven o'clock the next morning, a distance of twenty-five miles, without saddle or bridle.[9]

Soon after this, Colonel José de las Piedras arrested Bradburn and had him shipped to Mexico. Thereafter, the elections of Hugh Johnston and William Hardin stood as Frank had certified them. Colonel José Antonio Mexía conducted an inspection of the area and found "all quiet" in Texas.

This quiet period allowed William to return to his land-buying. Promoters were selling New Yorkers land no one had ever seen in this loosely held northernmost province of Mexico. William sold land to the Galveston Bay and Texas Land Company, which resold it for five cents an acre to Yankees who thought the company's scrip was as good as a deed until the Mexican government refused to honor it. On April 23, 1831, William had been issued a headright of 4428 acres that he and Frank had staked out on Buffalo Bayou, an area now within the city limits of Houston.[10] He also bought a piece of land near Anahuac in Burnet and Vehlein's colony, land which was under the auspices of Commissioner Jorge Antonio Nixon. He sold several pieces to Malanckton Smith of New York City in 1830 and 1832 and asked J.C. Dey, a New York City lawyer, to try to collect the notes for him.[11] William kept the respect of the local Mexican authorities and cooperated superficially with them, even though he wrote a long complaint about taxes to the governor in May of 1835. He rushed off to the States for a land deal, however, before he mailed it. William also complained, "One had to go to Nacogdoches for every little thing."[12]

Commissioner Nixon, a man of high integrity, appointed Frank the surveyor of the Atascosito District in 1835 (Ap. 17). Although Frank had learned to speak and read fair Spanish while he was in prison in La Bajía, the bilingual Nixon chose to write to him in English:

Commissioners Office
Nacogdoches, Jany. 8th, 1835

Dear Sir:

I hope you will pay strict attention to the instructions you have already received. . . .

I have given you the appointment you now hold and according to my instructions I am responsible for your conduct as Surveyor. . . .

I wish you to understand distinctly that I am determined to do justice to the Government and the people according to law [Ap. 13], and to the best of my ability, and I have that confidence in your integrity that you will assist me as far as you possibly can in making correct returns of the quality and quantity of lands you survey.

The 14th article of your instructions is that you will make no survey without conforming to the following law—

He, the Commissioner, shall issue in the name of the State the title for land in conformity with the laws and put the necessary colonists in possession of their lands with all legal formalities and previous citation of the adjoining proprietors, should there be any.

By which you will perceive, that it is necessary previous to making a survey, that you obtain from the adjoining proprietors, if there is any, their lines; and I am determined to make no titles where persons have their land or improvements taken from them without their consent. . . .

In the communicaton of the Government, it appears that complaints have been made of the surveyor not respecting the claims of individuals and particularly the Coushattee Indians, who are entitled by law to be respected. I hope you will not in any instance infringe on them or any other persons, as it is my wish as well as my determination to act in all my business according to law, and confidently hope you will aid me as far as you possibly can, in doing justice to the Goverment and the people, and I assure you, Sir, I am determined to do my duty strictly.

You will please also respect the survey made by the former Commissioners, Juan Antonio Padilla, José Francisco Madera, and Vincente Aldrete.

Respectfully yours,
Jorge Antonio Nixon
Comr.[13]

The calm period after the Anahuac Disturbances was the quiet before the storm. Mexican political upheavals had caused the frontier government to disintegrate, and the Texans were on their own to keep order in the fall of 1835. Because the Mexicans had not abided by their commitments, the Texans were furious at them. As early as that October, disillusioned and frustrated, Stephen F. Austin had already decided it was necessary to call for volunteer soldiers. He wrote to his trusted friends on the Trinity:

October 5, 1835

To Mssrs. Wm Hardin and brothers
Gentlemen,
    The enclosed paper will inform you of the progress of the glorious cause of Texas. Everything goes well. It could not go better. There is not one "peace" man that I know of in this country.
    All have studied for themselves, all doubts are removed, all are satisfied that we must either fight for our rights or leave the country or become an abject slave or a disgrace to the name of an American. No one here hesitates a moment which of these alternatives to adopt. All say, "Fight!"
    I have no doubt it is or will be the same at Trinity. I can not believe that any of you can be so blind and infatuated as to believe in the promises of the present military party who are in power in Mexico, nor in General Santana's profession of friendship for Texas. I am just from Mexico. I know them well. There is no faith in them.
    Public opinion has declared itself. The country has a cause, and a just and glorious one to defend. From this time forward those who are not for the cause ought to be treated as enemies. There is no middle ground, no neutrality. Those who are not for us are against us and are therefore enemies.
    The first blood that is shed—the first of Texas—I believe it is already shed. Report has just reached here that the Mexican troops at Gonzales have been defeated by the army of the people with the loss of forty Mexicans killed and no loss on our side. Bexar must be taken before the campaign closes. Every man is wanted. We expect aid from Trinity and Bevil's settlement. All Texans ought to move in one body for Texas to be free. We will establish a government before this campaign closes and drive the invader from our soil. Now is the time. We must be free.
    Everyone is wanted. Send all you can.

Yours respectfully,
S.F. Austin[14]

Later in that same month of October, fifty-six delegates met at San Felipe to ask that the irritating laws be repealed. Blackburn served as the delegate from the Atascosito District and was one of a very few who had lived in Texas for as long as nine years. William Hardin had now been elected the alcalde of Liberty. Certain Texas hotheads desired to kick the Mexican garrison out of Bexar and considered the idea lawful resistance to misrule. The Commission of Safety for the Municipality of Liberty issued a call to arms in a letter addressed to Joseph Bryan, the son of Luke, who was a member of the Permanent Council at San Felipe.

> Liberty
> October 24, 1835
>
> . . . Of those of our fellow-citizens who regard the sanctity of their oath of allegiance and allege it as a reason for opposing their country-men now in arms, we would enquire, what is the obligation of that oath? It is certainly to support the federal and state constitutions. But where are those constitutions? They have been torn and rent to atoms and their scattered fragments are to be traced in the lines of blood beneath the tramplings of the usurper's cavalry on the plains of Zacatecas.[†]
>
> Texas is but pursuing the noble but unsuccessful example of that highminded State [of Zacatecas]. She has resolved to sustain a legiti-mate government or perish in the effort to oppose the tide of military and ecclesiastical usurpation and roll it back upon the unholy league, and she looks with confidence for the aid of her adjacent sister states who have already experienced the bitterness of military misrule. For this purpose the sword is already drawn, our fellow-citizens are in the field, the banner of Liberty is unfurled and the high example of lawful resistance is exhibited in the gleam of our rifles and the thunder of our cannon before the walls of San Antonio. . . .
>
> Edward Tanner
> David G. Burnet
> Jesse DeVore
> Wm. Hardin
> B.M. Spinks
> H.W. Farley[15]

[†]Just before he crossed the border into Coahuila, Santa Anna had crushed a revolt led by Mexican liberals in Zacatecas.

Dr. Henry Farley's Harvard-trained literary rhetoric and logic are evident in this letter. In any case, the above signers and more were all answering the call of "the glorious cause of Texas." Frank, who had been made a lieutenant in the militia by the General Council of the Provisional Government, was one of the first to march. He fought in the battle of Concepción against General Martín Perfecto de Cós, Santa Anna's brother-in-law, who led five hundred Mexicans. On Lieutenant Hardin's muster-roll were his brother-in-law, Philip Dever, and two of the Bryans (Ap. ii).

On December 2, Frank was at San Antonio, and followed Ben Milam into a five-day battle for the town. Dr. Farley was a first lieutenant in Hirom's company of minutemen who were marching toward San Antonio but arrived three days late. During the attack, a sniper killed Milam, but Cós surrendered and was allowed to go back to Mexico on the condition that he would never return to Texas and would respect the Constitution of 1824.

The elegant General Cós traveled with a lot of very fancy equipment. He traded Frank his silver traveling candlesticks for provisions he needed to travel back to Mexico. Frank kept the sticks all his life.

The following spring, Blackburn was again delegate from Liberty at the Consultation at Washington-on-the-Brazos. The question was whether Texas should demand to be a separate state of Mexico or become a sovereign republic. All voted for the latter. Only on March 3 would the late-arriving Blackburn sign the famous Declaration of Independence.[16] But just before the leaders convened on the Brazos, an interesting trial was brewing in Liberty, a trial that would have significant impact on events at the convention. The story involved lawyer David G. Burnet, who, like other empresarios, had been left without a job when the Mexican law of 1830 closed the border to new settlers. The 23,000 acres he had been given by Mexico he sold to the Galveston and Texas Land Company. In mid-February 1836 he moved his family to Liberty, where his friend William Hardin had become the alcalde. Hardin was also "first judge" of the Atascosito District, and the two lawyers discussed how to handle the trials of two accused murderers sitting in the jail during this juridical limbo on the eve of independence and before any new legal system was implemented.

The indicted men were William M. Smith and his father, John M. Smith, a man who was known to be sympathetic to the Mexicans. The younger Smith was the one thought to be the actual murderer, and some Libertians, including Peter Menard, believed the elder Smith had been arrested on political rather than criminal grounds. The adamant and impulsive William Hardin had set the date for their trial for February 22 in the twenty-two-foot-square Casa Consistoriale in Liberty. Menard was in favor of trying both men but thought Hardin should disqualify himself as presiding judge because he was not at all impartial. Menard wrote his concerns in a letter to the General Council of the Provisional Government:

9 o'clock AM October 19 '35

Mr. President—

. . . Mr. Hardin . . . observed to me that he thought it was advisable and necessary to have a Mr. J.M. Smith also arrested. His reasons were as follows—"Mr. Smith has always been opposed to the cause of Freedom, he has whenever in his power, favored the Mexicans to the prejudice of our citizens. He has, Sir, injured the Cause of Liberty by giving all the information possible to enemies (that is to those that are now our enemies). He has, Sir, blackened the reputation of the best citizens in that part of the country by informing the Mexican officers and military, as well as those that belonged to the Custom House, of all that was said by them and a great deal more, all lies of his. He has to my knowledge, Sir, attempted to take the life of Mr. Chs. Wilcox for no other reason but only because he was favorable to our cause, and took an active part in the affair that took place at Anahuac.

"[Mr. Smith] has influence enough, Sir, to injure our cause matirealy. He is beside all I have stated to you of his character, a murderer. My reason for saying so is that a few days before I left home I was informed that he and his son have murdered a Mr. Carroll (Son-in-law to said Smith). The last accusation is not probably the business of this body but it is my opinion that as we had had no court in the district of Liberty since our country has been attacked therefore I think it is our duty to have him arrested, not only as a murderer, but as a traitor and an enemy to the Cause of Liberty." . . .

Peter J. Menard, approved of by Joseph Bryan—
Both from Liberty.[17]

They might call it bias, but Hardin called it "loyalty to the glorious cause." He assured Menard the men would get a fair trial because he had got the Smiths the best lawyer around, David Burnet, and Hardin intended to have a jury. Under Spanish law there was no jury, so this also underlined Hardin's determination for independence.

The young accused man, William Smith, testified that he had complained to his brother-in-law, Carroll, of his severe treatment of a Negro girl and that they had argued about a piece of land. Smith quoted Carroll as saying, "If it's land you want, I'll damn soon give you all the land you'll want in Texas!"[18] and picked up a gun while the elder Smith stood by. Young Smith grabbed a club and killed Carroll. The jury found William Smith guilty of murder in the first degree and named the father as accessory, but recommended clemency. The convicted felons were thrown on the mercy of the court. Hardin addressed the Smiths as follows:

After the most attentive and patient investigation of all the facts offered by you in defense, after having been allowed every latitude and indulgence which a regard for justice and humanity would permit the court to grant, after having the benefit of those exertions of the most able, eloquent and just counsel whose exertions deserve your warmest gratitude and whose abilities would have saved you if legal learning and ingenuity could have availed you, a jury of your countrymen have pronounced you guilty of the foul, awful and horrid crime of murder. When we consider the character of that jury—a jury comprised of men of our own choice whose characters for honesty, humanity and intelligence is so unquestionable the court cannot but conclude that nothing but a full, clear and indubitable conviction in their minds of your guilt could have induced them to render a verdict of condemnation. To the contents of that verdict the court is reluctantly compelled to add the sanction of its opinion.

The court has nothing left but to pronounce the sentence of the law, and here let me urge you to use the short time between this and the awful moment of your execution in preparation to meet a Just and Merciful but I fear an Incensed God, whose laws you have violated above imagining in your brother man you defaced. Let me beseech you to look to that God for mercy—he alone can save you—and I awfully fear from the apparent indifference which you have heretofore manifested that you are ill prepared to render an account at that bar where nothing is secret—where the secrets of all hearts shall be laid open.

And here I cannot but indulge the hope and belief that from the solemn and imploring scene which we have this day witnessed, from this awful example we may all be taught the necessity of taming our passions—and of controlling our tempers—and that the record of the court of this jurisdiction may never again be blurred and stained by the accusation of murder.

You, John M. Smith and William M. Smith, are to be taken back to the place of confinement, then to be kept in safe and close custody until the 25th day of March next from above—you are to be taken to the place of execution—where between the hours of ten and two you are to be hanged by the neck till you are dead. And may the Lord have mercy upon your souls.*

It was high-handed of Hardin to ignore the jury's recommendation for clemency, but to him it was terribly important for the fledgling republic to take a strong stand against Tories. This would make undecided, timid colonists turn out with the rebels. When Burnet complained to him about the harsh sentence, Hardin smiled and suggested that an appeal before the council at Washington-on-the-Brazos would be Burnet's golden opportunity to interview for a new job.

Beginning to see the judge's reasoning, Burnet and the elder Smith's wife saddled up the Smiths' horses and set out. At the convention, Burnet begged for his clients so persuasively that the delegates added his name to the list of candidates for president, and subsequently elected him interim president of the new republic.

One of Burnet's first acts was to have the sentence of the Smiths suspended until May 1. Shortly thereafter, he wrote the following letter to William Hardin:

Harrisburg, March 29

My dear sir:
. . . I must now in great haste, for my whole time is occupied in public matters, call upon you as a friend, and I am always happy to call all the Hardins my friends, to do me a private favor. There is nothing official in this.

You know that I served the Smiths faithfully as a lawyer. Since then my relations to them have undergone an important change. I can no longer communicate with them as their counsel. But it is still right, and absolutely necessary for me to pay some attention to my private interests, for I am poor. My business with Mr. Smith is unsettled. I went to Washington very reluctantly and did not do so without in-

*All documents marked with this symbol are located in the Sam Houston Regional Library in Liberty, Texas.

tending to charge. What was right then, cannot be wrong now. I want nothing but right.

Will you be good enough as my private friend, to say to Mr. Smith that he must send to me to be delivered at my house, the large bay horse which Mrs. Smith rode to Washington, and his mule Fan or his roan mule—that when he gets here, I will settle with him in full for my professional services. . . .

Your friend,
D.G. Burnet*

The judge could not persuade Smith to part with his horse or either mule, but he would keep in mind that his friend Burnet should be paid. Everyone's attention was focused on the news that General Cós, with President Santa Anna, was returning at the head of an army to Texas, and that the garrison at the Alamo desperately needed reinforcements.

Frank, as lieutenant, had personally recruited for Captain M. Logan a company of twenty men. Included in it were three of Luke Bryan's sons: Luke II, Christopher III, and fourteen-year-old Tom. In another company (Ap. 11) there were two more of Luke's sons, the brave Kindallis as lieutenant and young Pryor Bryan as orderly sergeant. Luke Senior soon signed up. On March 15 both companies were marching to San Antonio from Beaumont. Just before they arrived at San Felipe, they heard the terrible news of the massacre at the Alamo. Some men were so frightened that they deserted.

William Hardin had given up his Mexican title of "alcalde," but he still considered himself "first judge" of the district. He was worried about the protection of the coast and of the battles to come. He wrote to some friends not yet in active service:

Beaumont, March 21, 1836

To Messrs [John] McGaffee, Coats, [Joseph] Dunman,
[Burril] Franks and Neighbors
Gentlemen:

We received only yesterday an express from our Army giving an account of the defeat and probable massacre of Col Travis and his force of 180 men and also that it is expected that Col. Fannin shared the same fate.

Our army has retreated to the Colorado where they intend to give the enemy a fight. We are called on in the most urgent and pressing manner to turn out and go immediately to the aid of your friends and fellow citizens.

The people are generally turning out and I confidently hope that you will all do the same. The time has now arrived when we must all lay business aside until the enemy is driven from our borders. We had better let our business suffer a while than to be driven from our houses and compelled to sacrifice our property to the enemy.

All that is necessary to insure success and restore peace and safety at home is a general turnout. We now have a sufficient number of vessels to keep the enemy off by sea, and so long as we can do that we have nothing to fear, as it will be impossible for them to cross our rivers without being cut to pieces by our riflemen. The Indians are all friendly and nothing to be apprehensive about from them.

All that is necessary is a general turnout and I have no doubt that they will be driven across the Rio Grande in six weeks or less time. Don't fail to report to Liberty prepared to march for our army as soon as you can possibly get there.

> Respectfully your friend and fellow citizen,
> William Hardin
> First Judge[19]

In April, Frank's company was marching with Sam Houston and ever retreating before Santa Anna. Militarily, Houston was later proven correct, but Frank worried about the enemy's destroying homes and families on its march east. He wrote to the remaining Bryans and Farleys and the other two Hardin brothers, who were getting ready to send the three Hardin wives and children and slaves to a hideaway on Milton's plantation. Newton Swinney, a private designated as courier, carried an extra letter:

> Headquarters E. side of Brazos
> at [Leonard W.] Groces, April 14, 1836

Boys—

Mr. Swinney will give you in detail the news. I would advise you to be prepared for a move at a moment's warning for it appears that the enemy will be permitted to devastate our country. I believe they could have been whipped long before this time. I still have some hopes that we will check them before they get to Trinity. The army is becoming much disatisfied because we do not give battle to the enemy. We are now just at this river 15 or 20 miles below San Felipe and will, I have no doubt, march on to Harrisburg. You ought to have every gun and pistol put in order. I believe there is enough men in the jurisdiction of Liberty and Jefferson, if all would turn out, to whip them in crossing the Trinity, for there is not more than 1000 to 1500 of them. The movements of this army has lately been so contrary to my expectations, that I shall not now hazard an opinion of what will be our next move. Orders, a few minutes ago were given to prepare for a move, when, I have no idea. Show this to Capt. Johnston.

Frank Hardin *

Two days later, Luke II, Christopher III, and fourteen-year-old Tom Bryan, all in Frank's company, received a letter from their brother Joseph which told them he was beginning to evacuate the Bryan women and children from Liberty. Among them were Christopher's wife, Elizabeth Whitlock Bryan, and their two babies, and Luke II's wife, Sarah, who was Elizabeth's sister.

Liberty, April 14, 1836

Dear Brothers,

. . . I have not time to answer the particulars of your letter at this time, but will only say that we just received a letter from [President] Burnet informing us that 500 or 600 Mexicans have crossed the Brazis at Fort Bend without opposition and 1000 is on the march to Brazoria and that they wase expecting an attack at Harrisburgh instantly. I shall start the family together with Mrs. Whitlock's and Dr. Farley's tomorrow to the eastward. I think they will go to Brother John's [at Berwick]. Dr. Farley will accompany them, and I will probably remain [here] some days, and perhaps not leave attal.

Tell Felix [a cousin] that he need not fear for Julia [his wife] as his and her mother leaves hear tomorrow. Tell Tom Howdy for me and that he must act like a man [even] if he is but a boy.

. . . affectionately yours,
Joseph Bryan[20]

Dr. Farley was leaving early, before the Runaway Scrape became a rout. Joseph was right about the attack on Harrisburg, which Santa Anna burned on April 14. Desperate for troops, William considered the two men in jail, the Smiths, whose sentences had just been suspended by the new president. He agreed to release them if they promised they would go with him to fight the Mexicans. They agreed eagerly. The young one fought at San Jacinto alongside Frank, but the older one ran off to Louisiana with the Runaway Scrape, taking his horse and his mule, thus showing that William had been right about him all along. William had had the foresight to send old Smith's slave, Gabe, into hiding with the Hardin blacks.

On April 21, the cannon was heard so clearly in Liberty that many remaining citizens stampeded toward the Louisiana border. Immediately after the battle at San Jacinto, on Sam Houston's order, Frank turned his fast horse toward Lynch's Ferry to catch up with some of his fleeing friends and bring them the joyful news that they could return home.[21] Now it was the turn of those who had sided with the Mexicans to run out of Texas. Among the Tories that now took off for Louisiana was a local judge named John A. Williams, who left behind in Liberty his wife, Margaretta Dugat Williams, and their children.

Three months later, President Burnet was still in a quandary as to what to do with three hundred Mexican officers suffering greatly in a P.O.W. camp on Galveston Island. Suddenly he had an inspiration and wrote to William as follows:

Executive Department
Velasco 24 July 1836

To the Hon William Hardin
Sir:

We have it in contemplation to remove the Mexican officers from Galveston Island. There are two objects in view—security and economy.

It has occurred to me that they could be safely, conveniently and cheaply kept at Liberty. Will you be good enough to report to Col. James Morgan Com of the Island, whether you could conveniently organize a company say of [twenty men]—exempt them for the time from any call to the army; and also whether a suitable building or buildings at Liberty could be had for the accomodation of the prisoners, some 300 or more, and the guard and also whether provisions could be procured for government paper for their subsistence.

Col. Morgan will be instructed to send the prisoners or not, according to the nature of your report and I request you will makeout and forward the report as soon as may be convenient.

Your obl. Servt.
David G. Burnet

[Postscript]
My dear Sir:

I am very anxious to get Gabe. He would be very useful to Mrs. B. in getting along with her sick children. I beg you will send him to Col. Morgan as soon as a good oppy. may offer. What eventually became of the horse and mule? Present my best regards to Mrs. H.

Yours truly,
David G. Burnet

The writs of elections are at the printers and will be out as soon as possible. The Constitution is also being printed.—In haste   —B.[22]

William sent his answer to Burnet along with Gabe to look after Burnet's sick children. He said Burnet could bargain at the peace table just as well with one hundred and fifty prisoners as with three hundred. Anyway, William felt he would be able to accommodate only the smaller number. As to government "paper," Hardin said the locals would not accept it for foodstuff but he, William, would use his credit.

The prisoners had arrived in Liberty by the time Frank and his company returned to guard the Mexicans. Frank put the prisoners to work building barracks. Then he had them build a brick kiln so the Hardins could defray their expenses by selling brick and tiles.

Among the prisoners was General Cós. Every time Frank looked at Cós his blood would boil. Three months after giving his solemn word in San Antonio never to return to Texas, Cós had come back and ordered the murder of Frank's dear friend, William B. Travis [†] and other heroes. Now Frank's brother William had guaranteed this murderer's security. Cós had even managed to secure a brand new pair of boots through the Mexican consul in New Orleans.

The slaves heard Frank muttering about what a skunk Cós was. One night one of the young blacks told Frank not to worry because soon everyone would know about Cós. The slave surreptitiously made off with the new boots from beneath the prisoner's bunk and took them to a den of young skunks he had discovered. He introduced a male skunk into either boot and kept it there until it sprayed its scent. Then he replaced the boots under Cós's bed.[23]

[†] The Hardins are mentioned seventeen times in Travis's last day-book (a personal journal). *

That the rest of the prisoners fared better in Liberty is shown in the report made on the return to Mexico City in 1837 of Santa Anna's aide, Captain Pedro Franco Delgado:

> . . . On the 26th [of April] our property was sold at auction. It was hard to see them breaking our trunks open. . . . I saw my boots going while my blistered feet were wrapped in pieces of rawhide. . . .
>
> I have said that we remained on Galveston Island until the middle of August.
>
> On the 16th of that month we slept on board a schooner, the name of which I do not remember, and, on the 18th we landed at the town of Anahuac, where we remained up to the 25th. At 4 o'clock p.m. we started for Liberty, ten leagues in the interior of Texas, under the orders of Judge William Hardin of that locality. On our arrival, we camped in Judge Hardin's yard, in a small shady grove. There we breathed a pure air, enjoyed a milder climate, wholesome water, together with much more comfort and liberty. At last we were free from the rod of that pitiless Morgan and the incessant insults of the volunteer rabble.
>
> Soon, however, provisions gave out, notwithstanding the repeated and urgent applications of Hardin to his Government, which failed to attend to them.
>
> It is proper to say, to the honor and credit of Don Francisco Pizarro Martinez, Mexican Consul at New Orleans, that, when we were destitute of food, clothing and all other necessaries—most of us down, struggling with chills and fever, the prevailing disease in that country between the months of October and December— this worthy Mexican sent us a supply of excellent hard bread, sugar, coffee, blankets, and a plain suit of clothes for every one of us. I am convinced that nothing but the timely arrival of these gifts saved our lives. Had they been delayed only fifteen days, most of us would have died, as happened with fifteen of our companions who were laid in the grave, from exhaustion, before that supply reached us.
>
> Judge Hardin relieved our bitter condition by all means in his power, retaining for himself the worst of his houses, in order to appropriate the two others for our sick. Although ill himself, he went, personally, for a physician, medicine, or whatever we needed.

He listened to our frequent applications with remarkable patience; granted them if he could; if not, he felt deeply concerned. More for the form, he kept over us two sentinels at night, relieving them in day-time, and allowing some of us to walk about town. In the month of November he built a fine frame house at his own expense to shelter us from rain and cold. After a short time he became very much attached to us, and felt so grieved at our unfortunate condition that he withdrew entirely the small detachment that guarded us, and allowed us the limits of the town. Should some drunken man insult us, he went or sent some member of his family to drive him out. Meat and salt were our only rations and those often gave out. Then, even in the stormiest or coldest days, Hardin would shoulder his rifle and walk out to kill a beef, which he sent, ready butchered, to our quarters. When we were out of rations, which happened not seldom, his good and virtuous wife was kind enough to send us large pieces of seasoned beef, bacon, coffee, sugar, bread, and whatever was placed upon her own table. On one occasion she removed from her family beds five or six mattresses which were placed on the beds of as many of the sick prisoners. Again, on another occasion, she distributed among us half a barrel of hard bread, all that was left for her own use. The butter, potatoes and corn in the house belonged to the prisoners.

Oh! virtuous family! How great and how many your exertions have been to relieve the despair of our sorrowful and destitute condition! Oh, William Hardin! thy name, and that of thy noble wife will be imperishable in the hearts of the Mexican prisoners, who, victims of fate, suffered the unexpected disaster of San Jacinto! I vow that, although thou art among the criminal enemies of my beloved country, whether of thy own free will or because thy destiny so willed it, I will never cease to proclaim and praise thy meritorious and charitable conduct towards us.

A ball was given by the citizens of Liberty, on the 21st of April, 1837, to which all the neighboring families were invited.

The ball was intended to commemorate the bloody 21st of April, 1836, on which day so many illustrious Mexicans were immolated. These people had the effrontery to invite to that criminal entertainment General Cós, who, of course, declined. It was told to him by a man of some standing that there were alarming conversations about the Mexican prisoners. This report was not altogether groundless, inasmuch as the gatherings of those besotted people are invariably more or less influenced by means of liquors. In consequence, we spent a very uncomfortable night.

However, it so happened that Bacchus inspired them with gentler feelings. There is no evil that does not work some good. We were told that they deliberated at length upon the question of the prisoners, and that they resolved to send a petition to their Government, which was signed by even the ladies, asking it to dispatch us at once or to set us free, as we were eating up their meat and supplies. They added that their destitution was daily increasing, and that they would soon have nothing left for their families, unless the Government granted them prompt relief.

Hallowed be the hour when this petition was inspired! Its result was that we were set free, which happy news reached us on the memorable 25th day of April, 1837.[24]

Although the majority of the newly released prisoners headed for their homes in Mexico, the kind treatment accorded them by the Hardins induced many of them to settle in Texas.

As the new republic ground into gear, Frank's first job was to supervise the roundup of horses, mules, and cattle belonging to the government of the republic but in the possession of various individuals. Among his other duties, Captain Frank Hardin had to write out two dozen discharges for his recruits (Ap. 12). As veterans of the Battle of San Jacinto, each was entitled to a headright of 320 acres of land, and Frank's letter of discharge was important to verify their eligibility.

In this first year of the life of the republic, land sales were booming and there was a mountain of work for lawyers. William helped John K. and Augustus Allen purchase from a widow the land which is now downtown Houston; the Allen brothers paid $5,000 for it. William also got involved in one of the grandest land schemes in Texas history when he and nine other men arranged to buy the city of Galveston. Since the Mexicans had closed it as a port, Galveston had once more become a sleepy little village. William got clear title (Ap. 14) on a grant of one league and one labor of land on the east end of Galveston Island for himself and friends in 1837, and decided to move there.

In seven years, the families we have been following, along with others like them, had moved from the small exigencies of making their community an *ayuntamiento* to running a sovereign state. Each man had done his bit. William Hardin, as the spearhead of confrontation with

Bradburn at Anahuac, had probably speeded up the Declaration of Independence of Texas by several years. William's high-handed running of the Smith trial and the death sentences he imposed had given David Burnet his chance to become the first president. Frank and several Bryans as military men had bravely fought and won against the Mexican army. Now they were all catching their breaths before the awesome tasks of running their new republic.

Benjamin Franklin "Frank" Hardin (1803–1878), Swan Hardin's fourth son. Surveyor, soldier, rancher. Father of Shattee, Bee, Mimmie, Christy, Nannie and Pep.*

Cynthia O'Brien Hardin (1812–1889). Married Frank in 1839, reared two babies in wilderness along the Trinity while he served as colonel of Texas Militia; famous for her hospitality.

Pryor Bryan (1810–1873), son of Luke O'Bryan, brother of Luke, Kindallis, Christopher III, John, and Joseph; married Mary Angelica Merriman.*

Harriet Evans (1822–1917), moved from Maury County, Tennessee, to Texas in 1829. Served six generations of Hardins.*

Catherine Brien Farley Bagarley (1806–1872). Married Dr. Henry Wise Farley and moved to Liberty in 1827. Sister of Cynthia Hardin.

America Brien Stevens (b. 1817), sister of Catherine and Cynthia. Married sea captain Alfred Stevens. Lived in Louisiana except during the war.

CHAPTER THREE

A Berwick home

IN THE MID-1830s, GEORGE O'Bryan, the youngest child of Christopher and Katherine Kimberland O'Bryan, settled on the western end of the Bolivar Peninsula, where he was engaged in commerce (Ap. 6). On his trips back to the family place at Berwick, George was bedeviled by his niece Cynthia, Christie's daughter, to take her to Texas with him to visit her sister, Catherine Farley. Eventually the twenty-five-year-old Cynthia won out. When she arrived in Anahuac in 1837, she was amazed by the men's colorful and varied costumes. Some wore faded homespun, some buckskin outfits, some storebought formal black suits, others ponchos and charro trousers. One thing they had in common was boots with their trouser legs tucked into the tops to protect from mud.

At Anahuac her uncle saw her aboard the *Laura* with Captain Grayson. This boat took her as far as Lynchburg. From there she took a smaller boat to Liberty. As she went by Morgan's Point, she passed the entrance of Buffalo Bayou into the San Jacinto River, described by Joseph Chambers Clopper of Morgan's Point as "the most remarkable stream I have ever seen." The aftermath of the Battle of San Jacinto had shown the peculiar advantages of this bayou as a link between the interior and the sea. That was why the tiny village of Houston was made the capital of the Republic of Texas for a short while. That year, the Houston newspaper, the *Telegraph and Texas Register*, declared:

> Houston is located at a point on the river which must ever command the trade of the largest and richest portion of Texas, and when the rich lands of this country shall be settled, a trade will flow, making it beyond all doubt, the greatest interior commercial emporium of Texas.

This sort of vision, although given to William Hardin, who was the largest landowner dwelling in Texas in 1839 (Ap. 16), was not in the ken of young Cynthia O'Brien, who cared more for parties. She arrived at Liberty in time for the ball celebrating the first anniversary of the Battle of San Jacinto. She wore a dress of Swiss net and carried her white slippers and gloves in her reticule, putting them on at the door of the ballroom.

Cynthia was reunited with her Uncle Luke and his seven children, whom she had not seen for six years. Several of the children had married, and she was at ease with these double first-cousins, who made her feel at home, and she did not miss so much the close-knit band of sisters and brothers she had left behind. Her sister, Catherine Farley, was delighted to show off her sons Swazey and Brien—who could already read and write and planned to become doctors like their father—and the new son, Henry.

Curly-haired Cynthia had a ready laugh and was known as a spirited dancer. During the first year she spent with the Farleys, Frank Hardin turned thirty-six years of age. When he met Cynthia, he knew that this was the girl he had been waiting for. Later on, when asked how she met Frank Hardin, Cynthia would say that her horse had run away and that Frank had galloped up to grab its bridle. Then Frank would claim that Cynthia had kicked the horse to make him run, so that he would be forced to rescue the distressed damsel.

Frank was not often in Liberty because he was so busy with his field notes and map-making. John Borden, land commissioner of the republic, had given him the job of mapping the whole Atascosito District. To fulfill this difficult assignment, he had to surmount many problems. It was an enormous amount of work, and although Frank asked for pay several times, there is no record that the Republic of Texas ever paid him a farthing. Frank's letters to Borden reflected the frustrations he experienced (Ap. 18). (The almighty importance of the proper location of each family's parcel of land is attested to by the fact that in these three families, the Hardins, the O'Bryans, and the Berwicks, the most energetic member of each spent some years as a registered surveyor [Ap. 2d & e].)

No sooner was the date set for Cynthia and Frank's wedding than the Hardin family lost the one whom the faithful slave Harriet called "the flower of its flock." William Hardin died of yellow fever on June 28, 1839, at his new home on Galveston Island. Frank and his slave John arrived at his brother's bedside just in time to hear William's last words: "Take me to Liberty and bury me beside my father." Frank and Peter Menard arranged for the body to be sent up the river on a sailboat with John, a trip that took a week. Sarah Hardin and the two children traveled on ahead.

Judge John A. Williams took the occasion of the funeral to come back from Louisiana where he had fled because he had sided with Mexico during the revolution. He and his Liberty family and all the Hardins assembled at the gravesite on Watson Hardin's plantation, where Swan had been buried ten years before (Ap. 26).

Frank, who had been helping Henry Farley with his mail route to Calcasieu Parish,[1] told Cynthia that because he would now have to take over William's mail route to San Felipe, he could not go to Louisiana to be married in her parents' home. Ever-practical Cynthia settled for a quiet ceremony by the magistrate in her sister's home in Liberty in mid-August. Cynthia may have also been afraid that Frank would think that her frivolous and giddy sisters were a bore and that her brothers put on airs, caring more about social amenities than developing the land. Also, the sugar plantations in Berwick were suffering a severe depression due to a late freeze the previous spring. Her parents sent as a wedding present Cynthia's favorite black girl, Mary Cottontail, with a chest of linen, and this note from her mother:

We have made up some little presents to send you and Catherine, such as we could get.
  For Cynthia
    from Serena: satin dress, veil, wreath, ribbon.
    from Elvira, Virginie and America: bonnet.
    from Mother: linnen
We have in the cup about ninety dollars, I think, to send you and I wish it was more. . . . *

Cynthia's decision not to delay the wedding was premonitory, as it turned out. It had been two years since Dr. Farley had last gone to New Orleans to buy medical instruments and supplies; consequently, his supplies of drugs were running very low, and he needed to go back. He figured that the round trip to New Orleans would take him two weeks. Because the yellow fever was raging in New Orleans, he delayed for several months, thinking that it would have abated by then. Finally, in November, he set out from Liberty on the same schooner *Columbia* with Luke O'Bryan. The day he arrived, as he walked through the German section of New Orleans, some ruffians beset him and stole his purse. Bruised and disheveled, he was still able to buy most of his supplies on credit, and he returned to the dock. A captain told him that his schooner, the *Alexander of Macedon*, was about to sail, and he booked passage. The ship did not sail for two days, however, and in the meantime he wrote the following letter to Catherine:

New Orleans, Nov. 19, 1839

Dearest,

You have undoubtedly heard by Luke of my starting on the *Columbia*. Our passage here was pleasant and quick. In order to hasten my return I sought out a passage on some other vessel that started sooner than her. The schooner *Alexander of Macedon* was to start the next day after my arrival here. I hurried, made all my purchases, all that I could, in order to board her and not delay for the *Columbia*. I got everything on board including myself and we are not off yet. The *Columbia* is at Galveston long ago. The *Neptune* goes today. I thought you might get uneasy and send this by her.

I am tired, dirty, ragged, lonely and low-spirited but not sick. Kiss our sweet treasures a thousand times each for me. You will see me shortly after you receive this.

Believe me your unaltered, unalterable but stagnated husband,

H.W. Farley *

Just after Catherine received this letter, Captain Lynn of the *Columbia* arrived to tell her that her husband had died among strangers, of yellow fever, in the early hours of the *Alexander*'s second day out. They had buried him at sea for fear of contagion. Poor Catherine, who was still mourning the recent loss of a baby son, was now prostrate with grief. She decided to move back to Berwick as soon as her brother could come fetch her. Cynthia helped her in the sale of her household goods, and Frank applied for the military headright of land that was due Farley.

The O'Briens were happy to take in this returning daughter, as more and more of the family had moved to Texas.

Cynthia settled into a new and busier life in Texas. On her father's Louisiana plantation, life was relaxed compared to the code of strict discipline and hard work by which Frank Hardin lived. They had a little house in town, but their main home was a plain log structure situated on Frank's original claim, on the river nine miles north of the little town of Liberty. Indians lived nearby. Cynthia, having grown up with the Attakapas, had no fear of these Indians, whose drunkenness and thievery were becoming a problem. Besides, during the revolution, Frank had helped convince Chief Kalita (Ap. 1a) to stay neutral, and to ensure the chief's continued solicitude for his family, Frank told Kalita that he would name their first baby for him. Toward the end of Cynthia's pregnancy, Frank had to be absent, so Jerusha came across the river and stayed with Cynthia to await the birth. Although the baby was a girl, Frank still named her "Kaleta," and he reinforced the Indian quality of the name by nicknaming the child "Shattee," which is short for "Coushatta," the name of the tribe.

It is easy to imagine how much letters from home meant to Cynthia. Her mother, Ann Berwick, had married Christie Brien in 1802. Ann's children were Andrew, Catherine, George, Cynthia, Charles, America, twins Elvira and Serena; then Virginia, and finally Gertrude and Camilla, both of whom died in their teens. The three letters following have survived all these years in the single envelope in which they arrived. They show how closely knit the family was. Cynthia's younger sisters, America and Virginia, and the twins Elvira and Serena were obviously intimidated by the very idea of this authoritarian brother-in-law whom they had never met.[2] The first letter was from her mother, who had learned of Cynthia's pregnancy:

Tiger Island February 16, 1840

My dear child,

We received yours of the 20 January; and if Andrew has got out [through flooded roads—see Ap. 5] you know my mind in regard to Catherine's affairs as I wrote by him to you and her.

Cynthia, it seems like a long credit from now until next fall, but oh! if I can see you then it will make up for all the trouble and anxiety of mind I have suffered on your account; if you will only be more explicit in regard to your situation perhaps I may have it in my power to be with you at the time you need me most. Before this letter reaches you

I think Catherine will be on her way home if she is coming at all; and if not tell her I sympathize deeply with her and her calamities. The sleepless nights and melincholy days I have spent this winter [at the bedside of her dying fifteen-year-old daughter Gertrude] I never can forget on her account as well as my own.

In regard to your money I don't know how long it may be before we can send you a dollar. The crop is yet in the sugar house and no sale in New Orleans for sugar.

I will send you the keepsake you requested from your deceased sister's hair.

Adieu, I will say no more as the girls are both going to write.

Ann D. O'Brien *

Dear Sister Cynthia,

I do not wish to upbraid you. It is the most foreign of my wishes. All you can say about the girls is they are lazy devils or some such phrase, but the past must be forgotten in hopes of amends in future. If Brother Frank, if he will so allow me to call him, will only let us hear from him once in a while, even he has no real regard for us, to assure us a little merely for the gratification of his sister America it will compensate in a masure for the negligence of both. . . . Cynthia, you requested in your last letter that we all would think of you every day. Do you think there is a day or even an hour escapes without we are thinking or talking about you? unless we are asleep and then we dream, for it was only last night I dreamed of you and your better half— No, Cynthia, there is none of us newly married, so we keep our thoughts in bounds, that is I never suffer mine to go astray, but the least said honest mended. . . .

Cynthia, I think it likely if ever Brother Hardin and Elvira meet they will have a fist-fight, for she is jealous of your affections. She said you have forsaken all your friends for "F. Hardin." Serena replied she would not give a cent for you if you did not. I was neutral, being unacquainted with such matters.

Serena has weaned Mac and is as fond of oranges as she was when you left. Elizabeth M. has been fond of them but don't care anything about them now. She has altered several of her dresses. We have been to Bayou Boeuf and Dutch Settlement both on a visit within a month.

Farewell, my dear Sister.

A[merica]. S. O'Brien *

A[merica]. S. O'Brien *

Dear Sister,

You must excuse my negligence for not writing to you before, but now I will make up for lost time. I have been staying with Martha [O'Brien] most ever since brother Andrew left [to fetch the widow Catherine]. I came home yesterday. Elvira, Serena, Mac and Tut went the same day to the Black [Bayou].

Cynthia, you must overlook all bad spelling being I seene John every day last week and you know it puts me out of sourts. In your last letter you said the Lazy Divels must write to you. I agree. . . .

Did you and Brother Frank get the segars I sent you by Mary [Cottontail]? I sent them for you and him to have smoke rub and think of me. But dont think a-bad!

William Rachel has gone to Virginia with his sugar. America is reading now to Mother and Charles. I have not rolled [cigars] since January and I am in a grate hearry to "get in" segars and so you must excuse my writing. Give Brother Frank a shy kiss, but don't let him know, for me.

Virginia R. O'Brien *

Virginia did not marry the fellow named John who made her so nervous, but instead married the calm and steadfast William Collins, whose sister had married her brother Andrew. No letter came announcing Cynthia's baby's arrival, but Ann wrote:

Tiger Island, July 9, 1840

My Dear Child,

I have not heard a word from you sence Mr. Hardin's letter to Catherine except a flying report; your uncle George Brien left here yesterday with his young wife [Nancy Millard] on his way to New Orleans and she told me that you had three in family but he could not give me a satifactory account of you. So my child if you have become a Mother you will now be able to judge what a mother must feel for her child in a far distant country in the situation you have been in.

Your Uncle [George] told me another peace of news which has caused me still greater uneasiness. He told that the Mexicans and Indians have both become very troublesome in Texas. America wrote you a long letter immeadately on the recept of your last. My Dear child I do not like to advise but if in case of a war would it not be better for Mr. Hardin to bring you in to reside in this country until

peace? That you may not suffer what poor Catherine did during the last war.

You wrote to me in your last that Mrs. [Jerusha] Hardin was a mother to you. May heaven bless her if she proves such!

. . . Your father was at an election last Monday and he has been so deeply emersed in politics ever since that you can't get a direct answer from him on any subject . . . Andrew went out to the Bayou Black sugar mill to frame him a dwelling house. His children are going to school and Brien and Swazey with them. Catherine and Henry [Farley Jr.] are over at your Uncle [Joseph Berwick]'s on a visit. George and Johnson are running the saw mill as hard as they can. . . .

It seems as if I could press you and that dear infant to my heart it would fill up that vacancy that is preying over it. I want you to send me the name, size and complexion of our son or daughter whichever it may be and also a lock of its hare. Tell my son Frank that I shall not call him son any more if he does not say something to me soon.

Now farewell to you my dear children—

Ann D. Brien

Via New Orleans
Direction Wm Bryan, New Orleans Mgr. of the Texian Post. *

The warmth and emotion of the above letters contrast with the businesslike tone of a letter Frank wrote to his beloved Cynthia in the same year. Frank was writing from Galveston, where he had gone with John, that most reliable black who was a skillful sailor as well as a first-class cowman. Since Harriet did not mention John's coming with the family from Tennessee, he must have been a Texas acquisition.

Galveston, Sept. 23, 1840

Cynthia—

We got here on yesterday morning. John is now ready to start back—waiting for the wind to shift. It's impossible for me to return with him for he stays so short a time. The steam-boats are so irregular in their trips to Houston that I have concluded that it would be better not to trouble you sending a horse to Lynchburg for there is no certainty when I could get a passage to that place— consequently will risk getting up by small boat. There is frequently sail boats running to Anahuac. Col. Boyer tells me he expects to start up first of next week with his family on a steamboat to Liberty. I shall necessarily be de-

tained here until Monday next. If she starts soon after that time with them it would be a good opportunity. I think I shall have but little trouble in arranging my business here. I am very anxious to get away from here and will avail myself of the first chance after I get thru with my business. You had better not look for me until you see me. You must whip the little Indian for me if she cries. Adios.

Frank

Via John *

Frank was teasing Cynthia when he said to whip baby Shattee. Whether she was crying or smiling, he adored his little papoose. Over in Louisiana, Cynthia's mother was thrilled about the baby, and Ann Brien's grandmotherly intuition told her another was on the way.

Ann was now housing her widowed daughter, Catherine Farley, and grandsons Henry and Swazey, as well as about six of her own brood; Serena, one of her twins, had married at sixteen and was visiting at home with her husband, George Johnson, and baby Christopher. Serena and George were enjoying the easy life before returning to New Orleans. The only other married child was Andrew, who had wed Martha Collins and lived near Dutch Settlement on the opposite side of Tiger Island with the four children Martha had produced so far. Catherine Farley's son Brien was boarding at Andrew's house because Andrew had a fine tutor for his twelve-year-old daughter, Delia, and Brien was planning to go to Harvard like his father.

Restless like most returned daughters, Catherine went around visiting her Berwick uncles, the ailing Joseph and his Nancy, and Thomas and his Rachel, over on Bayou Boeuf. Catherine's big, strapping, twenty-five-year-old brother Charles had been home from the sea for the last four months recuperating from a ruptured appendix or some such grave illness.

In the middle of all this, the father, Christie O'Brien, was relaxing and exhibiting his contentment by playing the flute for his grandsons. As a young boy in Virginia he had attended school with Henry Clay, who about this time came to Berwick and had dinner with him. Later he noted that Clay said, "But for politics, I might have been a happy man." Christie was leading the quiet life of a sugar planter and had no regrets.

In her next letter, Ann began with a typical attempt to evoke sympathy for herself but was soon relating the cheerful, cozy daily events of her home on Berwick Bay.

Tiger Island, March 19, 1841

Dear child,

I am very happy to hear you are comeing in in the fall, but fear very much that I shall not witness the pleaseing sight.

Cynthia, the discription you gave me of your little girl makes me want to see her more than ever. I only have from hints to beleve that there will be more than one to speak of before long. I wish you in your next letter to tell us as much of our new relation as you know and tell us about all our relations in Texas as far as you know for they never write to me nor do we hear from them only through you.

Cynthia, I will now try to describe to you the situation I have been in for the last four months. You heard of [your brother] Charles being sick and starting on a sea voyage; he rolled on the sea sixteen days before he got to Mobile. It was about three weeks from the time he left before I heard from him and the news that came then was that he was laying at the point of death and I will leave you to judge what my feelings must have been. In the week following he was brought home nearer dead than alive and I have watched over him from that time till this, day and night, and not been further than the kitchen until yesterday I went over to see Mrs. Wofford. He is at last getting better of his complaint. Dr. Ryan has been his phasision. He is now able to walk across the house or get on a horse and ride a little distance and I think with care will soon recover. My first visit was to Mrs. Wofford because she has been a friend to me in time of trouble.

Catherine has just now returned from your Aunt Nancy's. She says your aunts and uncles are vary well but that your Uncle Thomas [Berwick] is almost blind. He can scarcely see to walk across the house. But, Cynthia, he is seventy years of age and I think he has lasted remarkable well. Delia is almost as tall as her mother. Serena is with us yet and has been through the winter but I expect she will go home soon. You never got a lock of Christopher [Johnson]'s hare because there was none sent. He is now almost large enough to carry it himself.

Your father just struck up a lively tune on the flute. The girls are mopeing about sewing some little things being it is Saturday evening. Mac and Henry are out doors playing and fighting occasionly. Dwoney Diles [Swazey Farley] is asleep. Heaven bless you and Frank and the little one. Farewell.

A.D. O'Brien *

Back in Texas it was a tense and serious situation. Because the Mexican and Indian raids were getting so troublesome, George Miles, chief justice of Liberty County, begged Frank to join the militia as colonel, and lead the men against the marauders. Frank was torn between his duty to his new country and his obligations to Cynthia, who was expecting her second child in June of 1841. Fortunately, Cynthia shared her husband's code of honor and was willing to let him go as soon as he had laid eyes on what they hoped would be a son. She could take her chances on the plantation of being scalped by Indians, or move into the tiny house in town. Cynthia shined up General Cós's candlesticks and reminded Frank how much he hated the Mexicans, especially General Rafael Vasquez, who was said to be inciting the Indians to attack settlers.

The instructions that Miles received to complete a regiment of militiamen were from that same excitable, dictatorial bureaucrat, George Fisher, who had been a Mexican customs inspector at Anahuac but was now just as strongly in favor of the Texas militia as he had been in favor of Mexican authority earlier.

> Headquarters 2nd Brig. T.M.
> Inspectors Depart.
> Houston 15th July 1841

To the Chief Justice of the
County of Liberty
Sir,

The whole of the County of Liberty as originally established including the territory of the "Northern Division of Liberty County and the County of Menard" . . . [is] attached to the Second Brigade T.M. and this Department [is] not being informed whether the said regiment has ever been organized . . . I am instructed to enclose you the accompanying military order, to the Commanding Officer of the said regiment should there be one, or in the contrary case, to require of you in the name and by the authority of the President of the Republic of Texas . . . to organize the militia of the said territory by election for company and field officers, in conformity to the several laws relative to the organization of the militia of the Republic. . . . It is the duty of the Commanding officers of the regiments to fill all vacancies in the regimental staff, by immediate appointment.

> I am respectfully,
> Geo. Fisher
> Brigade Inspector *

Frank accepted the appointment and kept it for three years (Ap. 19). He enjoyed the hours in the saddle, the strategies to be planned, and the preparation for battle. He also liked the idea of being a colonel as his grandfather had been, but he did not like taking orders from his superiors and filling out forms and rounding up militiamen who had gone back home. He headed west whenever his presence was needed.

Just before Frank left on his first campaign, he sent a packet of letters to his wife's family in Louisiana. The one he wrote to Catherine Farley, who had become his dear friend as well as his sister-in-law, was warmer than usual. In it he told how happy Cynthia was in her new life, with her two babies, and that she was the best wife a man could have.

At this time, Catherine was becoming frustrated over money problems; her family was paying for her sons' education, and being a dependent offended her pride. She wrote to her sister Cynthia about her financial worries, and her sister America included a letter to brother-in-law Frank. The letters were sent in a single packet to William Bryan, the head of the Texian Post in New Orleans. He sent them on by water to Liberty.

Dear Sister Cynthia,
. . . Brother tells us how happy you are and I hope you may even be what he represents you in his last letter. Though how I wish to be near you again! I am more anxious to get back than ever I was to leave. And back I will go!! I will be better satisfied to live on the support that was provided for us even if it is ever so small but the schooling of my children bothers me. Here they are at school. I fear thare I should not be able to school them. But I will risk it when I get the means. I would return this spring if I could have spoken to Andrew—as he does not wish me to go. I do not like to raise the children to depend upon others for support. I am too far off to get it from them and my mind is set upon going back. I have no money. . . . [torn]
C. Farley *

America O'Brien's letter to Frank showed that their life on the sugar plantation in Louisiana was a merry one:

Tiger Island
January 23, 1842
Dear Brother,
. . . Then came on what the Negroes call Christmas holy daze,

---

which occupied our time and thoughts for our house was crowded with company. Then on the 29th of December we gave a party and on New Years we attended a dinner and dance in the evening at W.C. Stansberrys, besides other frolicking between times. Now judge for yourself if our time was not well spent!

Oh how I wish to see you in that happy home you speak of with the dear children playing round you. I fancy I can see you so plain that I think in reality if I was to see you I should know you. But I have almost despaired of seeing you and Cynthia except in my imagination for it seems every year brings less hope to cheer the desponding hearts.

I see it takes two weeks for a letter from the U.S. to Texas which is outrageous . . . [torn] . . . It is almost as bad as the constant fear of the hostile Indians plus little-hearted Mexicans if there is any truth in the report. Forsake all such [military] plans and come to Louisiana where you can live in peace and plenty and we can all be together.

We made 80–90 hogsheads of sugar here this year which was very good considering the general turnout of the crops. . . .

Adieu,
America *

In March 1842, a party of several hundred Mexicans led by Vasquez captured San Antonio, pilfered it, and retreated. Texas declared war on Mexico, and in September, General Adrian Woll, who had participated in the campaign of 1836, and who was now at the head of an army of twelve hundred Mexicans, captured San Antonio for a second time. This time, district court was in session, and Woll captured all sixty-seven men in the courthouse and took them to Mexico.

Frank Hardin wrote to his sister-in-law:

Liberty
March 21st, 1842

Mrs. Farley,

I have had before this time no chance to write. Hope you don't hear too many appalling accounts from this country of War, Invasion, In-terminations, etc., etc. We indeed have had much excitement here for the last five weeks on account of about 1000 Mexican troops having taken possession of Goliad and San Antonio, we supposing it was the advance of a large invading army. But they immediately retreated to-wards the Rio Grande after plundering the places. The last accounts say about 500 of our troops were in close pursuit and strong hopes are entertained that they will overtake them before they reach the Rio Grande. If so they will be cut to pieces. The whole country was in arms and anxious to meet them. About 200 men had volunteered from this county and would have marched Saturday last but for the news of their retreat and orders to remain at home. Many believe yet that they will invade the country this spring. A few weeks will tell. I think now there is a large majority of Texas in favor of invading Mexico and I think before 4 months we will send an army into their country. If so we may suppose that the fate of Texas will be decided before 12 months. We will either lose our independence or force an acknowledgement by Mexico that we are a republic.

Cynthia was less upset than I expected. She was willing for me to go with the army saying that she would rather I would risk the dangers of a campaign than to disgrace myself by remaining at home when my country demanded my services in the field.

I see by the few lines you addressed to Cynthia short time since, that you have some notion of returning to this country. Nothing would be more gratifying to Mrs. than your society here and I feel that it would be a pleasure to me to give you all the assistance in my power. Your business here stands very much as when I last wrote. You have no idea of the difficulty of collecting debts. The fact is it amounts to an impossibility. Write to me soon and let me know your determination with regard to moving, when, etc. I have obtained the patent to your league of land. . . . It is a fine league, nice land, well watered, will someday be worth a great deal of money.

Pryor [Bryan] talks of starting to Louisiana in a week or two. Why don't some of your brothers [Charles, Andrew, and George] come out and see us? Cynthia says they are fond of hunting. Tell them to come out and we will take a big hunt or in case the Mexicans should invade the country we could take a few pops at them. Tell the girls not to believe all the war news they hear. In case of war we will write often and give the news about as it is. . . .

Kaleta and Billy are both crying to get to their mother. They are jealous little dogs. I do think Billy looks very much like little Henry [Farley] did when he left here—

Tell the girls the $1.50 marks on letters is Texas money no more.

F. Hardin *

The republic's big problem was money; there was none to pay or equip soldiers. Sam Houston tried unsuccessfully to get a loan from the

United States. He did not even have money to pay postage on important government papers. Letters sent to the States had to be paid for in U.S. money, as the scrip of the republic was no longer honored. Houston was embarrassed about the lack of funds but still ordered the postmasters to cover the costs:

> Galveston
> 28 April, 1842
>
> Col. Frank Hardin,
>   If at any time I should send an express with important news to your care at Liberty, I will expect you to have it sent on to its destination.
>   I wish you would form an association in your county for this purpose. Congress made no provision for mails, and I am without one dollar.
>   The people must support the government in its present crisis. I am truly your friend,
>
> Sam Houston[3]

General James Davis and General Alexander Somervell both knew the Texan troops were not prepared for an offensive war against Mexico. When Frank arrived at San Antonio in December of 1842, he realized this and considered the Mier Expedition to be harebrained. Until spring of 1844, Frank continued his military service in Houston, turning out his troops whenever and wherever they were needed to keep the Indians at bay.

In the fall of 1842, Catherine Farley had still not moved back to Texas. She wrote to her brother-in-law:

> Tiger Island, October 15 '42
>
> Brother Hardin,
>   If you think . . . at any time . . . I have neglected your kind letters, I do not do so intentionally. I moved here to Brother [Andrew]'s the last of May with the intention of return to Texas the first opportunity. I wrote to you accordingly and completed the letter to send and Brother objected so strongly to my returning or sending the letter, I gave up. . . .
>   Brother, you promised to let us know from time to time concerning the disturbances of the country. We heard accounts in the prints of San Antone being taken by the Mexicans while Court was in session and

the whole campaigns. I wait for your account. I don't put any confidence in hear-its.

They will commence making sugar in a short time. Then is your time to be here. Cynthia ought to come so she can see to her parents. The pleasures of again seeing their favorite child would be great.

Many has been the useless regret that I ever left my thoughts and came home. Too late! A step taken can never be recalled. There is no roof like a persons own. Hope is all that supports me. I look forward for something better. I have a support I lean upon at last—my Heavenly Father. I trust in Him and Him alone. My mind is easy in that trust.

. . . Brien works at the plantation and Swazey will when they commence making sugar. . . .

> I remain your sister,
> Catherine Farley *

Cynthia finally had the opportunity to visit her family and to show off her babies to all the relatives in Louisiana. The next year America, who was depressed over losing her fiance, and the widowed Catherine traveled to Texas together. Frank managed to get America a piece of land also, and Cynthia got her all spruced up with a grownup hairdo with a spit-curl in the middle of her forehead. On her return to Louisiana, America wrote:

> Tiger Island
> July 25, 1844

Dear Brother and Sisters—

. . . I write this evening in the few moments I have stolen from the busy scene of preparation for [Catherine's] children's departure to brother Frank, to return thanks to him for the valuable present of land which he made me. Dear brother—you need not think that I look upon your kindness lightly. . . . Elvira and Virginia say you have wrought a wonderful work for I am almost a belle. They can't get more than a side glance from one of their beaus. One will say, "They are holding out great inducements in Texas for you." Another will say, "All I want is a home in that beautiful country." All calculated to tantalize and vex a younger and more attractive sister.

I told Uncle Joseph B[erwick] of the claims I had in Texas. He appeared much pleased, advising me not to be too much attached to my home but go as soon as possible, which made me laugh—to think that he thought I would or could be justified in going and casting myself upon friends for support when I had not given up my claims to my parents roof yet. . . .

All I can say is Farewell! but whenever you welcome the hour which awakens the nightsong of mirth in your home, then think of the one who once welcomed it and would forget her own grief to be happy with you.

America S. O'Brien *

Once Catherine had time to settle into Liberty, her sons were sent to join her. The following spring, Ann O'Brien finally made her triumphant visit to Texas to see her daughter and son-in-law. After Liberty, she visited some of the Mississippi Shaws on Bolivar Peninsula and then went to Galveston to board a steamer back home to Tiger Island. Her momentous welcome home by Tom, the major domo, was recorded by many of the family:

Ann wrote [to Cynthia and Catherine]:
It is my turn now to speak. I cannot resist speaking of my enjoyment on Bolivar with my friends, riding on the beach in the company of you all. I found Amanda Shaw everything I could wish, an affectionate, noble minded woman in every sense of the word. She seems fully determined to visit us in the course of a year. She is vary solicitous for Catherine to spend part of the summer with her. (She, I expect, will write.) My dear child, I do not think you could be more happily situated than to spend the latter part of the summer in that healthy place.

I returned to Galveston on time accompanied by Pryor and Mary. There we met Uncle George O'Brien and spent the time vary agreably until Wednesday at eleven o'clock when I parted with them on the wharf and took their waves for a mile distance.

My dear child, you know not how my heart sank within me as your house faded from my sight in the dusk of the evening that I left you.

Catherine's son Brien wrote:
Grandmother arrived safe here on the 2nd. Her arrival was quite a tragi-comedy. It being about 10:00 o'clock at night, we were all in bed when we heard the steamboat making a fuss, hunting a place to land. Grandfather waked me up to go down to her. In a minute they were all up and dressed. Aunt Virginia was dragging me and saying, "I

know it's Ma! Brien, go see quick!" I went. The steamboat landed at the bay-tree; when I got there they was just shoving out the plank.

"There," says Tom, "I said it was Old Mistress." The next thing I heard was a voice saying, "Where am I? That you, Tom?" It was Grandmother. She kissed me and walked right to the house. Tom arrived first and told them all it was a strange lady. Anyhow, on coming out to the gate, they were undeceived by the voice of Grandmother saying, "Well, how are you?" Aunt Virginia kissed her, and they cried out, "Where is Cynthia? She is hid! Where is she?" At last they arrived at the house and got Grandmother's bonnet off. She looked round and said, "Make more light, I want to see your faces." She seemed quite confused but at last she got seated and gave us a history of what transpired during her route. Next morning everything looked natural to her.

Elvira wrote:

. . . Mother tells us you are to have a glorious camp meeting which we suppose you are partaking of at this time and which we hope you may enjoy, drink deep of, O, may you taste the sweets of religion! Do not think, dear sisters, though so far apart we cannot partake of your enjoyments at that camp meeting. We do often exclaim with the poet, "O, that to me the wings were given which bear the turtle dove to nest." Then would I fly to thee and in reality partake of your enjoyments at this time, for, sisters, you know that we seldom have the privilege of a Meeting here that is for worshiping God, but we have a great many to worship the "Ancient Harry." So, dear sisters, pray for the salvation of our souls. . . .

Mother reminded us of St. Paul. The day after she got home the anxious crowd surrounded her, which was almost the same as when you left. She stood in their midst with her jestures to suit her words, while we stood in breathless silence listening to her relation of that Lone Star State and its dear inhabitants. But stop! We go too fast! for it is not a "lone star," not according to the prediction of Mr. Custis.

Mother was under some excitement the evening of her arrival. She was in the act of embracing Levi, the negro that carried her trunk to Father, and didn't catch on who it was until he told her. . . . *

It was stylish for a young girl to be cracked on religion in those days. Elvira soon married John McMahon and moved to New Orleans. America married sea captain Alfred Stevens. The first Liberty Methodist Circuit was organized in 1841, and soon Liberty had enough Methodists to merit regular outdoor camp meetings with much hymn singing. Ann was sorry such big social events did not occur at Tiger Island. She came to rely more on God as she grew older.

Tiger Island December 22, 1845

Dear Children,

. . . I am so glad to hear that Catherine is comfortably situated. I recolect the house which she has purchased. . . .

I am very much pleased to hear of your privilege as regards to Camp Meeting and I hope that it will meet with encuragement there and that you may give up your whole heart to religious interests. My dear children, how necessary it is for all of us to live as we wish to die, for life is so uncertain that we strive to be ready to meet God without a guilty conciance.

Tell Sister [Catherine] that Mr. Danzer and his son is hear and I know if he was aware of my writing he would send his slave to her.

A.D. Brien *

Two and one-half years later, Ann was as newsy as ever:

April 16, 1848

Dear Children,

We received a letter from the girls [Elvira McMahon and America Stevens] this week which informs us that Capt. Stevens has started on his seasonal trip to Vera Cruz with his chief, Augusto, and I presume is in good business in that trade. They are very anxious that you should write to them and all you have to do is direct your letter to New Orleans. . . .

My blessing upon you.

Ann D. O'Brien

[In same envelope:]

April 21

Dear sister,

I am somewhat surprised to hear that you are still fond of balls and dancing. I should think you would be more steady in your habits and change from your former self, but I presume change is limited to this small island for I assure you there is great change here. First in the feeling ways of its inhabitants. Dear brother and sister, I am thankful to heaven to know there was a change in you, not so much in action as in feeling, to know that you have given your hearts to God instead of to the unfaithful and cold-hearted world. You say you are a Moralist! God forbid that you should continue so, I think of the results of it— think of those lovely children, all of whom are depending on you for instruction in the way of life. . . .

Virginia *

Frank called himself a moralist. That was like today's behaviorist. Frank believed in God but not in the Evil One and thought man had to look after himself, not expect God to do it. Frank believed in a structured, health-oriented life and in trying to learn the lessons it taught one.

Of the members of the O'Brien clan who for one reason or another had not moved to Texas, many had the desire to do so. One of Cynthia's many nieces, Delia, wrote to her of her dream:

Bayou Boeuf July 26, 1850

Dear Aunt,

Thirteen years has elapsed since I saw you. . . . I was but a little girl, but do not think that those years have wrought any change in my memory for I remember you as well as if you had departed but yesterday. I do not think you would recognize Cambria [sister] or me either if you was to see us. You cannot possibly realize what alterations have been made on this island since you left. This island [Avoca] has a thick forest, is thickly inhabited also, but the neighbors are not sociable.

Cambria and I have the Texas fever very bad and think if we had it in our power we would be there before this year rolled round. Although Father has given up the idea of going to Texas Cambria and I still retain the thought ourselves. If we could have the means and any person to go with us we would be there this winter. . . .

Delia O'Brien *

Delia and Cambria, Andrew's daughters, soon moved to Texas, Cambria as the bride of Ben Hartman, to live on the plantation adjoining Frank and Cynthia's. America would come twelve years later as a war refugee.

CHAPTER FOUR

Ursuline Convent, Galveston

AFTER THE ANNEXATION OF Texas, things went well for Frank Hardin. The plantations prospered and he bought more slaves to work them. In 1849 he bought George and Myra and her four-year-old daughter, Emma, from R.W. and Billups Gayle. George had talent for overseeing the cotton fields and sowing grain. Cynthia taught Myra to be an excellent cook. As the price of lumber increased, Frank built a sawmill on a piece of land across the river and worked strong blacks there in off seasons. Mule teams dragged tree-trunks to the mill where the logs were sawed into boards and piled onto wagons for transport to the river.

With prosperity came the ability to afford good teachers for the children. By now Milton, the youngest of the Hardin brothers, had become a wealthy cotton planter. He had a teenage daughter, Jane Jerusha, who had been brought up with many advantages (Ap. 15). When the prestigious Ursuline Convent opened a chic school in Galveston, he sent Jane there. She greatly patronized her cousin Shattee, who was three years her junior.

Ursuline Convent, Galveston
September 19, 1850

My dear cousin Shattie—

. . . I have enjoyed perfect health ever since I left home and I am very much pleased with the Convent, much more so than I expected. I would not leave it for any other school and I think you would be pleased also if you were here. We have a little pony and a little boat in which we go rowing nearly every evening. I would like to see you very much. I have not forgotten the many happy hours we have spent together. I am trying to improve my time to the best advantage for I have seen how necessary it is to obtain a good education. . . . I am looking for Pah [Milton Hardin] every day. Write often as it gives me great pleasure to receive a letter from you.

> Your affectionate cousin,
> Jane J. Hardin *

Two years later, twelve-year-old Shattee had enrolled with her friend, Laura Williams, the judge's daughter. Shattee boarded with her cousin Pryor and his wife, Mary Angelica Bryan, because they lived quite near the school in Galveston and their daughter Mary attended.

Shattee's siblings were Bee, a boy age eleven; Mimmie, a sister age ten; Christy (Tah), a boy age six; and Nannie, a sister age four. Bee and Mimmie attended a one-teacher school located a short ride from their home. It was run by A.B. Trowell and his son of the same name, who was Mimmie's first crush. Between terms their parents read with them and encouraged the fine art of letter writing.

> October 18, 1852

Dear Shattee,

Pah received your letter yesterday. George [slave] and I went and got it and came by the chincapin trees but found very few. Pah, Mimmy and Christy went again today after chincapins for you.

There was a Presbyterian preacher preached in town yesterday but I did not go. There will not be any Camp meeting (today) but a Meeting next Saturday and Sunday and Ma expects to go. Nanny and Emma [Myra's daughter] are now taking tea [supper].

Ma is making your dress. Ma wants to know if you attend Sunday School, if you read the Bible, and how you spend your time when you are not at school and if you go to Church. She thinks your letters are too short but very good what there is of them. We received your mottoes [stickers] and there was quite a stir till they were divided. We have been abroad [off the plantation] but little since you left.

. . . We went fishing last friday to the little lake. The fishing was rather dull though we caught a dozen or two for dinner. We enjoyed ourselves pritty well thogh you was absent. Mr. A.B. Trowell Sr. has not commenced school until today and I don't know whether we will go or not. Ma has not been to town but once since you left. We expected to send the rings by J. Wrigley but he left too soon. Ma wants to know whether she must pleat or gather the skirt of your dress into the body. Pa and George has got back from hunting chincapins and has got about a gallon for you.

Your brother, W.F.H. [Bee] *

And from her ten-year-old sister:

At home, October 25, 1852

Dear Shattee,
    You know this is about my first attempt in writing letters. Ma and Pa and I went to quartily [Methodist] meeting Sunday last. . . . We have no school now Mr. [A.B.] Trowell has gone to the school up country. Mah and Pah makes us learn our books. Sometimes I sew a little. I have hemstiched a pair of pantaletts for Nany and you know the doll has to be attended to. I have not been to Uncle Blackburns since you left nor have I seen the girls. Mah and Pah was at Aunt Mary's [Mrs. Milton Hardin] a few evenings ago. . . . I am going to hemstitch you a pair of pantaletts.
    I am very lonesome and often wish to have a play with you. Your hen has been sick and the one you pointed out to us the morning you left we took good care of her and she has got well. Anything that belongs to Shattee will be taken care of here! Whitefoot is seal fat. I will take good care of your lemon tree. You must write me a long letter soon and tell me all the Galveston news. Nany has taken your place at the table but will give it up when you come back. Shattee you must write to me how you pass the time when you are not at school and whether you are happy and contented on the Island. Have you bought a bonnet yet? I had the pleasure of wearing your bonnet to meeting.

C.G. Hardin [Mimmie] *

The letters from home were frequent and newsy:

October 26, 1852

Dear Shattee,
    I want to see you very bad. When the steamboats begin to run you

may look for some of us down. We expect to go and see the sugar works next Friday or Saturday at Mr. [James] Griffin's. . . .

Mah and Pah rides nearly every evening and once and awhile play cards to pass off the time. . . .

I must bid you good by.

Your brother, W.F.H. *

Liberty, November 4, 1852

Dear [daughter] Shattee,

. . . There was a small dancing party at Mrs. Preacher's last night. Bee and Mimma went up. They came home this morning, looking pritty bright considering they slept but little; Mimmie about an hour and Bee, I think none. . . . Let me know when your pocket money gives out and I will send you more. . . . Good-by, my little Shattee.

F. Hardin *

There were many parties for the children to ease the isolation of plantation living. Young teens might ride for miles to attend an all-night dance and slumber party, with music provided by a fiddle and sometimes a pianoforte. For such events, the girls wore lace-trimmed pantalettes extending below their adult-copy pinch-waisted dresses. They had pierced ears and wore rings and beads right along with their pigtails. Because it was the only way to travel inland, horseback riding was an integral part of children's lives.

Catherine Farley was living comfortably in her home in Liberty when her second son, Brien, attained the age of sixteen. The tender and compassionate Catherine soon found a beau—Blackburn Hardin, who had recently lost his wife. Their romance, however, ended abruptly when Brien was fatally injured in a fall from a horse at Blackburn's plantation. Mimmie had an indelible memory of creeping into the room where the body was laid out and where Catherine's flat trunk was stored. Ten-year-old Mimmie thought the trunk was the coffin in which her cousin would be buried.[1] Poor Catherine, again overwhelmed by grief, fled back to her family on Bayou Teche and left Frank and Cynthia for the second time to look after selling her Liberty house and land.

Catherine's son Swazey Farley, now twenty years old, was in medical school in Louisville, lodging with the Watkins family, whose son was a doctor in Liberty. To keep up Swazey's morale, Dr. Watkins wrote to him regularly.

To Swazey Farley
Medical School, Louisville, Ky.

Liberty, November 5, 1852

Dear Swazey,

. . . It is quite natural for you to feel a little homesick but that is of minor importance when you think of what you expect to accomplish by being from home temporarily. Our merchants are receiving very large stocks of goods from the East.

. . . Louisville is rather larger than Liberty isn't it? I want you to stick to your work not only for our sakes but to show what Texas can do. She has done poorly in a political way but I hope that as she gets older she will get wiser. I want you to write often, every week or so. Send me from time to time whatever you may find new in the proportions [of drug mixtures].

My love to my brothers and family. As ever your friend,

Dr. S.S. Watkins *

Doctors mixed their own prescriptions, so it was important to know how much to measure out in their little portable scales. The doctor carried his instruments in his saddlebags when he made a house call in the country. Mimmie was following in her mother's footsteps just as Swazey was in his father's:

December 5, 1852

Dear Sister Shattee,

. . . You must write to me how you like your little school mates and whether you have formed any acquaintences or not and if you visit any. . . . Mah's engaged making a couple of dresses for Nany. All the dressing we have bought since you left I will send you a piece of each dress. I am hemstitching you a pair of school pantelets. We like to sew for Shattee. I have to help Ma make up the beds as Myra has a little boy four days old. She asked Ma to send to you for a name for him. He is a 'pretty nidder,' as Nany calls him and he must have a pretty name.

[Mimmie] *

Shattee replied that they should name the baby Richard. Now it was four-year-old Nan's turn to write, with help from her father:

December 12, 1852

My Dear Shattee,

Pah is writing for me again. . . . Mimmie has been busy for several days gathering eggs for Christmas. She has now 27. You know she is a great hand to gather eggs.

Bee and Christy are getting tired of their [animal] traps. They occasionally catch birds but let them go again. Pah has promised to take Mimmie to town tomorrow to select some little presents to send to you by Uncle Milton who expects to start to Galveston in a few days. I have got the red ribbons you gave me before you left home.

Shattee, don't you think Ma pushed open a window the other day and knocked a board down and come verry near breaking my finger! Don't you think she is ugly?

Shattee, I have some good news to tell you. Your pullet is laying on the scaffold by the chimney! . . . Mah has to take her cane down to us pretty often. Tah [Christy] caught it yesterday morning but still I think we are all good children. Better than we were when you left.

Shattee, I have a heap of kisses laid up for you when I meet you again. I have not forgotten how you look. If I could see you now I am shure I would know you among a thousand little girls.

We are now eating dinner and I am at your place. Pah took a snack before dinner and can't eat any. Old Aunt Violet is in the cabin—the only visitor we have today. Mah is just telling of dreaming about you last night.

Shattee, you must not forget—

Little Nanna *

Aunt Violet Hobbs was a black who had belonged to Hugh Johnston, but by this date she was free to go where she pleased. She had the use of the guest cabin at Frank's because she was a respected midwife and roamed the woods to find all sorts of herbs and natural medicines. She collected the roots of chinkapin bushes, made sassafras tea, and even used voodoo charms on blacks.

Cynthia was very ambitious for her daughters to have fine social standing. She had an inherited prejudice against the Louisiana French and their Cajun dialect. Some French had moved to Liberty after annexation, and she was very upset when Shattee told how much time she was spending learning French at the Ursuline Convent. Frank explained to Cynthia that Shattee was learning a very different type of French.

Before Shattee could buy a new bonnet in Galveston, she got quite a suntan. Cynthia objected to her brown skin and immediately bought Shattee a bonnet and some bleaching cream.

January 13, 1853

My dear Shattee,

. . . This is a busy season of the year you know. I keep the children at their books. Minnie [a mulatto] is sticking Bee's shirt bosoms. The little girl helps me a good deal. The children are all very good and growing fast. Nanny is as fat as a little pig; she says she wishes I would take her down to Galveston to see Shattee.

Your Pa is out at Long Island attending to getting out some boards [timber]. There is none of us wastes much time. I feel more ambitious than I ever did in my life. I am so desirous to be able for us to keep our little girl at school, also to send Bee and Mimmie. I was very glad to hear we won't have a little French girl. Mother did not know you was studying French. I shall look for a French letter pretty soon. . . . Tell Ma what you are studying this quarter. . . .

It seems to me I have no taste for visiting since you left home. Mother sometimes feels very lonesome at your being absent from home, but feels a gratitude still we have you at school. You never mentioned to Mother whether you go to church or not. You know, my child, what the Bible tells us: to Watch and Pray, for the Thief cometh in the night. . . .

. . . Shattee, remember [to brush] your teeth and to wear your bonnet and gloves. I want to see my little girl bleached up when I go to see her. I know when you're confined at school all week you must feel very little like writing but once and a while you must write Mother a long letter. . . .

We have but one young calf up yet. I don't like to tantilize you Galveston folks talking about young calves for I expect milk is rather a scarce article in the winter. I expect you are getting to be quite an old lady, drinking tea and coffee. . . .

Mrs. Cade has given me a pair of turkeys and your Pa a pair of geese. He has promised to attend to the geese and I will attend to the turkeys. I will have roasted turkey when Shattee comes home. . . . Give my love to Cousin Mary and family.

Your mother, C.H[ardin]. *

As soon as a milk cow had her calf, she and it were placed in the barn corral so that she could be milked twice a day. When all six cows had calved and been put up, it required many hours of work daily to bring the fresh milk to the house for making into cream, butter, and cheese. All the children of both blacks and whites enjoyed the good things to eat, but also had chores to do in connection with the farm.

There were two routes to Galveston; the long one meant boarding a steamboat at Frank's dock and floating down the Trinity. The other was to have the black coachman John drive the carriage to Lynch's Ferry and then take the boat down the San Jacinto River. This was quicker unless heavy rain washed out the road, or the rivers overflowed their banks. Cynthia traveled quite a bit by now on shopping sprees, going as far as New Orleans, and she visited friends on neighboring plantations. She was adventurous and sometimes drove the horses herself, with John as outrider. The first time she took Mimmie by the Lynchburg route to Galveston, it was winter and Cynthia was pregnant. The buggy became mired in deep mud and then flooded. They were able to unhitch the horses and make their way on them to Mrs. C.D. Brashear's house in Dayton, which was called West Liberty then. Frank wrote to his stranded wife:

February 4, 1853

My dear Cynthia,

John has this moment arrived. I am sorry that you could not cross Cedar Bayou but it will only detain you a few days longer in getting down, which is nothing. I determined in a moment what I wish you to do: just take it easy. Get some person to go with you around the head of the Bayou. You can get in a day to some of the houses on the San Jacinto timber and next day get to Lynchburg. John says Andrews [Mrs. Brashear's black coachman] will go with you. Hire him to go all the way with you. Get him to take a horse along that will work in the buggy [traces] in case yours should give out.

You say Mrs. Brashear will go. Any person that you think, but I would like for whoever goes to go all the way. My greatest dread now is that you will make yourself sick with fatigue and anxiety, [but] I think there is not the shadow of necessity for my going over.

Tell Mimmie her first strike out in the world was pretty rugged. Tell her its good for her. I want her to learn a thing or two while she is young. . . . Let me impress one thing on you: that is, not to suffer yourself to be perplexed with a little disappointment. Take your time in getting over, and don't fatigue yourself.

If the weather appears like remaining good, you might, if you think best, remain at Mrs. Brashear's a few days for the Bayou to fall. Tell Mimmie we have three goose eggs and that I will keep her advised of the progress of the old goose by mail if anything should happen again. Send me word and I will come across on a visit for a short time. Don't be afraid of hiring, or spending money. I want you to get to Galveston as you have started. Tell Mimmie and Shattee I had to scold you for not driving to suit me going through the bottom. No more, but remain affectionately your

Frank *

After Cynthia reached Galveston, she received another letter from Frank:

At home in the gallery,
February ___, 1853 Thursday

Dear Cynthia,

You are not here to tell me the day of the month and I have to leave it blank. All well and busy—working with the potatoes, plowing in oats, etc. John got back last night just as we were talking of going to bed, say quarter to eight. We were glad to hear from you and that you were so fortunate in meeting a boat. We hope that no accident has happened to you and you and Mimma are now with that sweet little Shattee. We all get along firstrate during the day but when night comes I can assure you that I feel quite lonely. The cotton has to be hauled so you know John will go over in the morning.

How will you get back? I suppose you have seen enough of the Lynchburg route. The boats will be coming up frequently so that I think you will get a passage to Liberty. George [slave] has this moment called on me to sow him some more oats and I shall have to stop a few minutes.

Well I didnt sow the oats. Concluded to stop the plow for the evening and let them all work at the potatoes as it looks like raining again. . . .

That buff dress didnt go [in the valise]; I called in Myra [the cook] to get it. She rolled it up and layed it on your bed and we all forgot to hand it to John.

Well, Mimmie, now for the goose eggs: five in the nest. We are licking [laying more eggs than] the turkeys. I have been thinking seriously about taking them and setting them under one of your hens when one of them goes to setting down. You think it would be best?

The old goose, no doubt, would lay a good setting for herself afterwards.

Nana says I must "tell Ma about dem trees [budding] and better still that she had not p__d in bed since Ma went away."

. . . I had like to forget your Turkins. That old Turkey Gobbler of yours won't do. I heard a cry among the little negroes yesterday evening that "The old Gobbler was killing Miss Cynthia's turkey hen." I ran out and what do you think he was doing? Well, that is a mystery yet, but—that he had her in an awkward predicament is certain. It may be possible that she will be after making a nest soon. If not, he certainly had some designs upon her life. I am sorry you was not at home; you might have accounted for his movements, as you know something about matters and things in general, and perhaps a good deal about [sexy] Turkins in particular. I have heard you say that your Mother [Ann O'Brien] used to raise a great many of them—If there had been another old gobbler in the yard I might have supposed that he was chastising her for breach of faith, but that could not be, and particularly as my old gander stays in the pasture. If he had been my gobbler I might have attempted to chastise him for his rudeness, but as they belonged to you I thought I would let him and the old hen work it all out until you got back.

I am sure my old gander will not be caught at such a caper. When he wants anything out of the old goose he takes her off to one side and arranges everything peaceably. He is a civil old fellow. He takes after his master, but the gobbler, who can he take after? Make haste home, I want to see you just about now.

Your . . . [torn]
[Frank] *

Cynthia loved the social life of Galveston, and the chance to wear pretty dresses to social events. Her impression of Galveston was quite different from that of seasick young Lieutenant Jeb Stuart:

I was struck with the rusticity of the inhabitants and the extreme economy and simplicity displayed in their edifices, of which by far the most imposing and the finest was the billiard saloon and barroom attached to the Tremont House.[2]

Cynthia Cade, who is the "Mrs. Cade" mentioned in several letters of this period, was the handsome daughter of Mark Hardin, Swan's Tennessee brother. She had married Dr. Samuel M. Cade of Louisiana, whose plantation was located in High Island. Cynthia Hardin enjoyed the couple's worldliness and accompanied Samuel and Cynthia Cade to Sour Lake, a spa located fifty miles northeast of Liberty. Doctor Cade thought the petroleum and sulfur mud packs benefited his wife's sciatica. The hot packs were administered by a loquacious half-Indian, half-black who had formerly broken horses as a slave on the Cades' High Island plantation. He wore a tall white hat and a frock coat and was called "Dr. Mud."[3] Mrs. Cade was a first-class gossip and match-maker. She introduced her cruel nephew, Jim Hardin, to Ophelia Hardin three years later; their marriage resulted in tragedy (Ap. 22).

Here is a letter typical of Cynthia Cade, written to Catherine Farley:

Liberty Texas   March 17, 1853

Mrs. C. Farley
Dear Friend,

We has lost Judge [Billups] Gayle, Squire Rogers, [and] Mrs. [S.S.] Watkins [who] left a babe a few weeks old. . . . The most melancholy death was John E. Waring from the effects of liquor but not more so than was Lenbron White who died in a camp in the swamp entirely alone with the smallpox. . . . [Isaac Williams] said he was entirely cleared of the charges against him but regretted his conduct since that time.

. . . The [widowed] doctor [Watkins] has broke up housekeeping. Mrs. Jackson has his children and I have heard he was going to carry them back to Kentucky.

. . . Mrs. Clayton has bought the tavern and moved in. [Her grand-son Bill and she] gave $4,000 in land for the tavern. Everyone thinks they gave a very high price for it. . . . Don't you think they have a gay landlady at the hotel?

We have a new circuit preacher—Mr. [W.V.] Angel—you see he has a good name. He is generally liked. He is young—only been a Meth-odist three years and a preacher two. He stays two or three days with us every time he comes round. He thinks he has a hard circuit but is determined to go ahead. . . .

Your relations, Mr. B. Hartman and wife [Cambria O'Brien] are at the Col.'s [Frank Hardin's]. Cynthia met them in Galveston and they came up with her. He has bought land near Blackburn's, your old flame. If you don't make haste, and come back, I fear Blackburn will turn crazy and [re-]join the Catholics. They have had a priest up with a subscription to build a church in Liberty. The only evidence I have of his craziness is that he subscribed $100.00 [Ap. 23]. He has his daughters at home. It is said that Mr. Stephen Green is addressing Jerusha [Blackburn's daughter]. Miss Jane [Milton's daughter] is yet at the convent. Her mother I have not seen for three months. I dont think she visits anyone of late but your friend Mrs. Jackson. . . .

Miss Mary Smith is not married and, I think, entirely out of beaux. Her mother is making drapes yet. Philip [Smith] has declined coming home and is trying to get some office under [President] Pierce, so says Fielder Waring. . . .

I suppose you will think I am nearer being crazy than your beau from this "correct and well written" letter. I am sure you will have to ask hands to help you read it, but pray dont ask any except crazy folks.

> Your sincere friend
> Cynthia Cade *

In one letter to Shattee, Frank referred to her mother as being "too fat for comfort," his euphemism for her pregnancy. Unfortunately, Cynthia miscarried shortly after this, but she soon became pregnant again. It was obvious from his letters that Frank had a strong sexual attraction to Cynthia. When he teased her, talking about the gander and the goose, she knew that he meant that he wanted her, and missed her dreadfully. Frank was called away from home a lot during this year to lay out the new twenty miles of road between Liberty and Woodville to the north.

> April 8, 1853

Dear Sister [Shattee],

Pa is going to take another trip in the woods marking out the road to Woodville. . . . We had a fine ball at Bret [LaCour]'s. Mimmie and I went down Sunday morning and stayed until Tuesday. We had a crowded house and snotty American ladies. Ma danced and cut round the right way. . . .

Pa says you must put stamps on your letters. It is troublesome sending money to the office. . . .

> Your brother
> W.F.H. [Bee] *

> May 13, 1853

My sweet girl [Shattee],

I was glad to hear you enjoyed yourself at the May Spree. . . .

Mother is sorry to hear it is not convenient for you to attend the Sabbath School. . . .

We have rejoiced to hear such fine accounts from your school. Well may you want to see that sweet face of Nanny's for it is sweet indeed. She is very busy now getting something to wrap a "sick chicking" in two rags. She helps Mother take care of her young chickings. I have put out 200 and I have five turkeys. Your Pa and Mimmie have two geese, so that is the amount of our young poultry. . . .

Bee and Christy are going down to see a kind of Indian Ball played. [†] There has been about fifty or sixty Indians camped here. They left for town this morning.

. . . Shattee, your verbena is blooming beautifully and your Jackson rose. Also the sweet rose you set out near the Cape Jessamine.

Mother *

Cynthia loved her garden and shared its bloom with her daughters. Frank also felt great closeness to growing things, especially his children. He was proud to tell his sister-in-law that Cynthia was expecting again:

Sunday, Nov. 6, 1853

Mrs. Farley,

. . . I expect to go with Shattee to Galveston as soon as I hear that the [yellow] fever has disapeared from the City. I dread for the time to arrive as I am never happy when any one of family is missing. We often go riding, sometimes down the road, sometimes hunting grapes, etc. I took the boys and Shattee and Mimmie the other day into the bottom hunting among the wild cattle. We killed a fine calf. It was a real frolic for the girls. Cynthia and Nanna had to stay at home as they could not get through the cane brakes in the buggy for [pregnant] Cynthia has now grown so large that she cannot ride horseback any more. It would take two large American horses and two creole ponys to carry her.

I have found among Dr. Farley's old papers a copy of the discharge signed by Hiroms as Captain and F.W. Johnson commander at San Antonio. I think I can obtain a certificate for 320 acres Bounty land and perhaps a Donation Certificate for 640 acres.

November 11. You remember when I commenced this letter Sunday

---

† "Indian ball" was a two-goal game like lacrosse, requiring great physical endurance. The Indian players wore moccasins and breechclouts, sometimes with a panther tail attached to symbolize courage, and paint on their bodies. The ball was made of deerskin stuffed with hair and was caught in a cup made of sticks.

that Cynthia was off at town—well I went down again with her last Tuesday and she has just notified me that she will have to go again tomorrow. She is fitting Shattee out for school!

F. Hardin *

Frank supplied good illustrated books to his children and they loved them. He also saw to it that they had good horses to ride. The one called Talleyrand got his name because he threw his riders, just like the French minister by that name out-maneuvered both his sovereigns, Napoleon and Louis XVIII.

In the Hardin home, discipline was meted out by Cynthia's "regulator," a slim bamboo cane residing atop the cupboard. In another county there had been a bloody feud known as the Regulator-Moderator War. Frank believed in verbal chastisement, or "moderating," so he claimed that the children were caught between the "Regulator" and the "Moderator."

Frank had another way of pointing out the children's faults to them, by facetiously projecting them onto their mother. He accused her of reckless driving, window slamming, snitching, covetousness, greediness—thereby explaining these faults to the children without making them feel guilty. To teach Christy how to write letters, Frank penned the following:

December, 1853

My dear little sister [Shattee],

Pa has consented to write for me today. Now the question is what shall I say? I would like to interest my little sister if possible.

My horse is not broke yet. He is a splendid horse. We are all home now—no school, and you know that we keep up quite a stir about the house. Ma has her [regulator] cane hanging up in the corner yet and every once in a while she hauls it down upon us. They don't forget to draw me up for a lesson occasionally. Whenever I come to 'Old Mr. Post' they are sure to laugh at me. I should like to have a new book to get clear of Old Mr. Post. I wish you would send me one.

I have not rode Talleyrand since you left. He throwed me, and I have rode Mimmie's horse Splash ever since. Nanna is very proud of her tea set.

We have not been to the pond since you went away. It has been so dry that there has not been enough water in it. So goodbye, my sweet Shattee, from your brother,

Christy O'Brien Hardin *

The idyllic life that Frank and Cynthia's children led on the plantation was about to change. For the older children there would be no more summer days spent "bee coursing" with the prize the finding of a hollow tree in the woods filled with wild honey; and less time for trips to the Indian trading stump in the back pasture to place a bit of metal or a few beads on it in expectation of a return trip next day to see what the Indians had left in exchange in the way of basketry, wild berries, or shell jewelry.

At the age of seven each child was taken on his first trip to Galveston. Mimmie got her second glimpse of the cosmopolitan world of Galveston when she went to visit the Pryor Bryans and Shattee there. To her, Galveston was a grand city. However, as early as 1847 another traveler had been impressed with its cosmopolitan quality. It had "clean" and "spacious" streets and "a number of churches, a fine market house, town hall and offices for the municipal court and adjunct offices" and "very good American, German, and French hotels." There were brick buildings as well as many gleaming white frame houses. This German world traveler, Martin Maris, also commented that the shops contained "every article demanded by the necessities and luxuries of man." People there lived in "great comfort [in] the most delightful residences" set in "surpassingly beautiful gardens."[4] With such trips into the outer world as those to Galveston, the Hardin children were leaving the family nest.

*Kaleta "Shattee" Hardin
(1840–1884) daughter
of Frank and Cynthia.
Named for Chief Kalita
(c. 1785–1852) of the
Coushatta tribe.*

*Adah Isaacs Menken
(1836–1868). Poet and
actress whom Mimmie met
in Liberty in 1855–6.
Companion of literati, died
in Paris.*

CHAPTER FIVE

THE INDOMITABLE CATHERINE Farley suffered one tragedy after another. Again living back at her brother Andrew's in Pattersonville, Louisiana, she received a letter from another lonely man in New Orleans— her remaining son, Swazey, who was in medical training as an intern. The letter must have filled Catherine with an eerie sensation of *déjà vu*:

New Orleans, June 26, 1853

Dearest Mother,

. . . I will assure you that as far as it is in my power I will be prudent and cautious and by the will of Providence keep my health, not only on your account (yet that is a high, a holy and a sacred consideration) but on my own selfish reason for keeping it. For I do not fancy it to be very agreable to be sick, probably upon a death bed in a strange city and surrounded by strangers, alone. So, as far as I am concerned make yourself easy upon that point.

I feel just at present rather relieved, though I must acknowledge rather beat. In the last two letters to you I have rather inferred a reason which I did not express directly for changing my mind so suddenly; that was that there was about to occur a vacancy among the attending students at the [Louisville] hospital and I expected to apply for the place. But just at the good time when the situation was to be won or lost my opponent (for I had one) stepped in and is now being instituted into office. I, in the meantime being ignorant of how to proceed, and how, and to whom to make the application until it was too late, when he had by the aid of friends made the application and gotten the place.

Yet after all I feel myself as well qualified for the situation as he, for it was not questioned. In fact I hardly had a showing by being too indolent and ignorant of how to proceed.

I am told that there will be other [places] of the graduate resident students to have during the summer or fall. And although . . . [torn] . . . this time, I think it worthwhile to stay a month or two longer anyhow and try to take better advantage of another chance if it should offer. In the meantime I can very profitably spend my time. As I have told you I am writing for a physitian [Dr. Fenner]. In other words I am his student. In fact I have very nearly the same advantages of a resident student only on a more limited scale. Therefore you need not look for me soon.

Tell those that are desirous of knowing where I am boarding, that it is at Mrs. Harrison's on Common Street, between Carondelet and Baron Streets.

As regards acquaintances, I have but few. Only those I necessaryly come in contact with. I have no intimate associates. I am acquainted with a few young men at my boarding house and a few of the students at the hospital. I sometimes go down into the old lady's parlor and probably meet a few strange ladies to whom I am introduced, hear some singing and playing on the piano and in that way while away an hour or two of an evening, but that is not very often.

I am sorry to hear of Uncle William [Collins]'s affliction. I hope that it is nothing serious. It is bad about not hearing from Uncle Frank [about the Farley land]. I hope you will hear soon.

And now, dear Mother, if you have anything to propose in relation to me, or anything you desire of me, do let me know.

I remain ever your most affectionate son—

Swazey Farley *

The young intern's fears about falling ill were realized during the yellow fever epidemic which flared up that summer. His Aunt Elvira McMahon and her family had already left town. The helplessness of victims and doctors alike is vividly recorded by the eloquent local author of that day, Lafcadio Hearn, who had suffered through the brutality of such an epidemic:

> Midsummer in the pest-smitten city of New Orleans. . . . *Décédé, décédée, falleció*, died: on the door posts, pillars of verandas, over government letter boxes, everywhere glimmered the white annunciation of death. Lime was poured in the gutters, huge purifying fires were kindled after sunset. . . . [The stranger] stretched himself under the mosquito curtain. The venomous insects were thick;—they filled the room with a continuous ebullient sound. . . . It was strange!— he could not perspire. He rose up and a bursting weight of pain at the base of the skull made him reel—there was blood in his mouth. . . . Strong young men carried panting to the fever wards at sunrise; carried to the cemeteries at sunset.[1]

Victims of the fever turned yellow because of liver damage. Their intestinal hemorrhaging caused the so-called "black vomit" symptom. The virus was brought over from Africa but once arrived here was carried by a common mosquito that lays its eggs in or near a building occupied by humans, especially in cisterns. If the mosquito bites an infected person during the first three days of his illness, the virus then incubates in the insect ten to fourteen days. After that, the mosquito's bite is more lethal than that of a rattlesnake. As urban populations increased, the stage was set for epidemics. Many arriving slaves and old-timers had frequently suffered a light case of fever, which conferred some years of immunity, but the disease decimated the Indians, the newly arrived Europeans, and those who had been away from the coast for four or five years. The death rate among those who contracted the disease varied from ten to fifty percent, and due to unsanitary conditions, the fever was frequently followed by cholera.

Another fever, malaria, was endemic, and its chills and fever weakened the populace so that children, especially, easily fell prey to secondary infection. Almost every house and cabin in the South had a chinaberry tree because its fruit was believed to ward off the fever. The well-to-do slept under "mosquito bars," and all people closed their shutters at night to keep out the "miasma." Nothing was effective against "yellow jack," however, so long as the port traffic carried on as usual. Ships from the Bahamas or any other warm port were carriers of the virus. Quarantine of infected ships did not help if the mosquito flew ashore.

All Dr. Charles Fenner could do was write to Catherine Farley that Swazey was buried in the old Girod Cemetery.[2] The widowed Catherine was now childless as well, having lost all her sons. To lose so many children was not as unusual in those days as it is now, and orphaned children were also more common. Back in Pattersonville, one of the O'Brien brothers died that winter, leaving two children, Theresa and Thurlow. America Stevens and her husband, Alfred, were their official guardians, but Catherine mothered them as well.

A letter from Frank Hardin told that he was still settling her affairs in Liberty. As usual in his letters, Frank was unemotional and factual. The Ben Hartman he mentions below was married to Cynthia's niece Cambria O'Brien. Frank thought that Hartman was lazy, but he nevertheless allowed Hartman to be caretaker of Catherine's large piece of land. Frank was good at sizing up people's character. Another in-law he disliked was Alfred Stevens because of his cunning poker-player manner. Stevens was also impulsive and unreliable.

Home, February 3, 1854

Mrs. Farley—

We are truly sorry to hear of the deaths in our connection at Pattersonville. . . . As soon as the boats commence running we will send your trunk as per your request and also the profiles [†] as per request of Mother O'Brien.

There was a charter by the Legislature for a railroad from Galveston by way of Houston to Marshall in Henderson County. It is said the road will run on a direct line from Houston to Marshall; if so [it] will pass through or very near your league of land on Big Creek. I give you this information to prevent your selling your land until the course of the [rail]road is known. Hands are at work now on the road between Galveston and Houston.

[Ben and Cambria] Hartman and family are well. He is working away on his place. I have some faint hope that he will do pretty well as a guardian. Would not hurt him (say nothing about this). . . .

Cynthia says I ought not to have written so plainly about Hartman. She says he will do first rate. Well I hope so. . . .

Old Mrs. Green, Mrs. [Jas.] Knight and Widder L. have turned

[†] Ann had requested silhouettes of Frank and Cynthia.

Mormon; have sold out their negroes and other property and will
start to Salt Lake in two weeks.

Be cheerful and happy. Good bye.

F. Hardin *

On Christmas, 1852, Eliza Green Knight had given "a big fandango"[3]
hoping to find beaux for her daughters. A year later the widow Knight
was planning for her family to join the Church of the Latter Day Saints.
Washington Lafayette Jolley came through Liberty on his mission to
gather a group of Mormon converts to travel by wagon train to Salt
Lake City. One requirement was to dispose of one's slaves and land.
Jolley baptized Eliza, her widowed mother, her daughters, and her
friend, the "Widder L.," among others. They believed that in order to
be "saved" all women had to be "sealed," that is, married. Jolley also
taught that polygamy was a practical way "to make possible the procrea-
tion of spirits who were waiting to be reincarnated." Eliza's nineteen-
year-old son, John, refused to convert. The wagon train set out on the
arduous seven-month trek and along the way both of Eliza's daughters
married, one of them to Jolley. Six years later, Jolley made another
sweep through Liberty and brought the remaining Greens news of the
family. Young John Knight was still bitter, saying that he did not wish to
see Jolley and his assistant unless "he had the power to hang them."[4]

By relating the information about the three widows, perhaps Frank
was suggesting to Catherine that since a widow's life was hard anywhere, she was better off with her family in Louisiana. At any rate, the
underlying political unrest of the times surely had its effect on popu-
larizing the new religious sects.

As irrepressible as Easter, in the course of the next year, Catherine
married again, this time to a jovial gentleman named Hezekiah Bagarley,
a physician who seldom practiced medicine. Cynthia and Frank were informed of the marriage by Bagarley's mother. In her letter of congratu-
lation to Catherine, Cynthia mentioned, among other pieces of news,
that young Sam Cade and widower Blackburn Hardin had exchanged
angry words over Blackburn's fifteen-year-old daughter Cornelia. The
issue was Blackburn's not allowing her to attend the dances for teenagers. Ever since his first wife, Mary Elizabeth, had come to Texas in
1838 with no husband and several children (Ap. 23), Blackburn had begun to withdraw from social events. His first son was bitter toward his
father. Blackie felt that his father had betrayed his mother and himself
by marrying again in Texas. Blackie accepted money from his father but

tried to embarrass him. Shortly before Cynthia wrote the letter that follows, Blackie was suspected of being one of those who set fire to a public building.

November 2, 1854

Dear Sister [Catherine],

We have had the pleasure of receiving two letters from Mrs. Bagarly, Sr. to hear you was married. It was very pleasing to us all and seems to be to all your friends. You beat old Black [Hardin] for he is not married yet. The old fellow keeps very close. I very seldom see him. Sam Cade and him have had a blow-up about Cornelia [Blackburn's daughter].

Sister, I am quite alone as Frank and the girls went up to see Mrs. Long, and Bee is on a hog hunt with William Cade. I have to steal time while Peppy Berwick [new child] is asleep to write.

Christopher [O'Brien] has rented the hotel and is doing very well. He bought Letta and Napoleon's children at Nancy Brien [Berwick]'s sale.

Mr. [Isaiah C.] Day married Mrs. [Tilpah] Orr—he lit upon quite a fountain!

Tell Mother I am desirous of receiving her daguerreotype in miniature form and Father's if it can be taken from his portrait. Also a piece of Father's hair. I have some of Mother's. I want to have them put in a locket or pin.

We have hired Harriet out for a few months. Myra cooks, and it leaves a little more sewing for me to do. That is when I am not playing cards with Frank and sometimes drafts [seven-up].

Since I began this letter every old acquaintance of yours I'm telling, "Well, Mrs. Farley is married!" and they seem to be highly delighted. I wish you would bring Mr. Bagarly out on a visit shortly. I can't see what would prevent you. Oh, I wish the time would roll around and the means with it that we can go on a visit home. That I can be seated in the parlor where Mr. Bagarly was when he wrote his last letter. Oh, there is such charm for me there, that is the sweetest spot on earth! . . .

If I had a large carriage, some of these dry fall days I would bundle up all the family and pay you all such another visit, for I cannot give up the idea of going.

Cynthia *

The letter carried news about Tilpah Orr, who was still attractive although in her fifties. Back during the days of the republic, George Orr's eye had fallen on another woman, and he had told Tilpah to move out since they had never had a marriage ceremony. Tilpah, however, appealed to Congress, which decided that she was entitled to half of the property and that her children were legitimate heirs of Orr. Soon after this, George Orr remarried and took up residence in Liberty near the church. Tilpah bought a house on the other side and so literally as well as figuratively the church stood between them. Then one day God intervened. While George was felling a bee tree to rob it of its honey, the tree fell on him and killed him, and Tilpah decided to remarry. People felt old Isaiah Day would have his hands full after high-spirited, garrulous Tilpah gave him the nod.

One of the deaths in the O'Brien family that Frank had mentioned in his last letter was that of Nancy, the widow of Joseph Berwick. A sale of her slaves was held and her nephew Christopher O'Brien III (Luke's son) went to Berwick for it. Nancy's faithful old couple Letta and Napoleon were given their freedom, but their teenage children were acquired by Christopher and brought to Liberty to staff the City Hotel, which he had leased. It was customary to keep the slaves in the same extended family. At times Christopher hired Letta's children out to masters in whom he had confidence. Likewise, Cynthia hired out Harriet once for a few months, and Frank hired out Jim to Mrs. Moseley Baker in Huntsville.

Dr. Bagarley owned a summer house on Last Island, "the most fashionable watering place of the aristocratic South,"[5] a charming village of cottages and a two-story hotel located on a small island sixty miles southeast of Berwick and girdled by a beach of dazzling white sand. He and Catherine invited the two little orphans, Thurlow and Theresa, to visit them for the next two summers at Last Island. Thurlow is a boy's name which had been in the family for many generations and went back to the battle of Clontarf in 1014 A.D. when King Brian Boru of Ireland whipped the Danes (Ap. 2c). "Thurlow was Boru's youngest son, only 15 years old, and he fought alongside his father, the mightiest warrior of his day."[6] The ancient names were perpetuated in the family through retelling the legends of early Irish history.

Since America and Alfred Stevens were the legal guardians of Thurlow and Theresa, Captain Stevens was the one who responded to Dr. Bagarley that he would be happy to have the children spend the summers with them. The second summer, the Bagarleys had three other guests, the Misses Hartman and a preacher.

Pattersonville, La.   March 9, 1855

Sir [to Dr. Bagarley on Last Island]—

Having an opportunity I thought I would drop you a line and say to you that the family are all willing that Theresa and Thurlow should come to the island and stay with you on the terms spoken of and they are further willing that you can take them to Texas if you should go there. I have full charge of them until they arrive at the age that they are allowed to do for themselves. I think we will be able to spare you two hundred in advance. . . . Am glad to hear that you are all well and that you have plenty of work to do [fixing up the house] as the old proverb has it idleness is the mother of mischief and you cannot do anything "wrong" under such circumstances.

Now say Adieu and remain your friend,

Alfred Stevens *

It was a glorious trip for the two children. The writer Lafcadio Hearn knew this coast intimately and expressed with great sensitivity the beauty of the island in his novel *Chita*, which commemorates the island's destruction:

> The trip to Last Island may be made south more rapidly and agreeably on some one of those light narrow steamers, built especially for bayou travel. . . . she crosses the river, slips into some canal mouth . . . to puff her free way down many a league of heavily shadowed bayou . . . through the immense silence of drenched rice fields. . . . whichever of the five different routes be pursued, you will find yourself more than once floating through sombre mazes of swamp forest—past assemblages of cypresses . . . into wastes of reedy morass. . . . there are other vessels which make the journey also by night . . . threading the bayou labyrinths winter and summer: sometimes steering by the North Star—sometimes feeling the way with poles in the white season of fogs—an oasis emerging—a ridge of evergreen oaks—a chenière. With its imposing groves of oak, its golden wealth of orange-trees, its odorous lanes of oleander, its broad grazing meadows . . . pretty islets . . . where dwell a swarthy population of Orientals—Malay fishermen. . . . The charm of a single summer day on the island shores

is something impossible to express, never to be forgotten. Then slowly, caressingly, irresistibly, the witchery of the Infinite grows upon you.[7]

All went well at the Bagarleys until the night of August 8 when the severest hurricane ever to hit that area washed away the hotel, all the cottages and the oaks, and cut the island in half. That afternoon, before the storm's arrival, it was strangely still and oppressive. The three house guests were irritable, and Dr. Bagarley offered to take them to a dance at the hotel two miles away. No sooner had the four of them set out in the surrey than Catherine went back into the house, where she found Sterne, the butler, quivering and muttering that he could feel a terrible storm brewing. He had predicted a destructive storm once before, so she took him seriously. From living in Berwick and from the Liberty storm of 1837, Catherine knew first-hand the awful devastation that a hurricane could wreak with its reversing winds and powerful tidal wave. The thought of losing her beloved Theresa and Thurlow struck her to the heart. With the strength of old King Brian she took charge of the desperate situation. Shaking her fist at the sky, she swore, "You won't have them; I won't let you." Then she ordered Sterne to unhinge the big barn door made of half logs bolted together, and leave it flat on the ground. She took the new rope that was used to haul the water up out of the well and had Sterne, with an expert sailor's knot, secure one end of it to the barn door and the other end to the iron frame above the stone well curbing. It was raining, and the west wind was beginning to blow hard when she brought a coil of rope out of the house for Sterne to make four loops over the wide puncheons of the door. Then they all went inside to wait. She took the smoked ham out of the larder and stowed it along with tins of biscuits and a blanket in the oven that was built into the side of the fireplace, and locked the iron door on it.

The house was shaking and creaking as the wind and the rain tore at it, and the children were whimpering. It was black dark outside now, and there was no light in the house. Catherine and Sterne could tell that the house was beginning to move off its foundations. Then the eye of the storm passed over. During its calm, they rushed outside and lashed the children and themselves to the barn door. Now the wind began to blow fiercely from the east. The water began to rise, and the ocean made a terrifying roar. Pushing everything before it, a fifteen-foot storm surge smashed over the island. Somehow, the buffeted barn door held together, and the four half-drowned people managed to stay on it. Catherine was praying and telling God that she had suffered all any wife and mother could bear already, and he must spare her and the children. Their raft began to balance more evenly now, but just as dawn began to break she saw an enormous treetrunk bearing down on them. Its branches would surely kill them all. She told the children to pray as hard as they could, and she herself called on King Brian Boru to protect his namesake. When the trunk was only a few feet away from them, it suddenly veered off, and they were safe. When the water receded, they were set down on a bare beach of sand. The house and the barn were both gone. Only a part of the chimney stood.

Earlier, Dr. Bagarley had been watching his guests glide about the hotel dance floor when the wind began to make the building shiver and sway. The band continued to play as a rivulet of salt water spread across the floor, wetting the ladies' satin slippers. Bagarley decided to take his chances on a steamboat that had just moored alongside the quay. He urged the Misses Hartman to let him guide them through the rain, but they and the preacher refused to go out into the storm. Hezekiah dashed aboard the *Star* just as the boat broke its lines and dragged its anchor toward the mainland.[8] Eventually the *Star* snagged on a chenière during the storm surge. A handful of those aboard survived, Bagarley among them. The hotel and all its guests perished.

Two days after the storm some Malay fishermen looking for loot found Catherine, Sterne, Theresa, and Thurlow surviving on ham and biscuits. When Catherine learned that her husband was alive, she decided that God was indeed through punishing her.[9]

CHAPTER SIX

WHILE THE HARDINS WERE DE-scended from French Huguenots (Ap. 7) and the O'Bryans were Protestant Irish, the Davises, who now join our story, were descended from a Welshman. Like the Hardins and the O'Bryans, the Davises had their American beginnings in Virginia. They were farmers, and an argumentative and humorless bunch who nevertheless had an inborn love of language and came to know the power of words. Though alike in physical appearance, with their straight, blond hair, blue eyes, and cleft chin, the Davises were strongly individualistic and lacked the clannishness of the Hardins and O'Bryans.

The first of these Davises to make his voice heard on the pages of history was John, who was born in Virginia in 1762. After marrying Mary "Polly" Easten and fathering several children, he moved from Richmond, Virginia, out to Winchester, Tennessee, where he suddenly heard the call of God and was ordained a Baptist minister. In 1818, John Davis moved to Muscle Shoals, Alabama, where Polly and her black maid Sarah were two of the thirty-one original members of the Russell Valley Church, which he founded.[1] In the Baptist records, John is described as follows:

As a minister, Elder Davis was laborious. His mode of preaching was plain and pathetic. Experimental religion was the theme on which he mostly dwelt. . . . he was Calvinistic in his doctrine, and however much he might warn sinners, he gave God all the glory for the graces of repentance, conviction and regeneration. . . . He never seemed to forget God's merciful dealings with him. . . . Elder Davis was a man of strong natural mind, without much literary culture, but strong in thought and clear in perception. . . . He was downright and straightforward in his preaching, and gave himself the name of 'Flatfooted John Davis.' The amount of his usefulness will never be known nor correctly appreciated in time.[2]

John's eldest son was probably William Davis, and there were eleven other healthy siblings. The youngest child, Reuben, recorded memories of his father in a book:

When I was about five years of age, my father removed from Tennessee to North Alabama. . . . The land had been recently purchased from the Indians, and many of them yet roamed the dense forests of that section. I well remember how I hunted with these wild companions, and was taught by them to use the bow and arrow. Even now, I can recall something of the emotion excited in my youthful breast by the wild yells of a party of drunken savages passing near my father's house. Occasional deeds of frightful atrocity were committed in the immediate neighborhood. Long before I was competent to reason upon it, the problem of race hatred was forced upon my observation. The fierce antagonism of one race for another and the frequent rising of the conquered against the conqueror were met then as practical questions, as the fashion of the day was, without much speculation or moralizing.

Although a Baptist minister of high standing, he occupied himself during the week with ordinary farm labor, and could never be induced to accept any compensation for his services in the church. It would have been, according to his belief, "serving the Lord for hire."

Clearing land and opening a farm required constant and severe labor, and I, with my five brothers, performed my full share. . . . my brothers and myself, assisted by six colored hands, cultivated the land and attended school only about three months in the year. . . . having few books and no excitements in life, my mind naturally exercised itself upon the life around me and the wonders of nature.[3]

As the boys wanted more education, and inclined toward a study of the law, they clashed with their father's narrow-minded views:

> My father held stubbornly to his peculiar theories on that subject. It was very clear to him, he said, that lawyers were wholly given up to the devil even in this world, and that it was impossible for any one of them ever to enter the Kingdom of Heaven. . . . he also entertained strong doubts as to the final welfare of medical men in general, but admitted that some few might be saved, provided they used their best endeavors not to kill their patients, and resisted all temptation to prolong illnesses with a view to pecuniary profit.
>
> It was to the moral fiber of these pioneers that we chiefly owe the wonderful success they achieved—our first settlers have too often been characterized as a set of ruffians and desperadoes whose courage degenerated into ferocity, and whose freedom was license and debauchery. . . . the great body of settlers were sober, industrious men, who met hardships and toil with patient courage, and whose hands were as ready to extend help as they were to resist violence and oppression. They took life jovially, and enjoyed such pleasures as they could come by. Although a God-fearing people—for infidelity was unknown—there was nothing strait-laced about their religion. They attended divine worship in a reverent spirit, and endeavored to do their duty to God and man, so far as they saw it. Even the strictest of them made no scruple about a social glass, or a lively dance, or a game of cards, or even an honest hand-to-hand fight under due provocation. Minister as he was, my father never doubted it was part of his Christian duty to knock down any rascal who happened to deserve such discipline. . . . As the world has of necessity grown colder and more selfish, as those primitive days recede into the dim past, and in grasping all things, men let happiness slip out of their hands.[4]

Reuben's older brother William Davis married a girl named Eliza Cooper and settled in the Edgefield District of South Carolina. Two children were born of this union, Sini Ann and John Isaac, but Eliza Cooper Davis died, and William left the children to be brought up by a relative of his deceased wife, a Mrs. Fudge. Sini Ann at age sixteen married a cotton planter of substantial wealth, John P. Wise, from the adjoining Barnwell District. John Isaac played the violin at his sister's wedding reception, held in nearby Augusta, Georgia.

In this same Barnwell District, John Isaac met and married Sarah Moody Green in 1830. They produced three children, Caroline, George, and Sallie. John Isaac did some legal work near his grandfather's home in Russellville, Alabama, and his clients failed to pay him. In 1840, John Isaac moved his little family to Macon County, Alabama, to a family place called Fort-Davis. This was not a fort but was a village named for the two prominent families there, the Forts and the Davises. The following letter from a maternal relative of John's is addressed to Franklin, Alabama, but that is the same place found on the map today as "Ft. Davis."

Berlin, Ga., December 10, 1845

Lockheed P.O.
Franklin, Macon Co., Alabama
John I. Davis, Esqr.,

I have been delayed writing longer than I anticipated— pardon my neglect—Have settled in the above place. . . .

I regretted not seeing you while out there [in Russellville]. Will return in January, then dun those people every day until they pay you. Say to Mrs. Davis that I know she dislikes such brief letters—but suffice now. . . . Tell her to kiss the girls [Caroline and Sallie] for me and you treat George to a pony. Accept my regards and best wishes.

My respects to the Captain and family and tell Amanda [Green, Sarah's cousin] to let me know her answer. Oh, those blue eyes haunt me so much!

Yours truly,
George S. Cooper [5]

John Isaac's eldest uncle, General James K. Davis, had left Fort-Davis earlier for Texas and in 1834 traveled with Sam Houston up the Trinity River on a boat. Both were looking for and found places to build their homes. James chose a hill rising 265 feet above the plain, on the west side of the Trinity, while Sam chose the east bank (Ap. 27). James Davis's salt dome is to this day called Davis Hill. Being a military man, he calculated that, with a cannon on top of the hill, he would be able to protect the whole Trinity basin from invasion.

In 1848, General James Davis was a delegate to the Democratic Convention in Baltimore (Ap. 27). On his way east, he informed his Fort-Davis relatives that he had found and purchased some splendid acreage at Cold Spring, Texas, and suggested that John Isaac bring his family there, where he could make a lot of money growing cotton with the elder Davis.

John Isaac set out with Sarah, the three children, and her cousin Amanda, who was offered a teaching job in Keatchie, just south of Shreveport, Louisiana. It took a while to get Amanda settled in Keatchie and the girls enrolled in nearby private schools. By the time John Isaac, Sarah, and their son George arrived in Cold Spring, it was December and the land had been leased to someone else by James's son. The son's Boston wife treated Sarah coldly and hurt her feelings. Without even seeing James, who was ill down at Davis Hill, John Isaac and Sarah took the stage back to Jefferson, where they boarded a boat bound for Keatchie.

For the next two years George Davis, now a young teenager, worked alongside blacks on a big plantation. One day he had an accident in which the tendons of his right hand were severed and the two middle fingers became paralyzed. With much encouragement from his mother, he was finally able to hold a quill between those fingers and practice his handwriting. The following Easter he presented his mother with a copy of Robert Burns's poems. On the flyleaf he painfully scrawled, "Mother's book—Nihil desperandum. GWD."

Two years later the Texas fever was on John Isaac again. The family came to Walker County this time, except for his daughter Caroline, who had a beau and a teaching job in Keatchie. The new plantation was near Huntsville, and John gave it the name of Mount Prospect. The prospects, however, were dim, because to raise cotton many slaves were needed, and their price had soared. John hated the scrimping and saving and hard work that had become his lot.

There was a lot of talk among Texas cotton planters in the year of 1856 about reopening the slave trade. A diminutive fireball by the name of General William Walker advocated seizing Nicaragua, "the new land of opportunity," which would be the landing place for Africans.[6] At the time, this was a very popular idea. Prominent men like General Sidney Sherman, Oscar Farish, David Burnet, and Governor Hardin Runnels urged citizens to give funds to the "patriot" Walker. If Walker were successful in taking Nicaragua, his backers would receive large land holdings in Nicaragua and be able to import slaves directly from Africa. John

Isaac invested all his spare cash in outfitting the invasion, but he lost it when disaster struck the General. The majority of Texans turned against Walker as "not a liberator but a slaver."[7] Shattered by the affair, the depressed John Isaac probably tried to assuage his pain with the bottle. At any rate, his home was not a happy one, although Sarah did the very best she could to provide a social life for her son and daughter.

George Davis had his twenty-first birthday in time to vote in the 1856 presidential election. He took politics very seriously. The burning issue was whether the Territory of Kansas would enter the Union as a free or a slave state. George's father would vote for the Democratic nominee, "Old Fogy" James Buchanan. George learned from his Uncle Reuben, who was involved in Mississippi politics[8] that if Buck became president the Republicans would tear the country apart; so George favored the American Party, called the Know-Nothings because when asked whether slavery was right, they answered, "I do not know." Their candidate was ex-president Millard Fillmore, who said that blacks should be able to vote but that he did not know when. George conveyed his opinions in a correspondence he had begun with his mother's nephew, Frank Green, a young man his own age who still lived in Barnwell District, South Carolina. Frank's answer showed Frank was completely occupied with girls:

Barnwell, Feb. 9th 1856

Dear Cous. [George]—

I got your last this evening—been wandering for more than one month. You take on desperately about Buck's election, and ask something about "bleeding Kansas" too. But my mind is too far from the subject to say anything now. Since I wrote you last I have been back to Athens [Georgia], busted up an engagement—paid all my debts, and took a last farewell. Since my return have courted a Miss Turner of our District—succeeded in making an engagement, which time will consummate. She is good looking—finely formed—sufficiently intelligent—has a head and a heart. She possesses no fortune—worth about 5000 dols.

Of late I have done nothing toward entering my profession. This neglect was occasioned by laziness partly, and by a want of opportunity to be admitted earlier than December. . . . I am now reviewing Blackstone and reading Real Estate. I think I shall do better since my mind is at peace about women. I shall never marry any woman only the one I love best, fortune or no fortune. Glad that my former engagement was suspended. I advise you to take that woman you love best, caring nothing for blood or wealth.

I want you to tell me if you think Texas a great place for young lawyers—a great place for farmers, etc.—give me a description of the land and price in your vicinity, and also of that higher up on the same latitude as Augusta, and two degrees higher. As soon as I am admitted to the bar here, I intend to go to some part of Texas—read statutes and be admitted there for practice.

All are well—no news in this section. Love to all— write soon.

Cousinly,
F. Green[9]

George did not write, and their correspondence terminated with this letter. George was disgusted with his cousin's dilettante interest in politics at such a crucial time, whereas the cousin thought George's vote for Fillmore was a vote against the South. There were rumors that to belong to the Know-Nothing Party one had to take an oath of secrecy by which hatred of Catholics and foreigners masqueraded behind the pious face of freedom for slaves. Frank complained to Sallie about her brother's politics in his growing correspondence with her.

Snow Hill Oct 3rd 1856
Barnwell Dist., S.C.

Dear Sallie [Davis],

The satisfaction you have in your Texas home, as is manifest through your letters, causes my heart to beat with stronger impulses and steals a content over me whose influence I would not for anything be deprived of. When your letters are far between I become uneasy. If it is impossible for us to know each other, and enjoy social communion still we can feel and wish for each other—elite rays are plentiful (so mother says) with which, and in pen, thoughts can be borne with almost electric speed. I never want you to stop writing unless you want to. It is a great pleasure to hear from you.

George must be dead or offended at some of my remarks about his political principles,—can't hear from him—am sure I wrote the last two letters. It was not my intention to offend—my remarks may have been rough, but positively I cannot believe K Nothings are sincere and reconcile it to reason. To vote for Fillmore as he now stands for our suffrages is madness gone crazy. I am proud of Texas—in the Democratic constellation of states she is a star! Democracy is "one of her institutions." It is surprising, Sallie, that you still adhere to such heretical doctrines when there is not even the "ghost of a chance" for their success.

"And the company got eleven deer!"—that is nothing. [I] had six dears following me yesterday, and we can beat you "all hollow" in the grape line—ask your mother about it.

I was not "fancy free" when I wrote you last, but have been kicked since to freedom. I am still before the people! I expect to go to the village in a few days to commence in earnest the pursuit of my profession. Among the folks nothing is occurring worthy of serious notice—health good— crops are being gathered. . . . I want to hear from you right off! Love to all.

Cousinly—
Frank [Green]

If Frank could use a girl as a go-between, so could George. When he heard that his Florida cousin, descended from Mrs. Fudge and named Carrie Clark, had been on a visit to Aunt Sini A. Wise in Barnwell, he asked her to report on his indolent and frivolous cousin Frank:

Monticello [Florida] Feb. 7th '57

Dear Cousin George,

I am so disappointed in hearing that your engagements are such that you cannot visit us, for I had flattered myself with the hope that I would prevail on you to do so either this winter or some other time during the present year. I expect there is some particular object there whose attractions are so great that you cannot get a consent to leave. You know young gentlemen are always in love first with one young lady then another, and so on till they get married. If you are now bound by the "chains of love" I hope you will be fortunate enough to make your escape some of these days. If you should you must come right to Monticello—we have any number of young ladies here. You can select any type you wish unless you want a perfect beauty. I believe we have none of those, fortunately they are rare things. If our ladies are not beautiful they are not ugly, you know

> "Tis not the fairest form, that holds
> The mildest, purest soul within."

I had almost forgotten your inquiries. Speaking of my visit to S. Carolina you say, "Give us your opinion of things in general." I must confess I was a little disappointed— perhaps I had set my mark too high. I expected to find the neighborhood very thickly settled and very fashionable but instead of that it is thinly settled and very little sociability among the people.

You wish to know how I like Mr. [F.M.] Green and his family: They lived ten miles from Aunt [Sini Ann Wise]'s so that I didn't become acquainted with any of them except himself. I saw his sisters [Emily and Mrs. Prior] at church once, I was very much pleased with their appearance. I was also very much pleased with Mr. Green, like him better than any gentleman who visited Uncle Wise's while I was there. He talks a little too much nonsense sometimes, but I suppose he thinks the ladies can't appreciate anything else.

You want a description of cousin Emma [Wise]; she has dark hair, grey eyes, fair complexion, her features are very good. She is rather dumpy—modest and retiring in her appearance. I suppose her age to be about twenty.

"Who is this Mr. Harley whom you mention": I had no idea you were so ignorant of your kinfolk's affairs or I would have explained matters. He is Aunt S's son-in-law, he married her elder daughter. Now you understand why he was entrusted with Emma.

The family send their love to all of you. Remember me to all.

Yours truly,

C.E. [Carrie Emily] Clark

Seeing Emma as a potential rival, Carrie was quick to downgrade her. Both Carrie and Frank had learned how to flirt in the accepted Victorian manner, and Carrie came across as more imperious and condescending than a modern girl. On the contrary, George's sister Sallie was quite a serious girl. The big diversion for Sallie and her mother at Mount Prospect was to go into Waverly to hear the Methodist preaching of the charismatic Thomas Wooldridge, who hailed from Abbeville, South Carolina, near their old home. Unlike the early Texas arrivals, these later ones tended to seek out those from their former U.S. homes and stick in enclaves with them.

Along with his teaching job at the Waverly Institute, George had time to meet young ladies. He was seldom at Mount Prospect. One day in Huntsville, George met Shattee, who was returning from visiting family friends. He was immediately taken by her strawberry-blonde beauty and bright wit. She was excited to meet a man with a mind against which she could spar. When he asked if he might call on her in Liberty, she said her parents would need to know more about him, so he wrote her this pedantic epistle, without a flicker of a smile:

[1858]

Mistress Hardin,

When I first entered a school room I could spell such words as "black, small" etc (which knowledge my kind mother had imparted to me in an old-fashioned primer at home). This was in the latter part of '43 while my father was living in Ft. Decatur, Macon Co., Ala. By 1845 tho' I did not attend school regularly during the intervening time, my knowledge of Geography & the 1st principles of Arithmetic & Grammar was pretty good for one 9 years of age.

In this year's latter part father removed about 8 miles from the village to the neighborhood of Lockheed Post Office in the same County. In this neighborhood was a specimen of pedagoguery execrable, to which of course I was sent because, yet, of no better choice. At this school the instruction tendered me only served to prostitute & enervate what I'd before learned. It is true I learned by rote. . . .

My former instructor at Ft. Decatur, Thos. A. Morris—a man whom I shall always revere . . . happening on a visit to my father's [he] discovered the course in which I was persisting & solicited Father to let me accompany him to Montgomery, which had very recently become the Capital of the State. Father reposing so much confidence in the worthy little gentleman consented & I took my seat in the railroad car for Montgomery about Oct.'46 . . . procured boarding in the kind family of Mr. Jas. Jones Stewart . . . entered school directly. In Nov. Andrews and Stoddards "Ist Lessons in Latin" was handed me to study in order that I might by extra efforts catch up with a class that was then just commencing to construe simple sentences . . . this I did & soon began to with flattering accounts to my parents etc. But in Jan. following, my course in town was ended. An Academy, called LaPlace, had been scared up in my old neighborhood, a good teacher employed named Jno. P. Panny . . . & Father had come for me to go hither. At this Academy I remained two years & a half.

In that time I reviewed & laid aside English Grammar & instead used Adam's Latin Grammar with Andrew's Reader (bad arrangement). Finished Reader, Caesar (4 books) then Virgil's Aenied (ist 6 books) & Cicero against Catiline, "For the Mamillian Law,"[†] "Pro

[†] An oration demanding civil rights for slaves.

Murena" and his "Oratio pro Archia Forta"; & learned to construe a little Greek according to the plan of this same author.

During latter part of Nov.'49 we embarked from La.—arrived Loganport and over into Texas across the Sabine and back in Dec., at Shrevesport—thence to a plantation about 30 miles distant from Shrevesport where we located in Jan'y '50.

Excepting 3 months study or review of Mathematics, in which, during my stay at LaPlace I had advanced thro' Davis Elem'ry Algebra, my sphere was the corn & cotton field until the 2nd day of Jan '51.

On this day unfortunately, while chopping a log my foot slipped—supplanting me in such manner that this right hand fell with the wrist across the keen blade of my ax.

As soon as able I entered a "high-school" at Pleasant Hill [Louisiana], about 40 miles from home . . . I was then about 16 years old & the month was March 1852. . . .

In July of '53 we came to Texas . . . located near Livingston where I engaged myself in the capacity of pedagogue again & remained 5 months at little more than 4 dols wages per month . . . all of which I've not yet rec'd. Feb. 1854 I entered Soph. class at Huntsville. . . . One month [into junior year] I accepted the Tutorship tendered me by the authorities . . . held this position till June last when I resigned . . . having now $450. due me for my services.

During August [1855] myself and a number of companions procured a little two-horse wagon & made a visit to the Tuscalousa Sulphur Springs on the Trinity river—hoping that by our mode of living & drinking that water to have our health much benefited. Indeed some others' actually needed such more than mine for I had just recovered from an attack of chills and fever. We experienced some of the hardships (real pleasures) of camping out—killed many deer—fished—in brief enjoyed our trip yet I was forced to return not much renovated in point of health, in the course of eight or ten days.

. . . I resumed my seat as a student again at Austin College . . . and took up an idea that I would strive to be the first honor man at the next commencement . . . as we were just admitted to the position of seniors. . . . The prize was easily gained and not very esteemed, perhaps on account that the Valedictory was awarded me by the Faculty; but I prized far more the appointment by the Clay Miner Lita Society as its representative speaker. . . . My valedictory, which was thirty-five minutes long rec'd a news paper encomium and gave general satisfaction. May 1856 I rec'd Diploma—left college two or three days after to find the "work for every man to do."

. . . Before graduating, I had . . . engaged to take the position of principal of the Math Department of [Waverly Institute] on the 1st day of June 1856 in consideration of $800 salary for a term of service equal to ten months. . . . I became sick from eating plums. Continued with the flux for at least two weeks, employed Dr. Spiller, and after a real hard time, I got able to stir and went down to the Sour Lake, Jefferson County, where I believed great curiosities, enjoyed myself, and reported this to a Huntsville editor.

. . . The 1st Sept. 1857 again found me pedagoguing at Waverly—the year passed on and closed again with sickness, caused by the measles . . . the Select Board was pleased with my services, and we parted in peace and goodwill toward each other.

. . . It had always been my design to study, if not practice, law—in keeping with which I had read some portions of Blackstone and Kent's Commentaries . . . I commanded law in earnest when I arrived at Independence and not before—even then my health [was] impaired by measles. . . . My love of the science tho' increased instead of waning as long as I stayed. . . . in less than two months. . . . I have gained two definite ideas: one, of my ignorance of the law, the other of the sublimity or profundity of the science. The Moots Courts were highly entertaining but my knowledge was too limited to authorize me to participate in the practice of them. Indeed I felt really ashamed of my ignorance, so gross it was in this particuliar. . . .

Be this as it may! It matters not—when my humble lot is cast what cause I may advocate or profession espouse, whether revelling on the mountain tops of Pleasure, sipping the nectared sweets of a luxurious life, plodding along the medium plain in the dignity of labor, or sulking in the dismal vale of sorrow struggling against the friends of Hispania[†] with the cup of bitterness humbling my life—it will ever be to me a source of inspiriting delight while revisiting the happy reminisces of the past, by the light of a sacred memory, to review and dwell upon the felicitous circumstances which led to the glorious privileges whereby I am enabled to subscribe,

Your friend and admirer,
G.W.D. *

[†] A reference to his father's losses in Nicaragua.

Dr. Samuel M. Cade, planter, who lived at High Island, Texas, before moving to Liberty in 1850. Father of Sam and of William, who married Betty Day.

Cynthia Cade, wife of Samuel Cade, daughter of Frank's Uncle Mark Hardin, sister of Toney Hardin and aunt of Jim Hardin. Died in late 1850s.

William Joseph "Joe" Hardin (1831–1861), only son of William Hardin and brother of Ophelia. Died at his mother's home in Bell County.

Jane Ophelia Hardin, born 1833 to William and Sarah Looney Hardin of Kentucky. Married in 1856 to her third cousin, Jim Hardin.

THE DAVISES

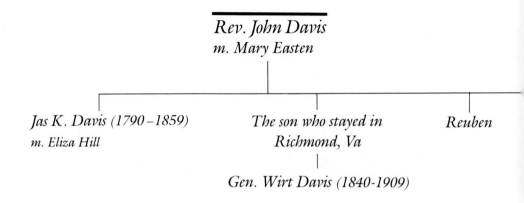

Rev. John Davis
m. Mary Easten

Jas K. Davis (1790–1859)
m. Eliza Hill

The son who stayed in Richmond, Va

Reuben

Gen. Wirt Davis (1840-1909)

Sini Ann
m. J. T. Wise

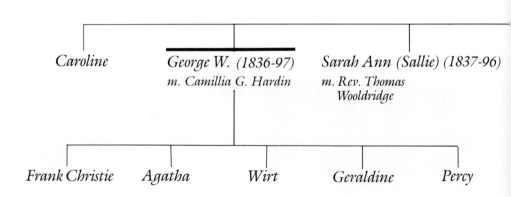

Caroline

George W. (1836-97)
m. Camillia G. Hardin

Sarah Ann (Sallie) (1837-96)
m. Rev. Thomas Wooldridge

Frank Christie **Agatha** **Wirt** **Geraldine** **Percy**

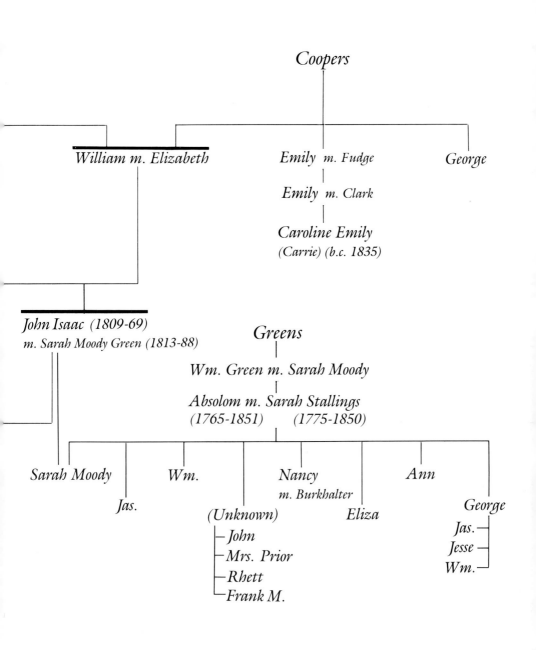

John Isaac Davis (1809–1869), born Edge-field District, South Carolina, nephew of James K. and Reuben Davis, brother of Sini A. Davis (Mrs. John P. Wise).

Sarah Moody Green Davis (1813–1888), of Barnwell District, South Carolina. Married John I. Davis and bore Caroline, Sallie and George.

Reuben Davis (1813–1890), youngest son of Rev. John Davis, born in Winchester, Tennessee, grew up in Muscle Shoals, Alabama, married at nineteen.

Sarah Stallings (Mrs. Absolom) Green (1775–1850) of Augusta, Georgia, and of Barnwell District, shown with a daughter of Sarah M. Davis.

CHAPTER SEVEN

Seven Pines *

IT IS EASY TO UNDERSTAND why George yearned for the warm coziness of the boisterous, loving Hardin family. This family shared so many *bon mots* that they had a sort of private language of jokes. Unlike the Davises, they felt when separated a strong urge to communicate the daily incidents of their lives and to enlist the loyal support of their correspondents. They felt about their home the same way Cynthia did about her old home in Louisiana: "Home is the sweetest spot of all."

On his plantation nine miles north of Liberty on the river, Frank lived like an English squire, hunting for sport as well as to fill the larder. As his sons grew up, he outfitted each with a fowling piece. The daughters also rode and hunted game. They spent many happy hours shooting ducks, quail, prairie chickens, pigeons, plovers, snipes, and geese. Fresh beef could be obtained any time of year by shooting a calf in the woods. In season, pork and venison were obtained the same way. The wild hogs were descendants of those released by the Spaniards. There was a smokehouse in which excellent meat was salted and cured. The orchard contained peaches, pears, citrus fruit, and figs. In the spring, wild fruit was plentiful, such as mayhaws, plums, and blackberries; later in the year, there were muscadine, mustang, and scuppernong grapes, and, finally, persimmons. There were walnuts, pecans, and chinkapins.

The Hardins always had a big vegetable garden and no shortage of potatoes, yams, and rice. They ate wild dandelion greens and pokeweed and found many uses for sassafras. The tree's young leaves provided the filé herb for thickening soups, the roots made a soothing tea, and the twigs were masticated for toothbrushes. There was plenty of wild honey and sugarcane syrup. Flour was usually made from corn, but wheat flour was often available. Lye hominy and pickled beef were staple foods for slaves, but slaves also enjoyed all the vegetables, dairy products, and poultry; catfish, crawfish, and perch; rabbits, squirrels, and opossums. Cynthia laid a bountiful table.

Frank had cleared much land along the Trinity (Ap. 16). The Hardins had their own dock, a large main house, and two rows of cabins for the field hands and for storage. Their blacksmith shed was well equipped because Frank was convinced the future of Texas depended on the axe, the plow, and the hoe. Horseshoes, nails, and all sorts of iron items were made there. There were also a big stable and a barn, two corrals, and a milk house.

In good years Frank made quite a lot of money from crops, cattle, horses, and timber. Both blacks and poor whites hoed the fields and picked the cotton, which they no longer seeded at night around the hearth because now there were cotton gins. Frank stored the amount of corn and cotton seed necessary for planting, and the rest was shipped to Galveston.

There were chores for everyone on a big plantation. Domestic fowl were new to Texans, and Cynthia was excited about learning the best ways to raise chickens, geese, and turkeys. She also grew perique tobacco for her little cigars. The two eldest children were now off at school. Bee was at Austin College in Huntsville. Shattee had graduated from the Ursuline Academy and was attending Andrew Female College in Huntsville.

In the following letter, Frank was trying to cheer Bee up about girl problems.

At home, Jan. 11th, -56

My Dear Boy, Bee,

We are alone at home. Ma, Mimma, Numa [Gillard] and Pep went to Liberty yesterday morning and sent your letter up [to plantation] last night by Jim [Paine]. We are looking for them home this evening tho it is bad weather. We were glad enough to get your letter. . . .

There is one thing we all ought to do; put the best construction on everything and look at the bright side. It's been so cold that we have stuck close to the fire. I have not got up my Smith hogs yet. I was down hunting for them a few days ago and found three sows with about 30 pigs. The pigs were so young I could not drive them home. I expect to go down again soon. Tah's fighting blue sow was one of them. He says he wants to go down with me and help drive them up— the blue you know would be the inducement for him to go.

Tah says that I must say to you that Worthy is in about as good order as any of the horses [Ap. 16] and that he will have him fed every time he comes up [to the barn] which is pretty often, and also that he is afraid to ride Summerset yet and that John [slave] still has him in charge. The little dog [Tah] has just taken his gun and gone out to try to shoot some crows by the back patch fence. Tell Shattie that White-Hoof is fat, that we have never had him hitched to the carriage yet, but that I think I shall have Bob broke soon and have him and White-Hoof to take the place of Smoky and Old Fox. Tah has just come in; missed the crows but fired on some black birds, killed two. Bee, I will stop for the present and pass the balance of the evening looking down the road for your Ma.

[P.S.]   Saturday evening 12th

Well, Bee, your Ma and the little girls did not come yesterday evening. They got here today after one o'clock. They brought us some apples. They say there are three steamboats laying at the Liberty landing waiting for the river to rise to go up. Dr. Alexander has left Liberty going to settle at Richmond [Texas] but we have another M.D. in this place named Fatheree. He may be as good a physician as Alec but I doubt whether he can spin as long a yarn with himself as the hero. . . .

I have been ahead of your Ma playing chess for some time. She has been pretty hostile several times. . . .

They say now that we will have a female school in Liberty soon, Mrs. Dr. Fatheree. I should think that we would send Mimma. . . .

Give our kindest love to our sweet Shattie, and you and Shattie must try and keep well. Sickness is the great dread.

Good-by my dear Boy,
Your Pa *

My dear Bee,

Have not commenced planting, nor can I until better weather. If you have as much rain above as we have here you and Shattie must have a bad time going to school—so much mud about Huntsville when I was in town. . . . No hunting stories to tell as the fowl have mostly left—and the hog hunting pretty well over and Tah and I have been too lazy to take any of those turkey hunts yet. You know, Bee, I am a poor hand to get up early and Tah not much better but however, hold on, you will hear yet perhaps of our being at Battise's [Coushatta chief's] timber on Long Island near Daisetta before daylight.

Bee, if you were at home now you would have fine swimming in the pasture pond. It is deeper than you ever saw it. I want Tah to learn to swim before you come home. The little dog, he is such a coward I fear he will not do it. . . .

We are just starting Jim back to town. . . . Tell Shattie that her Ma says she is going to raise a great many turkeys and chickens for you and her to eat when you get home. Tell Shattie also that I have never found her old black sow and shoaty yet; I think they must have gone wild. But say to her that we will have a big hunt after when she comes home. Bee, I don't think you have any hogs, have you? You will have to squabble with Mimma for some of hers when you come home. Tell Shattie we all think she is a mighty sweet girl and I guess we think Bee is some good, too. Good-Bye, my sweet children.

Pa *

The town of Liberty was growing up and the young Hardins along with it. Shattee was sixteen, Bee, fifteen, and Mimmie, fourteen, in 1856. As Frank had predicted, Mimmie was enrolled in Mrs. Fatheree's female school, but she had to board at Christopher O'Brien's hotel because the Hardins' house in town was not yet completed. The plans had been drawn up several years earlier by William Bledsoe, who was a cousin of Frank's, and also the brother-in-law of Sam Houston. Bledsoe died before the plans were finished, and Frank let the project drop. With continuing prosperity, however, Cynthia revived it. Using two slaves as carpenters and lumber from their own trees, they built the house on their block south of the courthouse. They moved into their new winter-season town house in the fall of 1856, but the carpenters would not complete work on the dining room and kitchen until the following year.

Joe Hardin, mentioned in the next letter, was the son of William

Hardin. He was a great favorite with the girls and he had just given Shattee the right to use the Jerusha Hardin brand on her cattle. Shattee had not returned to Andrew for breaking behavior rules and had been "convicted" to stay home for a year. It seems she defied authority.

In a previous letter, Minnie, the mulatto girl who did sewing for Cynthia, has been mentioned as "sticking his shirt bosoms." Among Cynthia's many jobs was overseeing the making of all the family's clothes, right in the home, including the men's shirts, but not their coats, trousers, or hats.

The following letter was written in the hotel by candlelight by Mimmie to Bee, who was back at college:

Great town of Liberty
Sept 17 [1856] Monday

Dear Bee,

Just returned from the store, been trying to get a pair of shoes . . . [old ones] do not fit, too small as usual. . . . I started to school first day of September, as well pleased as could be expected away from home boarding at the Hotel.

. . . Tah was as cute as ever when I left home. He has no one to tease but Shattee now; you know that will not be very hard to do. I would send our convict [Shattee] up to the Penetenture in Huntsville but I think that she would like it too well.

I see the young lady that stitched your shirt bosom everyday but can never think of telling her what you said about it. I shant neglect it tomorrow. Well I must go downstairs now and see what they are all doing down there and will finish my letter some other time.

Goodbye,
Mimmie *

The City Hotel was located on the northeast corner of Main and Webster streets. Mrs. Fatheree's fine teaching nearby opened wonderful long intellectual vistas to Mimmie, but there was one young hotel guest that she found even more stimulating. She was an eighteen-year-old New Orleans beauty, fresh from a ballet tour in Havana. She had come to Liberty at the invitation of Henry Shea to write a column for his weekly newspaper, the *Gazette*. Sixty years later, Mimmie wrote in her daybook her recollections of this belle:

We knew her as Adelaide McCord then, although I speak of her

---

as Adah Mencken. I was boarding there then and met her daily at the table d'hote and saw her eat so daintily and heard from some of the boarders on the gallery [porch] that she found me 'a beautiful child' with 'such lovely eyes.' She did not tell me these things, but I remember well that she much embarrassed me by gazing at me. She was a lonely woman as I remember her then, a little above medium height, very light hair which she wore in innumerable curls around her face and to her waist, beautiful grey-blue eyes. The eyes cannot be described—full of light and love. To my surprise, reading [Algernon] Swinburne's[†] poem, 'Dolores,' I found—'eyes greyest of things grey, bluest of things blue.' All of his references to her disposition, temper and personality are exact. She was always sighing, and the ladies said, 'Miss Adelaide is so sad.' She gazed into the distance as if looking into futurity. She had a wonderful soft musical voice, a lovely graceful carriage and step—feet and hands to match. She dressed well. I suppose she was not a rich woman by any means. Her sojourn in Liberty seemed to be a part of the tour of Texas and Mexico which her biographers mention more than once. Her companion was her sister, Josephine, a quiet plain woman who seemed to love Adah and need to be loved by Adah.

She was also much entertained in company with Henry Shea by a young attorney and my first sweetheart, A.B. Trowell. Adah accompanied them up and down [the square] and to the courthouse evenings when she gave readings of Shakespeare. . . . She showed taste for the nude. A schoolfriend and I searched in vain for a nude photograph [of her] hung in the newspaper office. I suppose Henry Shea took it with him to Houston when he sold the *Gazette* and went away just then. Or the treasure may have been removed by some prudent soul.

In 1851, when I was nine years old, my mother took me to Galveston to visit my cousin [Laura Bryan]. Someone said, "Let's go to the theatre." We went, and the actress was Adelaide Bertha Theodore (Vaudeville name of Adelaide McCord). She performed on the tightrope in pink tights. She did all to the satisfaction of her audience—Josephine being a dancer, stage managers being their parents, Mr. and Mrs. McCord. [††] I am forgetting to mention that Adelaide McCord had a row of lovely brown freckles across

[†] Swinburne was one of Adah's lovers.
[††] The McCords were not Adah's real parents, nor Josephine her sister.

112

her nose, and also she did not walk a tightrope, but balanced herself in midair, seemingly without support.

Kalita Hardin, my sister, once had her book of poems, *Infelicia*, with dedication by Charles Dickens. She was using Adelaide Dolores then as her pen name.

I fell out with Adah when she married the pugilist Benicia Boy. That was more than I could stand![1]

Mimmie became disgusted with Adah because she married a real brute of a man, and her third husband. By 1860, after Adah's departure from Mimmie's life, Adah was one of the most famous actresses in the world. New York and London newspapers called her "the most talked about woman of the day."[2]

What made Adah sad and unsmiling in Liberty might have been her dark secret, known to no one in Texas. Her birth certificate said that she was born to "a freeman of color," a wheelwright by the name of Auguste Theodore who lived at 35 Bagatelle Street in New Orleans. The reader who knows her secret can appreciate the piercing pathos of some of her musings in the column "Vaporings" that she wrote for the *Gazette*:[3]

What dear, quiet, amiable friends books are! Their information is pleasing, because communicated without petulance, or affected superiority. They are great, grateful and noble; yet humble and generous. They never intrude themselves. You must even take some trouble to find out the knowledge you wish to acquire from them. They are generally to be found at home, and their access requires but little court. They know no station; they are friends to the lowly, as well as the high born. Dear, beautiful books! How dark and dreary this world would be if deprived of your soul-elevating influence! Yet, alas! there are many, who are incapable of appreciating your gentle ways and sweet companionship when the dark shadow of sorrow is over them.

Public opinion is a terrible tyrant—cruel are the sacrifices it demands—many the hearts it has broken.

A man discovered America, but a woman equipped the voyage. So everywhere; man executes the performance, but woman trains the man.—Every effectual person, leaving an impress on the world is but another Columbus, whose mind was trained and furnished by some Isabella, in the form of his Mother, Wife or Sister. Will men never learn to be grateful?

In a young lady's education, every accomplishment is to please the opposite sex. To win for herself a wealthy husband is the lesson. She is taught all the feminine arts that woman is capable of teaching and learning, and every thought is concentrated in this all-important event. It matters not how the poor fellow is secured, so he is safely bound with the hymenial [sic] halter. Daughters should be trained with a higher, a holier motive than that of securing wealthy husbands. In fact, they should not be taught to secure them at all. Oh, mothers! believe me, there are other missions in the world for woman than that of wife and mother. Train your daughter to piety and usefulness; cultivate her mental faculties; train her heart and soul to rise in their majesty of heaven-created power! *

In this last paragraph, Adah came close to discussing her problem. Like many New Orleans octoroons, she had received a fine classic education, spoke both Spanish and French, but her heart burned with rebellion and defiance. She wanted to be part of that prohibited world of the whites. She had learned well how to snare a man, but it was against the law for her to marry any of the men around her. On the subject of interracial marriage, the law read: "No suit is needed to declare the nullity of such a union. Either party may disregard it, and neither can pretend to derive from it any of the consequences of a lawful marriage."[4] Six months before her arrival in Liberty, she had been presented at an octoroon ball in New Orleans, and found a protector by the name of Ben Russell. She was not submissive enough, however, to put up with Russell, because he was "a nobody who mistreated her."[5]

Ever since she was a little girl, she had used other people's names and passed for white. In a moment of confidentiality with Joaquin Miller years later on a California beach, she muttered, "I was born in that yellow sand—somewhere in the deserts of Africa, maybe."[6] And later she averred that, "I cannot, as the daughter of an octoroon, symphathize with the cause of the Confederacy."[7] And finally for her gravestone she requested the line from Byron's "Cain," where another Adah said,

---

> Thou knowest . . .
> The errors of our parents.[8]

At eighteen, her secret made the brilliant girl an alert opportunist. She was determined to marry a congenial white. When the *Gazette* closed, she shipped her "sister" home and went to Houston. A week later she took the stagecoach to Livingston. On the same stage was a young Jewish musician named Isaac Menken. A whirlwind courtship followed, and on April 3, 1857, they bought a marriage license at the Polk County Courthouse in Livingston,[9] and were married. They traveled on to Cincinnati to meet his family. Many years later, a mutual friend, Celia Logan, recalled: "Our family was intimate with theirs . . . there had been trouble about his marrying Adah, the reason of which I was too young to understand, but the old folks had concluded to make the best of it."[10]

Mimmie did not know about all of this drama, but she did gain from Adah a love of the theatre and passion for literature that lasted all her life. Meanwhile, the Hardins were concerned with more mundane preoccupations, such as the continuing work on the house in town and Bee's college career.

> Austin College
> Huntsville, September 27, 1856

Dear Pa—

I should think it was about time you were moving to town for winter quarters. Have you any male school in Liberty?

Pa, you and Tah will have to begin to prepare for duck hunting pretty soon, but you will not be so convenient to them in Liberty as you like. There is nothing that makes me feel more like going home than to think of the duck hunts we used to take winter before last. Tell Shattee to let me know if she is more lonesome in the great town of Liberty than in the country. Tell Tah to think more of his books than hunting. As to Mimmie, she will do her best without any warning. I have not commenced my Greek yet. My teacher thought it would be best for me not to commence it until I got a good start in Virgil and then take it week about. . . .

> Kiss all,
> Bee *

By this time the Frank Hardins owned about twelve slaves. Some were field hands, but a few of them were like a part of the family, and treated that way. It was said of Frank Hardin as it was of Benjamin Lundy, "He treats his slaves very much like other people." Black and white children grew up together and learned to read out of the same books, sharing the same writing slates. There was a strict pecking order among the blacks. Some of the older ones had authority over the young blacks and young whites as well. These respected older ones were called Aunt and Uncle by the whites and blacks.

In the next letter, nine-year-old Tah was reported to have been found under the meat-salting shed talking to the head carpenter, Jim Paine, and to Aunt Harriet's son, Henry Rowe. Shattee had been to call on George Davis's aunt in Cold Spring before coming to the new house in Liberty:

October 9th, 1856

My dear Bee,

We are at last in the great Town of Liberty! Ma and I arrived from Cold Spring and found them here corning under a shed. Tah is under the shed now talking to Jim Paine and Henry Rowe. He has quite a lively time scolding aunts[†] and chasing stray pigs. Prissy [Stuart] is now studying her lessons by the table. We find the house quite comfortable. The workmanship though not scientific is very good. We have removed very little of our trumpery from the old stamping ground. . . .

Mr. Henry Shea has been to Livingston on his nag. Up between Mr. Woods and home, his horse threw him; then he was compelled to ride behind Mr. Potter. Pa lent him the roan after he got to our house.

Mother and I made some very pleasant acquaintances while in Cold Spring. Called at the Gen'l. [James] Davises on our way home [Ap. 27]. There met the Miss Hendersons [the General's grandchildren], quite pleasant and accomplished young ladies.

. . . You attended Congress I suppose—indeed it must be interesting! They have a debating society in L[iberty] but it is secret, suppose the gents are timid yet a while. . . .

Kaleta *

Bee had indeed been on a visit to Austin and attended the legislative

---

[†] Tah was ordering about the older slaves, in imitation of his father, and was not being taken seriously.

session, in which his father would serve the next year. In back of the new house in Liberty there was a group of cabins for the servants, and a carriage house. The original house on the property was now used as a guest cottage and called "Hopkins" by the children. There was a profusion of fruit trees and flowers, and in front, the seven pines planted by Henry Rowe along Milam Street. The new Seven Pines was a square structure with a high-peaked roof. The middle part of the house was a story and a half tall, the back wing one story. The beams of the underpinning were handhewn oak fastened with pegs and set on oak blocks. Exterior siding and the roof shingles were made of cypress. Besides the kitchen fireplace, there were two double-faced bedroom fireplaces. A long gallery stretched across the front of the house; its roof was supported by six four-by-four posts which would later be replaced by columns.

Bee and Shattee were having the usual teenage problems of asserting themselves. Shattee covered her timidity with some caustic comments. It is no wonder Bee was timid about going out with girls, because he was the youngest boy in his class. It frightened Bee to think of the responsibilities which were ahead of him. He would have liked to remain a boy.

[Austin College, Huntsville]
Trio Hall, April 2nd 1857

Dear Sister Shattie,

I received your letter of the 17th yesterday. Am glad to hear that you spent your time so pleasantly while at Livingston; but sympathize strongly with your "beaux" if you treated them as you profess to have done. I speak only from observation as I have not been so unfortunate as to have any experience in the matter thus far. I think myself that it was hard that you should be so near me and we should still be unable to see each other, but two months will pass away. You must do your best toward getting to Huntsville at the last of the session. You shall be well entertained for we are preparing for a magnificent party at that time. Your young gentlemen of Liberty seem to be making bad progress in the way of marrying, letting strangers come and take off the young ladies without making any opposition whatever.

I am truly glad to hear that the Misses Leona and Ellen [Johnston] are progressing so rapidly with their studies but would be more so if I was not so far behind them. I suppose I will have to give up all claims now. It would be vain to attempt to prevail on one of them to wait a year or two. I shall be quiet though and look on the bright side of the picture until it reveals itself entirely. . . .

Bee *

Huntsville, May 2, 1857

Dear Pa,

I had a bait of fish yesterday. They are so scarce here that it is quite a treat to get a sight of one. I will try to satisfy myself when I get to Liberty. I am sorry to hear that Worthy has not stopped jumping yet. I can not see what we are to do with him. I was in hopes that I would have a chance to ride him when I got home but you know Ma would never consent for me to ride him if there was the least danger.

Pa this is my sixteenth birthday. I have but five more years in which I can call myself a boy. And if I keep as busy during that time as I am in hopes I shall do, they will seem but one. It causes anything but pleasant feelings to think that I am approaching manhood so briskly. But I have no reason to complain if I spend my future life in as much happiness as I have my past. I could ask for no better.

Give my love to Aunt and tell her that I am very anxious to see her. Tell Tah that he must prepare himself if you have any good jokes to tell on him. Kiss Helen and Ma.

Bee *

The next letter was from Shattee to her friend Betty Day, who was still in school in Huntsville. They were not sisters, but Shattee thought of her as a sister because they were such close friends.

Liberty May 22nd 1857

My Dear Betty,
. . . Dull as is this little benighted town, "The Comet" is creating some excitement. We hear of our becoming crazy on the subject of its coming in collision with this "mundane Sphere." We must be living in the wilds and very superstitious at that ! [11]
. . . We have at last sixteen cows up. Make butter to use. John rides Worthy after cattle. He still jumps and is very wild—considering that he was once gentle.

Pa is having lumber sawed to build a dining room and kitchen which will make the house large enough for the present. . . .

George is shearing the sheep today, what few there is left. The wolves very nearly destroyed them. . . .

W. Dugat is pilot on the *Betty Powell* which is now making semi-weekly trips. She gets cotton every trip. Wagons are constantly coming in and going out.

. . . Liberty is nearly equal to Huntsville in point of the number of saloons, gunsmiths, jewelers, barbers—also a market. Tis true it has no penitentiary.

All send love, nothing more this time.

Your affectionate Sister,
Kaleta *

She had outgrown her baby name of Shattee and signed herself "Kaleta" now. Jim Wrigley, whose brother John married Sarah Hardin, began a four-horse stagecoach service meeting Thomas Peacock's *Betty Powell* three times a week when the side-wheeler came up from Galveston to Liberty. It took the mail up to Crockett. Wrigley boasted that letters regularly made the trip in forty-five hours. Liberty was growing by leaps and bounds.

There have been several references to the Baker family in Huntsville. Bee would soon attend the funeral of Daniel Baker, the founder of Austin College. Bee boarded at the house of Mrs. Mosely Baker, Daniel's daughter-in-law. There was another son, the Reverend William M. Baker, who had become a spiritualist and later on published a spiritualist newspaper in Houston called *The True Evangelist*. The mania of spiritualism swept the United States in the mid-1850s. It began with the unexplained raps on the walls of the house of Mrs. Fish in New York City, where her little daughter said one rap meant "No" and three raps meant "Yes." Mrs. Hayden of Boston carried the mania on to "possession," including the wonders of trancespeaking and involuntary dancing.[12] In Huntsville, a "Colonel Hay" had joined a "spirit circle" and desired divine revelation, but apparently table tipping and hearing phantom voices was as far as he got. The "politics" that Bee was caught up in in the next letter to Kaleta were the fugitive slave law and the general future of slavery in Texas:

Huntsville, May 29, 1857

Dear Sister,

. . . the idea of getting home counteracts everything else. Politics seem to be the order of the day here at present. . . . Mrs. Murray requested me to write to you to come and stay with her if you came to Huntsville . . . I suppose you could not be better situated.

Col. Hay has turned spiritualist. He holds meetings here every night very nearly. I have not heard whether he has made any converts or not. They say he is completely changed. He appears to be a strong believer. I don't think from what I can hear that he gets the spirits started very often. . . .

Bee *

June 1st 1857

Dear brother,

. . . Suppose you are studying hard for the examination. Always let "excelsior" be your motto, and climb slow but steady the hill of science.

Mrs. O.J. Shelby has at last moved to Liberty. Tis like the Jews rebuilding Jerusalem—all the old inhabitants returning to the "Diggins" where they have experienced alike so many joys and so many sorrows—may the change remain pleasant to them!

Is Huntsville improving any at present? Jim [Paine] would scarcely know Liberty, at least after they get the new Courthouse built which will equal the one in Huntsville. . . .

See Jack [Williams] once and a while. He does not mix with the beaumonde much. Suppose the study of his legal profession engages a great portion of his time. If it does not it should, as to acquire any eminence, study we must. If the mind is spirited that sprightlyness should be cultivated. If to the contrary, it takes more application. . . .

Your affectionate Sister,
Kaleta *

Jim Paine was the slave who was driver and carpenter. He later married Harriet Hobbs. At this time he had been hired out to Mrs. Baker in Huntsville. The next fall he would accompany Frank to Austin as body servant and courier.

Aunt Harriet and her children lived at Seven Pines. Harriet was very sure of herself and had great dignity. She called herself Harriet Evans, but her children took their fathers' names—Henry *Rowe*, Calvin and Melinda *Green*, etc. Harriet became the family historian because she lived to be over ninety years old and could always recount how the various people were related, not only where they lived up and down the river, but whose blood they had in their veins. In her last years she continued to live in a house in back of Seven Pines with her granddaughter Lizzie and Lizzie's husband.

Many of the slaves of the Hardins and O'Briens enjoyed a special status in the respective families. Back in Louisiana Ann O'Brien had Tom, Maria, and Victor, plus lesser lights like Levi. On his plantation Frank had Myra as cook, and her two children, Richard and Emma. Jim Paine was a good worker, but the man in whom Frank had greatest confidence was John, the cowman and sailor. If John were in charge of a cattle drive, Frank knew the cows would get to market and the money would get back to him. Frank had owned John for twenty years, and after a lingering fever that ended in the slave's death, it was with great sadness that Frank buried John in the black section of the family cemetery (Ap. 26).

Monday night Oct. 19th '57

Well Bee,

Some bad news to write. Alas! John died yesterday afternoon. We buried him today. We all feel like we had lost a friend. He came home three weeks ago yesterday from a cow drive with a fever which continued until it took him off. The Drs. say it was Tiphoid fever. . . .

I wrote to Shattee last week and sent her in the letter $30 to bring her home via Houston. I hope she has received the money. You have heard no doubt of the great money panic north and the sudden fall in cotton. I see it's extending south. Some of the southern banks have suspended payment tho there is no fears here that any of the banks south will break. I think I sent Shattee New Orleans money. I have some fears that she may have some difficulty in getting it off in traveling. They have confidence in it here, for your Uncle Blackburn exchanged today some New Orleans money for gold, tho I know that the further you go into the interior the less confidence the people will have in any paper money. . . .

Goodbye my children
F. Hardin *

In those days paper money was backed by gold and you could exchange it at the bank for gold coins. Each bank was allowed to publish its own individual specie, and was allowed to make a decision whether or not to pay off the specie. Frank thought there was no danger in a New Orleans bank refusing to pay, but country people in the interior of Texas only needed to hear of a panic to refuse any paper money. There were no federal regulations to keep the prices of commodities up. A sudden fall in commodities could wipe out many investors.

Kaleta was back at Andrew College in Huntsville. As frequently happens with teenagers, these wished to be called by new nicknames. Bee was referred to as "Lun." Mimmie was sometimes called "Spin" and more often "Pet." She received that name at the branch of the Ursuline Convent which had now opened in Liberty and where she had enrolled. One of the teachers, Mother St. Ambrose, thought that in spite of Mimmie's delicate looking exterior, she had a core of steel, and called her "*Pétal de Métal*," which her friends shortened to "Pet." Cynthia was still called "Nannie" or sometimes "Nance." To people she wanted to impress, Shattee was "Kaleta." The baby name of Tah had been discarded by the younger son who was now "Chris" or "Christy." Helen, the baby, was called "Pep." Frank was now in Austin serving in the legislature, and he did not come home for Christmas.

> Town of Liberty
> Christmas Eve [1857]

Dear Lun,

Pet and Nannie have their stockings hung ready for "Santa Claus." Guess he'll reward them. Chris is out shooting fire crackers; is enjoying himself finely. The darkies are in fine glee. Henry [Rowe] is as noisey as ever. Martha has a fever so not enjoying it much. We don't anticipate much fun tomorrow. We will have a turkey and some egg nog. Mrs. Mosely [Baker] ought to treat you to something extra being it's Christmas.

. . . They say some [weddings] will take place in our town soon: Cornelia [Hardin] and [Jeremiah] Van Deventer, Fannie DeBlanc and Jefferson Chambers, Memie LaCour and Jerome DeBlanc, Jr. We'll have enough of fun when all the above mentioned matrimonial alliances take place. Don't seem to be any chance for Phil [Smith] or Absolom. Jack Williams has been sick for three or four weeks, lingering fever and chills is the complaint. And I have not seen him since my arrival at the "great Town of Liberty." Wonderful is it not!

> Shattee *

Absalom was a nickname for one of the Smiths, who were neighbors of the Frank Hardins. Shattee referred to one of them as Absalom because, like King David's son, he was always rebellious. Jack Williams was the son of Judge Williams, who had to run out of Texas in 1835 for supporting the Mexican side. Judge Williams had married Margaretta Dugat, who stayed behind in Liberty with the children. Williams did not return except for William Hardin's funeral, and he was ultimately called upon to meet the obligation of his "marriage contract and bond" by deeding over seven slaves worth five thousand dollars to Margaretta. There had been three children by that marriage: Laura, Jack, and Watson Dugat Williams. Margaretta then married Dr. Stanwood and produced Eugenie, who soon appears in the letters and who ultimately took Bee as her second husband.

Shattee was having so much fun that frivolity hid the fatalistic, self-blaming, and escapist side of her. When she met George Davis, she was as attracted as much by his literary bent as he was by her beauty, dazzling wit, dignity, and legal turn of mind. Although she covered it up with defiance, in her heart she rejected all the beaux. She felt a lot of pressure, but naturally her father was unaware of this. Only Bee sensed that she was lonely in the midst of people.

In the Texas legislature, Frank was made chairman of the Committee on the General Land Office.[13] He sponsored an act defining the duties of county surveyors, favored the one plainly marking the boundary lines between "the State of Texas and the U.S.," and one for better protection of the frontier. This legislature also established the University of Texas and the first state institutions for the handicapped. It passed an act permitting "free persons of African descent to select a master and become a slave." This was one way to circumvent freedmen from being harassed. Strict laws were enacted to regulate treatment and mobility of blacks. Frank wanted more liberties for them.

The new year brought with it a very rainy January. Frank was concerned about how he would get across the river back to Liberty when the legislature adjourned.

From Austin—Legislature in session
January 29, 1858

My dear Cynthia,

I have not received a letter from home either and I suppose on account of high water.

I am in hopes of leaving the 8th or 9th [of February] if not before. The legislature is still squabbling about the final adjournment. We have a bill before the House for an appropriation for clearing the snags from the Trinity below Liberty. When that is disposed of I shall feel at liberty to leave but if it continues to rain I expect to have an awful time getting home. The fact is the river may be so high that it cannot be passed. It is now almost impossible for the stages to get through.

I am beginning to feel extremely anxious about my home business. I am fearful that our next year's supplies will fall short if I am not at home soon, but we must submit to fate. Come what will, I reckon there is no danger of starvation. I set out to write only a few lines. I don't feel like spinning a long yarn about nothing. As the time approaches to go home, I feel more and more restless.

Goodbye to all,
F. Hardin *

All his life Frank had sedulously avoided political office because of the vicious name-calling (Ap. 20) the politicians indulged in. He had overcome his repugnance and agreed to serve in the legislature because he was so anxious for surveying laws to be revised and for stringent laws to be passed to stop the harassment of free Negroes.

Frank stayed on in Austin as long as there was hope of passing the Trinity navigation bill. He was still there on February 20 when a surprise tribute was paid to him by the House. A bill was passed to make a new county out of the east part of Liberty and the west part of Jefferson counties:

> The following limits . . . shall constitute the county of Hardin, named in honor of the Hardins of Liberty. The county seat thereof shall be called Hardin.

There was a tiny post office by that name on Milton's survey near the northwest corner of the Big Thicket. The community was expected to grow because a railroad was projected to pass through it. Bee and Shattee were especially proud of having a county named for their family.

CHAPTER EIGHT

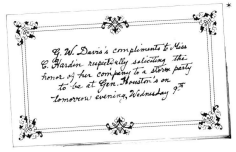

* THE HARDIN CHILDREN continued to develop distinct personalities and pride themselves on being unconventional. Shattee became even closer to Bee, who outwardly seemed less timid with girls than he had been earlier. His grades were excellent in Latin, math, philosophy, chemistry, and church history; a bit lower in speech and composition. Mimmie ("Pet") had developed a strong desire to learn French at Mother St. Ambrose's Convent School in Liberty. No doubt Frank had told her that the Hardins were originally French Huguenots named Hardouin from Rouen.[1]

Another French connection was the arrival from Louisiana of Uncle Charles O'Bryan and his French wife, Felide Salles, who settled at Magnolia Grove, a plantation east of Liberty. Charles and Felide had ten children. He was six-foot-four and loved to hunt the 200- to 400-pound black bears that roamed the Big Thicket. The way he did it was to have his black, Uncle Amos, pole him through the swamps in a pirogue at night, both wearing fire-pans on top of their heads to shine the bear's eyes. Bears fed on acorns in the fall, and the trick was to find a bear on a tree branch overhanging the bayou trail. One cold night Charles fired at a pair of eyes overhead, the kick of the gun knocking him backwards onto Amos. Amos hung onto the pole as the pirogue shot forward and floated under the branch just as the wounded animal released his grip and fell into it. Charles somersaulted into the water and he and Amos clung to the pole until the bear was through thrashing about. Finally, they dared climb back into the boat and head home with meat for the pot and up to twenty gallons of fine oil to be rendered.

This was 1860—the year Charles O'Bryan sold his Louisiana plantation, supposedly for $50,000.[2] He later claimed he could have sold it to a Yankee for gold but that he preferred to sell it to a Southern friend and take Confederate money on the installment plan. In Texas, he behaved like a "grand seigneur," entertaining lavishly and, during the Civil War, opening his home to an unending stream of refugees. Mimmie and Shattee also visited Wash O'Brien in Beaumont, where he had moved from Bolivar. His father and Cave Johnson had planted an oak tree in front of his house. It grew to be the largest oak in the State of Texas and finally had its own little concrete-enclosed island in the middle of a big paved street.[3] It was called the "O'Brien Oak" and reminded people of the way the family had proliferated in Texas.

As the town of Liberty began a new decade in its young history, it was changed forever by the construction from Beaumont of the Texas and New Orleans railroad. The tracks ran through the south side of Liberty, just one block south of Seven Pines, bringing jobs and fancy merchandise with them. The bridge across the Trinity was a major construction job. Within a year the railroad was complete from Houston to Orange, on the Louisiana border. This is the way Shattee described it to Bee:

Liberty, Feb. 8th, 1860

Mon cher frère,

The depot is not yet commenced. The hands are grading on the east and west side of the Trinity. The people chose Dr. [Gus] Loving's field as a proper place for a depot. The superintendents of the road say the cars will be through Liberty by April. They will run on "Eclat St.", the cognomen given to the one between here and Ed [Jones]'s by Phil Smith.

. . . Since Amanda [Wynne] left it seems an age. So dull! During two weeks we had company every eve: Mssrs [Phil] Smith, [A. B.] Trowell, two [Jim and John] Skinners, [Gus] Preacher . . . . Johnnie Laurie seemed to be quite fascinated with Miss Wynne. She also became the possessor of Absolom and Phil's ambrotypes. Trowell occupied the better part of two days endeavoring to get his uneven phiz passably conveyed to glass. But alas! the attempt was unavailing. It came out very semi—resembling a thunder cloud in hue and a misery-stricken wretch in expression. Phil, strutting like a turkey gobbler when "Lord of the Seraglio" came out with his arms extended, eyebrows raised, his high intellectual forehead bearing quite an important part in the fiasco of features. Amanda could not persuade Skinner to spend the almighty three dollars for his. Then Pet, after some wringing, teasing, entreating, and at last tear dropping, exacted a promise that she should have his. But I tell her I am afraid he'll come on me for the cash, being I am her sister. John Skinner has never paid me a visit since that eventful Sunday afternoon he spent from dinner till dark.

Fred Kimber has returned from college. Wonder if the study of the classics has polished him. Pet pronounces the idea of anything improving him "outré." Mimmie has finished herself a dress, and today is cutting my "silik" as [Wm] Meyer [merchant] says.

Phil, from all I can hear, is not improving. He still makes the ten-pin alley his resting place at odd times. Gus went up home today cow-driver like, riding homeward. Pa has gone up-country. Christy goes to school very regularly now.

Mrs. Branch has possession of Wright, tooth and toe-nail yet.

So now be it.
Shattie *

Phil Smith had become an alcoholic. That was why he made the ten-pin alley his resting place. When Gus Preacher arrived home, "cow-driver like," that meant that he was very stuck-up, cocky, and carefree, the way cattle drivers were after they had sold a herd. He was swaggering over his conquests of girls.

Liberty, Feb. 25, 1860

Lun,

As toll the days away in their rapid course, human events pass with them human actions, ending in fiasco. Petty ills and great ones all sink into oblivion, and what happened yesterday is forgotten in today's bliss or misery. I for one am in a state of blissful recollection of yester-days, as there is nothing exciting enough today to sink into the night of chaos of the past.

Sallie [Hardin] and [Ab] McMurtry were married [at her father Blackburn's plantation] . . . . Miss Leanna [Johnston] and Mr. Jimmy

McMurtry were the waiters [attendants]. The ladies looked exceed-
ingly well. Jimmy is a perfect Apollo. He and Miss L. perhaps, are in
love with each other. Miss Leanna's first attempt at the tender passion
surely. "There's nothing half so sweet in life as love's young dream".
. . . We all went to the wedding. Had quite a nice supper. Plenty of
champagne, also plenty to try its effects. Phil was the only gent from
town. Fortunately for the expectations of Liberty, he "touched-not,
looked-not, handled-not."

Uncle Charles and family arrived last Wednesday week. They are
snugly ensconced at home on the prairie wide . . . . Found them all
well and tolerably satisfied.

Mr. [A. B.] Trowell has a brother from Tennessee on a visit, Tom,
about twenty years of age, much better looking than A. B., but not
near so intelligent . . . . Pet had a gallanting spell with him. You know
report is she had a great predilection for the name . . . . Evening spent
in conversing. You may know that my tongue gave out early in the
action. Pet talks more than she used to.

Liberty is the same, only filled with drunken Irishmen, hands on
the railroad . . . . Christy, after the wedding, remained with Pa. They
will not be down until Sunday morning. Expect they will go turkey
shooting.

Chris Bryan has rented out the Hotel and is no longer a member of
the [Methodist] church. Left it because the church intended trying
him for keeping a grog shop.

Shattie *

The two sisters took turn about writing to Bee. Now it was Mimmie's turn.

Liberty, 8th March '60
Dear Lunny,
. . . Have not used my feet in a dancing capacity since I saw you
last, but once . . . . Do the Thespians still give entertainments in
Huntsville Institute? Of course you will have a commencement party
at the last of the sessions!

Jim Skinner is now in New Orleans purchasing spring goods resting
quietly in the bosom of the Methodist Church. Last "Distracted Meeting" saw him abandon the world and its ways. I think it is better for
him, only [I] will have to get a new partner for euchre.

Phil in status quo except he is getting tight every night—all think him a gone case, poor fellow. Such a pity that he should drink.

Jeff [Chambers] and Mimmie [Eleanore, Phil Smith's sister] are navigating the sea of life without a <u>ripple</u> as <u>yet</u>, to mar their happiness. Mr. Trowell is "still one of us" although he intends starting to Tennessee soon—about the 1st of April—with brother Tom.

I will send you two Gavettres—notice "Jamais" production. We recognize the author in the person of Ben Wrigley. I thought he was a better writer having been an editor. Kaleta and I take two papers and a magazine: *New York Ledger*, *Harper's Weekly* and *Monthly* (not at a loss for something to read).

Court [at Liberty] will be in session Monday week. Then I hope to have a lively time.

Prof. Wright intends building a school house. Don't think he is as fond of the Branches as formerly . . . . Divers reports are floating about concerning Bettie [Branch] and [Prof.] Wright[4]—some in which the words "marriage-engagement" and such like are prominent. Others say Bet was fickle. I is for rather the old lady [Mrs. Branch, Bettie's mother]. For the life of me I can't tell which is right, but suppose the latter.

It is supposed the [railroad] cars will be here in 6 or 7 weeks. The embankment between here and the river is finished, passing through the street south of us.

All send love,
Spin [Mimmie] *

Hopkins Cottage, April 23, 1860

Lunnie dearie;

. . . Heard from you through Mr. [George] Davis, who saw one of your classmates— . . . He now winds his way to Wallisville, business the cause of his trip. While here he was inspirably entertained at the "Owls' Nest" by us worthy proprietors who accompanied him there . . . .

Gus [Preacher], Pet, Mr. Trowell and myself went mulberrying last week . . . . We had a turkey. Suppose you can devine the cause of Mr. T's visit for a day.

We have just received tickets to a party given at the Liberty Hall. . . . The one given at the City Hotel was pronounced a brilliant success by all. Had ladies from Beaumont who came on the cars to within twelve miles of Liberty—a number of ladies whose husbands are connected with the railroad. Among them a Miss Truesdale, who is quite pretty. She boards at the Planters Hotel—which is kept in style. Price of board per day is $2 ½, living excellent, so they say. I tell you, Lun, Liberty is coming out! . . .

Shattee *

"Hopkins Cottage" was the old house, now used by the teenagers. The Owls' Nest was their tree house, where they discussed macabre and forbidden subjects. Trowell was Mimmie's beau, and he gave her a green silk dress and proposed just after this. She turned him down and he married another girl. He was not intelligent enough and did not have enough strength of character to suit Mimmie. She began to like George Davis.

In the next letter Mimmie, though younger than Bee, took a bossier tone with him than did Shattee, and Mimmie prided herself on being devilish. The railroad tracks had reached Kindallis Bryan's property just east of Liberty.

May 9, 1860

Dear Lun,

. . . Suppose you intend graduating this June. Take care now and do our ancient house no dishonor, else you'll be turned out as a vagabond. Think you'll turn Lawyer, and stick up a shingle on some corner of some town? and thereby, be the means of salvation for the widows and orphans? . . . Probably, "young-America-like," you'll wish to marry and present Kaleta and I with a lovely sister-in-law! You'll have to remove the darling from our reach, as you know of our love of convention. Turn merchant and go halves with the Skinner boys? Mine and Kaleta's influence will secure you the place. . . .

The cars are at Cousin King's—will be here this week.

Sorry to tell you of the death of Jack Williams—every one had despaired of his living—even his own family. Died in West Liberty day before yesterday, where he had gone, thinking the change would improve him. Had been sinking ever since he left. Was buried there at, I suppose, a family burying ground.

Don't know as any of us will go to Huntsville soon, although I would give a fourth of my existence to be at the Commencement. . . .

Pa wishes to know how much money you need, as he wishes you to settle all accts. before leaving.

Your affectionate sister,
Mimmie *

Dear Bee,

. . . There is a fishing party at "Gum Lake"[†] tomorrow. Miss Mary Smith is on a visit from Galveston. Suppose it is a "complimentary benefit". . . .

Liberty is quite crowded with strangers now, tho' the Railroad Company Irish and all are at Beaumont.

Gus [Preacher] is to give you a description of the Branch vs. Wright case when you come down. Tis a <u>rich</u> affair from beginning to end. <u>More</u> are in the <u>stir</u> than you think. But the Prof. stands higher in the estimation of the Citizens than when engaged to the <u>delectable</u> Betsy Branch [age sixteen]. The Lady Branch has had <u>Wharton</u> [twelve-year-old son] carrying a gun to protect her as she says the Judge would <u>not</u>—Mrs. Stone's [divorcee] stock is below <u>par</u>. She retains her predilection for the <u>same one</u> [Professor Wright]. I think he has somewhat changed for the better.

Gus has gone home to spend a few days of retirement from "amidst the hustle and shock of men," to dream of Lizzie more likely. Rumor says they are engaged. . . .

Kaleta Hardin *

Huntsville, May 29th, 1860

Dear Mimmie,

. . . I was very busily engaged preparing for our examination which came off yesterday . . . . There were very few to hear us. I suppose I will get my "Sheep-Skin," but I shall say to my friends "Approach very near for I am still one of your number." I would like very much to go home before Commencement. . . .

Kaleta tells me that you have a new supply of beaux on hand. You will probably succeed in getting her out of your way now. She seems to have her mind directed toward Mr. [George] Davis at present but that is very likely a flirtation. He spoke rather lovingly about her when he was here last. . . .

Gus says that he pays very little attention at all to the girls; did not hint that he was in love. I do not want him to marry yet.

The Wright difficulty seems to be creating considerable excitement. Liberty is improving in every respect. It must be quite a lively place

---

[†] This lake was filled with tupelo gum trees.

indeed. The old [Branch] lady's rage has been no doubt terrible in the highest degree. . . .

Give my love to "all inquiring friends."

W. F. Hardin [Bee] *

Bee wanted to go home before Commencement because he was so worried about secession. It was all his roommate, Bill Storey from Caldwell, Texas, talked about. Frank sided with Sam Houston, saying that Texas should not secede. Shattee, out of defiance, was strongly in favor, so much so that she did not wish to accompany George Davis to the "Storm Ball" given for anti-secessionists at Governor Houston's house in Huntsville.[†] Mimmie went in her place.

Frank devoted most of his time to his farm. He loved to take the girls, as well as his sons, on duck shoots to ponds on outlying lands he owned. Each child also had his own horse and saddle. The girls rode sidesaddle when there was company involved. Cynthia still enjoyed riding with Frank. He had increasingly voluminous correspondence with people who wanted his advice on land trades, and he was also executor for several estates:

Paris, Tex., Nov. 26, 1860

Col Frank Hardin,

Dr. Snow of Honey Grove having learned that I have been requested to act as your agent in the transaction of certain business pertaining to the sale of Mr. Tilton's lands, called on me a few days ago to ascertain whether I have any recent communications from you relating to the transaction and more especially relative to a deficiency in the survey, of which probably he had notified you. He seemed very desirous that I should address you upon the subject as he wishes the transaction should terminate soon—that he may know how to arrange the improvement of the same land adjoining. As to the reported deficiency, I know nothing except that our county surveyor who executed the work is a very reliable man and would not intentionally commit an official fraud. I wrote you immediately upon receipt of yours requesting me to act as agent informing you that I would serve you. Please write me soon. I will take pleasure in attending to your request as far as I can.

Very respectfully,
E. J. Shelton *

[†] See sketch at beginning of chapter.

The new year dawned with terrible political events. One by one, the Southern states began to secede from the Union. Jeff Davis was elected president of the Confederacy on February 9. During this time of hopeful waiting and fearful tension, George Davis wrote calmly to his newly married sister, Sallie, from his family home in Walker County. Sallie had lost her heart to the Methodist circuit rider, Thomas Wooldridge, even though he was her mother's age and had three children by his first wife. George had hoped for a better marriage for his sister, but gave his consent rather than see her heart ache. In George's letter words like "lugubrious" and "sorrowful" and "dead past bury its dead" show how he felt about it.

Mt Prospect, Jany. 12th 1861

Dear sister,

I am again at the old homestead, but alas—all are here except you! In vain does memory of numberless happy greetings from you upon the event of past visits to "the old folks at home" well up in my bosom and for a moment shed light of pleasure over my lugubrious spirits.— "Thou are gone!" It is written in every nook and corner—in the face of our sad mother and silent-thinking father—the whole household, the very framework in its loneliness echoing the solemn sorrowful thought. Had I known how deeply your absence would be felt and mourned I scarcely believe "my consent" could have been given so readily as it was. But "let the dead past bury its dead" if possible. It is with the present always that we have to deal.

I reached here on last night after supper, having come via Waverly. The surprise was as complete as I ever made it[†] . . . . We all rejoice together to know of your safe peregrinations, health and happiness in the [Methodist] "Modern Circuit." That you are not wholly a stranger in a strange land that is rather more than we had expected:—May you continue to find acquaintances and eventually to make friends.

Sam Keeland has called and told us the whole story without dismounting (as is his custom). Priscilla and her father and mother [neighbors] have been over and also spent some time. The other nearer neighbors have visited mother oftener. Though upon the whole from what I can gather she has not been oppressed by calls either of the *bon ton* or the backwoods style. But nevertheless she seems to endure the solitude of Mt Prospect better than you might guess. There

---

[†] George enjoyed surprising his mother by quietly putting his horse in the barn and tiptoeing through the back door and into the room she was in.

has been so much typhoid fever in the vicinity it may account for the paucity of her visitors.

I prevailed on mother to try Larkin, by riding over to Mrs. Chance's this evening, which she did. He is the very thing for her and as soon as I can so arrange I will send him over from Livingston for her special riding animal. The exercise on horseback seems to have eased her head. Since supper she complains but very little.

I spent Christmas day at Mrs. Tooke's—had a splendid dining— really aristocratic affair—enjoyed myself over syllabub and a discussion of the doctrine of state secession. Today a week since I went to Moscow [Texas] to speak upon this subject in case our candidate H. Maxcy, should be opposed by Dr. Paul Livingston. The doctor however refused to speak and I was out of place so called on Mrs. Johnson [Wooldridge cousin]. She insists that you have enslaved her cousin! Sends you many wishes for happiness etc. and just here did I attempt to mention all those who professed a similar interest in your welfare I should have to fill another sheet. When you come down Mother will relate to you.

All join me in love to you and Mr. Wooldridge. Tell him I shall be pleased to have a chance at his business. You can write as previously— just whenever you please. I must leave in the morning.

Your Bro
George W. Davis[5]

Before George left, he wrote to his father's aunt in Florida the news of Sallie's marriage to Thomas Wooldridge, who had come to Texas back in 1841 and had served in Robertson's Company during the Indian problems. He had once chased four Indian braves who had kidnapped a little brother and sister and murdered the girl.[6] George liked the man and all he stood for. In his letter, George had rambled on about his own ethical principles and enjoyment of social events. His Cousin Carrie responded.

Monticello, Florida
Mar. 16, 1861

My dear Cousin George,
Your letter was received. . . .
The family did not care if you were not a business man, etc. I did hope that you were one of those who never indulged in eggnog, champagne, etc.

So Cousin Sally has married a preacher! and a widower!

Do you know that you have the honor of being related to President Davis? Cousin William Davis can tell you all about it. I think he was a little proud of the relationship two years ago and I suppose he will be still more so now.

I know Aunt [Sarah Davis] must be lonely since Cousin Sally's marriage. Mother's health is as good as usual.

She joins me in love,

Yours truly,
Carrie Clark[7]

In accepting pretty Sallie's marriage, George showed he was accustomed to making the best of a bad situation. Mimmie on the contrary had everything her way. She loved to travel, and back in the fall of 1858 she, Shattee, and their mother had gone to visit in Franklin, Louisiana. From there they had taken a boat to New Orleans where Shattee and Cynthia alighted to buy things for the new Seven Pines, but Mimmie continued on the boat to Ocean Springs, Mississippi, to visit Lydia, a friend of Aunt Serena's who took in paying guests. There she met a brother and sister from New Orleans who were there to escape the fever season. They were Clem Schneider, who was exactly Mimmie's age, and her brother Louis, six years older and working as bookkeeper in his family's New Orleans grocery store. Soon Louis was called back to his ledgers, daybooks and journals, only to find a new assistant sharing the high desk in the back of Schneider and Wise. The sixteen-year-old girls stayed on the beach and became close friends. A week later the pompous Louis wrote to his sister:

New Orleans, October 16, 1858
Saturday evening

Dear Clementine,

. . . True, I have read the newspapers and accidently noticed amongst the many advertisements, the one issued by the superintendent of the First District Schools. It was a Want for a principal for the Girls High School to fill the vacancy occasioned by Mrs. Wilson's (Miss Loughery) resignation. I then subsequently saw it announced that your former teacher and friend Miss Perry had been honored with the Station.

I forgot to mention to Mimmie that Mr. J. E. Fischer and whole family have been, ever since our departure for the West, located at

Biloxi. Mr. F. came to the city about a week ago and remained a few hours, he visited us at our store and requested me to present to Mimmie the respects of both Mme. Fischer and himself—they will only return to the city when they know that the Yellow Fever has been deprived of its power and dwindled into mist.

Mr. Auguste Blaffer is now in our employ and will in future be an assistant at the Books—during the few days he has been with us he expressed his satisfaction and delight with this kind of business and is willing to make an engagement with us for one or two years.

Since my visit at Shakespear's [later mayor of New Orleans], I have not seen them, but will call on them again very soon, perhaps tomorrow evening.

I must not forget to tell you that I am the fortunate owner of a pair of slippers you had intended for Father—they were too small for him, and he presented them to me.

A few days ago Father gave me the Five Dollar bill that I now enclose and requested me to give you his love and that this little sum was a contribution to your Pin Money.

Mr. Wise [business partner] wishes me to remember him to you, and from me you will receive my love for Mimmie and yourself, and present Lydia with many good wishes from your Brother.

Adieu

Louis *

Auguste Blaffer was delighted with his job and stayed on, with the exception of a year out for war duty, until he married Clem Schneider, his boss's daughter.[8] Mimmie's friendship with Clem continued after the war.

After the railroad was completed to Orange in 1860, Mimmie very much wanted to ride the new cars there and take the new fast boat from Orange to Berwick, where she would entrain again to New Orleans. Frank finally agreed that she should go and visit Aunt Virginia Collins and the O'Bryan cousins in New Orleans. Mimmie was lucky to make the trip because the war soon cancelled all pleasure travel. New Orleans fell to the Yankees in the spring of 1862. There are no Hardin letters between Bee's graduation in June 1860 and February 1862, when his second period of enlistment began.

William Franklin "Bee" Hardin (1841–1898) graduated from Austin College in 1860. Became a judge after the war; finally married Eugenie Stanwood.

Christopher O'Brien "Tah" Hardin (1846– 1866) served in C.S.A. Brother of Bee, Mimmie, Nan, Shattee and Pep.

George Washington Davis (1836–1897) son of John I. and Sarah; arrived in Texas at age fourteen. Practiced law in Livingston and Galveston before moving to Dallas.

Camilla G. "Mimmie" Hardin (1842–1926) daughter of Cynthia and Frank; attended Ursuline in Liberty and Andrew Institute in Huntsville. Married George W. Davis.

Myra, born c. 1828, purchased from R. W. Gayle, with her daughter Emma, born 1845. She was the cook on Frank Hardin's plantation.*

Aunt Mary Cottontail, belonged to Ann Brien in Louisiana until she came to serve Cynthia Hardin in Liberty.*

Aunt Mary Iredell. Surname indicates she was from Louisiana. *

Henry Rowe, son of Aunt Harriet Evans, father of Lizzie. He planted the seven pines and spent his long life with the Hardins. *

*Harriet Hobbs Paine,
child of Violet Hobbs. Accompanied Mimmie on
move to Mount Prospect in
1869.**

*Maria Nashville, born in
1853 to Rehoden and Jane
Nashville, who were part of
the Saunders Hardin
household. She was born in
Alabama.**

CHAPTER NINE

Eugenie at Hempstead

LIKE MANY OF HIS FRIENDS, Bee enlisted for a six-month hitch in E. B. Nichol's regiment, where he held the rank of lieutenant. After that he was recruited by Jim Wrigley to join T. N. Waul's Second Battalion of the Texas Legion, which was assembling in Galveston. The horror of war hit home when Dugat Williams swung off the cars in Liberty just after the news had arrived of John Wrigley's death in the army in Virginia. He had brought the body home. "The Masonic fraternity with a large concourse of citizens"[1] turned out in the drizzling rain, along with the young widow, Sarah, and the Hardins.

Cynthia, who did not care about secession or states' rights or whether the remuneration for freed slaves was the responsibility of the government, or about any political arguments, was wondering how to get the safest place in the army for her eldest son. As they left the cemetery, she slipped some money for Bee into Jim Wrigley's pocket.

Early on, the port of Galveston was blockaded by Union ships to keep cotton from going out and supplies for the civilians from coming in. A sizable force of Confederate troops was posted there to keep the Union army from planning an invasion with a small force. Pelican Spit and Fort Pointe were two of the military installations on the island. Commander Leon Smith was making himself a reputation that later on put him in charge of the navy at Galveston. With a big sack of sausage and potatoes, Bee took the train as far as Houston, and on arrival in Galveston, wrote to Cynthia:

Galveston, Feb. 9th 1862

Dear Mother,

I did not have time to write by the first mail, I was so busy getting my things from the depot to camp, which I did not succeed in doing until Monday. I had very little trouble with them in Houston. Got a wagon from the Q.M. to haul them from one depot to the other. I stopped at the Soldier's Home and fared tolerably well. There has been an order issued stopping furloughs for the present. I suppose the expedition [First Texas Cavalry] that is fitting out in N.O. is the cause. The [Union] blockaders have had some employment within the last few days, shelling two steamers that ran ashore near the City while attempting to get in. One is a total loss. The other, after the Yankees had fired a hundred or two shots at her and struck her once, got afloat and came safely in in spite of them. Com. Leon Smith was aboard the latter.

The 25th [Regiment, Texas Cavalry] has not come down from Houston yet. I sent a pair of saddle bags of Christy's [brother] over by Mr. [I. P.] Filkins [Lynchburg ferry boatman], also a letter. We have very comfortable barracks here about two miles from town. There are but three companies here. The rest are in town but will come out as soon as barracks are finished for them. We have been feasting on potatoes and sausages, have some on hand yet. I could not get any clothing in Houston. Have [received] drawers, a pair of shoes and socks since my arrival here.

Bee *

Fort Pointe   March 7th 1862

Dear Mimmie,

. . . The sausages and bacon came duly to hand and was very gladly received. . . . We were awakened yesterday morning about 4 o'clock by the firing of cannon at Pelican Spit and the report came that there had been an attack made there which proved to be false. The firing was at seven deserters who made good their escape. They went to the block-ading vessel. Most of them were on guard at the time. It has been the report here for several days that an order had come from the war department to disband all the twelve and six month men. I can't say how true it is.

I am getting quite fat. I think I am fleshier than I have been since I first left home. . . . There are but few officers down here and they keep me on duty about half the time.

I have left off reading novels for the present. . . . I looked at Allen's [Houston bookstore]. Could not find any of [Sir Walter] Scott to read there, though I could not have got them had they been there. We have had some amusement that I was about to forget: the theatre, which I have attended several times. The performances are passable. They played the "Traveler" a few nights since. If [B. F.] Norvell had been present he would have no doubt been highly pleased. . . .

Wm. F. Hardin *

Mrs. Sarah Davis did not have Cynthia's problem, as her son-in-law, Tom Wooldridge, was excused from going to war because he was a preacher, and her son, George, would not be conscripted because he did not have the use of the trigger fingers on his right hand. Even though George was against secession, feeling was so strong after the war began that he felt he must enlist to keep in favor with Shattee and other patriots.

When Sallie was confined toward the end of her first pregnancy, word was sent from Limestone County for Sarah to come. She set out in her carriage with her driver, John, and his wife, Tommy, to help Sallie for two months. On Sarah's return home, she wrote to her son:

Mount Prospect, March 19th 1862

Dear George,

. . . I got home a little over a week ago.

Found all well, except my garden. As I expected, everything was killed dead nearly. . . . Planted a great many seed, worked 3 or 4 days—made myself sick as usual, am getting better now.

I came home safe and sound with no other company but Tommy and John. Got home in two days and didn't stay all night with our old friend either. Left Sallie and her fine daughter doing tolerably well, the child has the thrush. Its name is plain Sarah Davis. . . .

George, sometimes I think I can stand it and then again I cannot. You know what I mean, your going to the war. I know that I am no better than other mothers but it will be hard for me to stand it if you do go. But with the help of God, I will try to do the best I can. Stephen [slave] says tell you, "Don't go," that you have but one hand and that is your left. You must remember that he wants to go with you and that he will stay close by your side.

Well, as to marrying, if you do of course I had rather it would be to someone that I know, but if she suits you and you love and marry her, I know that I will love her too. If you think you can make her happy and she you why, I say, "Marry, It's nobody's business but your own". . . .

Be sure to come at the appointed time.

Your Loving Mother SMD[2]

Like all the Davises, George had a cleft chin. He was a gangly youth with blondish, lank hair, a cool-blue, appraising eye, and a serious mouth from which issued an unending stream of rhetoric. As he was very close to his mother, he gave close attention to her counsel. He decided that if a uniform meant more to Shattee than the moral persuasion of its wearer, she was not the girl for him. Instead of going to war, he was elected district attorney of the Fifteenth District, which post he kept for three years.

A letter from Bee in the early summer of 1862 told about the election of officers in his regiment. In the early days of the war, they were voted in by the privates. This proved not to be a very good system because the most popular men were elected and they were not necessarily the best officer material. In his first six months' enlistment, Bee had been an officer and had a sword and a grey uniform. His sisters had been very disappointed in both his enlistments because he had not joined a cavalry regiment, and they thought all gentlemen went off to war on horses. Bee did own a horse befitting the cavalry, named Jim Miller, but had left him in the stable on their farm.

Camp Waul June 5th 1862

Dear Mother,

. . . We arrived safely in Houston about 9 o'clock Tuesday morning not sleeping a wink. We left there at 12 o'clock [by train] and arrived in Brenham about sundown.

There I met with Robert Hardin[3] . . . who told me to make his house my home while in Brenham. The two Tracys [Gibson and his son] and myself spent the night with him. He has two or three sons in the Army. I saw there the wife of Joseph Hardin who was on a visit. She favors very much Miss Fields—She must be her sister. I did not inquire. I suppose Pa knows.

I had an excellent night's sleep, making up for what I lost the night before. The next morning (yesterday) we started out on foot for Camp about 8 miles from Brenham. Our baggage was brought down on wagons. The most of us walked in without stopping ten minutes, in two hours and a half. I was fatigued but very little. I feel as well after it today as ever in my life. We have no tents yet. Our only shelter is a few brush sheds. There was a long train of wagons got in this evening. I think they have brought a number of tents. As long as this weather continues we will have no use for them. There are eighteen companies on the ground and I believe more to come. The command will be much larger than I had any idea it would be.

This is the most beautiful country I have ever seen. I shall not attempt to describe it. We are camped on a creek. There are a number of springs near us. The water is passable cool but tolerably limy. However, I think the locality must be a healthy one.

We had an election of Officers this morning. Mr. A. B. Trowell made Herculean efforts for the first lieutenantcy but failed. Wm. Dugat was elected by a handsome majority. We had to work hard to keep Trowell out. He begged votes on all sides. The other two officers are myself for second and Ed Jones for 3rd Lieut. Bill Skinner was my principal opponent. Trowell and he were working together. Bill asked almost every man in the Company to vote for him and begged some to nominate him for 3rd Lieut. if he was beaten for 2nd. Such men are not fit to fill any office. [B. F.] Sterling ran for first Lieut. He received but eleven votes. I suppose I must have my trunk which you will have an opportunity of sending as some of the Company will probably go home soon. I hardly know what I want. You may send several shirts and some handkerchiefs and what other things you think necessary. My cap and sword of course I must have. You may also send my Uniform coat but not the pants. I have no idea how long we will be here. No one seems to know anything about it. I think it will be at least two months.

Bee *

Bee was surprised and overjoyed at being elected 2nd Lieut; and more surprised that William Dugat was elected 1st Lieut. He and Bee were both ten years younger than A. B. Trowell or B. F. Sterling. Sterling

147

was married to Mary Jane Bryan, Bee's first cousin.[4] Bee's criticism of Trowell and Skinner reflected disapproval of their "politicking."

Before Cynthia received his letter, Shattee had written with the news that Mimmie was now busy decorating bonnets. As ribbons and flowers were no longer available in the stores, she used berries, walnut shells, gum balls, dried flowers, small palmetto leaves and scraps of material for the bows. Frank had let various army units have all but one of his horses as he and the slaves would be breaking more very soon.

June 6th 1862

Dear Bee:

We have not been very lonely since your departure. Ma has been quite cheerful. . . . Mimmie is now engaged in trimming a hat for Laura Bryan. Peppie is holding the ink for me, singing, "The eyes of her love." . . .

There is a fishing party given for the benefit of the soldiers tomorrow. We will not go. Mimmie is not able—and there will be but one horse.

John Guise and some others arrived last night from Nacogdoches bringing news that the Yankees 20,000 strong men were marching to Shreveport. Col. Ricks with the men mentioned have come for some cannon that are at Virginia Pt. [near Galveston]. They said, just before they left, Carter made a speech to his men saying that he expected to have 19,000 men to meet the enemy with—Pa says he don't believe that part.[5]

So at that rate you may have to leave Brenham immediately. Pa says let him know right away whether you can use a horse so that he may send you one. . . .

Present our regards to the gentlemen who stayed with us. Tell them we hope they done full justice to the provisions, specially the chickens. . . .

Shattee

[P.S.]

Mimmy says send her a lock of your hair in your next letter. Tell Mr. Yeagher that we deputize him to do the clipping. *

June 9th 1862

Dear Bee,

The Cars have just whistled. . . . Had church yesterday. Mr. Loomis officiated. His sermon was better than the Sunday you heard him.

Mimmie and I have been to call on the [Oscar] Farishes. Met his niece, Miss Green, found her quite a pleasant young lady. . . .

You know Uncle Blackburn went up with [son] Swan to Nacog-doches. I heard that they had returned and Swan had a discharge. Mr. Van [Deventer] and Mr. [Jim] McMurtry came back the other day. Suppose they came with Col. Rick after the cannon.

Did you hear—Mr. [J. N.] Dark was elected Major of the Battal-ion—and Militia Gen'l. [W. M.] Neyland the Lt. Col. So you see Capt. [E. B.] Pickett was knocked out entirely. He ran against Neyland for Lt. Col. They say that Dark could have beaten either one of them but he only aspired to Major.

Uncle Bagarly is down [from Cold Spring] for the purpose of buy-ing salt.

Shattee *

The Farishes were refugees from Galveston. Old Mr. Oscar Farish, a San Jacinto war veteran, was blind and his daughter was "puny." J. N. Dark was a member of the 25th Regiment, Texas Cavalry. This dashing officer courted Shattee and, like all petticoat patriots, she was crazy about cavalry officers. She spurned any civilian suitor, including George Davis.

Uncle Hezekiah Bagarley bought salt in Liberty, which was shipped in from Louisiana, and hauled it in his wagon back to Cold Spring. It was one of the first war-time scarcities and very much needed to pre-serve meat.

Captain William and Aunt Virginia Collins had left New Orleans for Texas when General Benjamin Butler first took over the city. They were lighted on their way out of town by the fires consuming the cotton and corn stores, which had been torched to keep them from falling into the hands of the Yankees. General Butler was accused of various thefts in the city including $800,000 from the Dutch consul's office. When some Confederate belles insulted some of his more aggressive soldiers, Butler had placards posted saying that any woman showing contempt of the U.S. soldiers was to be treated as a woman of the town plying her avocation.

Butler immediately closed the port of New Orleans, but there was no way to stop the blockade-running down the bayous, whose every trail, Indian trace, and overland shortcut between Louisiana and Texas were known to the O'Bryans, who enjoyed outwitting and outfighting and outmaneuvering any Yankees who tried to stop the trade. Captains Alfred Stevens and William Collins both tried their hand at blockade running. Another problem for the Southerners was the Yankees' attempt to ship slaves up East. To prevent this, slaves were being moved inland, away from the coast. Their masters brought quite a few of them all the way to Liberty.

A succession of letters from Bee Hardin contained much news about the men serving from Liberty.

Camp Waul, June 15, 1862

Dear Shattee,

. . . We have eleven tents about eight feet square, two to be occupied by the Officers. You can imagine how a hundred men would fare crowded into them! They are made of Huntsville towels which I think the rain will penetrate very easily.

We have built arbors which we occupy all together. Bill [Dugat], Ed [Jones] and myself have bought cloth enough to make us a fly for our tent by means of which we hope to keep dry during a rain. We have engaged Mrs. Bolling and Miss Eugenia [Stanwood] to make it. We have been living well since we got here. We buy eggs and butter cheap and have milk and vegetables given us when we send after it. Abe [Trowell] cooks for our mess. He goes round the country almost every day and brings in eatables. Our Mess is composed of the four officers, Dr. Chas. Brashear and Orderly Sergeant Robert John.

We have the pleasure every day of beholding members of the fair ladies of surrounding country who come to witness our evening parade. Miss Eugenia and Mrs. Bolling visited us yesterday. They speak of going to Independence Wednesday to attend the Commencement exercise of the Female School there. I should like very much to go myself but it will be hardly possible as we have a great deal of drilling to do. . . .

We have no arms and at present I can see no prospect of getting any soon. Though I hope we will be able to procure some of some description by the time we need them. Tell Pa I cannot tell now whether I will want a horse or not. Mr. Gibson Tracy will probably be at Liberty soon and I will get him to bring one up if it is necessary. . . . Tell Ma I have gotten a pair of shoes from the Quarter Master. I did not get any clothing in Houston but think I will be able to get what I want. Write often.

Wm. F. Hardin *

Camp Waul, June 23, 1862

Dear Shattee,

. . . We have just completed a reorganization of the Company which resulted quite differently from the former one. [B. F.] Sterling was elected first Lieut., Robert John 2nd, Ed Jones selected 3rd. There began a movement in a very short time after the first organization to bring about another and Capt. [Jim] Wrigley being very much opposed to Bill Dugat and myself procured an order from the Col. [Waul] declaring the election null and void. I am constrained to believe there has been an underhanded game played from the beginning. Capt. Wrigley told Wm. Dugat that he was at first dissatisfied with the result of the first election but after considering the matter he had come to the conclusion that he had as good officers as any in the Legion, told him to run again and that he would like for the organization to remain as it was. He went immediately to other members of the Company and told them that he would leave the Company if we were elected. That will give you some idea of how things have been carried on.

I can assure you that I feel perfectly comfortable at the result. Mr. John is a very sober young man. Is a graduate of the Bastrop Military School and will make a good Officer. The others you know.

There will be four cooks appointed to cook for the company, and there is a man going along with us whose wife will accompany him and do the washing for us. So I will have nothing of that kind to do. I will return my trunk the first good chance. . . . I think I will hardly have any use for a horse. If I find that I will, there will probably be a chance to send one. We are as much in the dark as ever in regard to the length of our stay here. . . .

Wm. F. Hardin *

Camp Waul, July 20, 1862

Dear Shattee,

. . . Four of the Companies belonging to the Legion have left. I suppose they will rejoin the command somewhere on the route to Arkansas. I think the whole Legion will be on the march by the last of the month. . . . Bill Dugat and I have a project in view by means of which we hope to have a longer time to stay at home, which is to get leave to go by home whenever the Legion moves and overtake it somewhere on the road. . . .

We will endeavor to get Capt. Wrigley to aid us. He exhibits considerable eagerness of late to serve us in any way we desire. I believe there
was a ball in Brenham last night. Ed Jones was in town, I suppose he
attended. I think Miss Eugenia is enjoying herself finely at Brenham. I
do not know when she will return to Liberty. She has visited our
camp but twice. . . .

Bee *

July 24, 1862

Dear Bee,
    . . . We are very much in hopes you and Bill [Dugat] can get your
furloughs—'tis useless to say how [much] we want to see you before
you leave for Arkansas. . . .

Bill's friends and yours are indignant at the injustice with which you
and Bill were treated. Uncle Milton and Saunders [Blackburn's son]
are the maddest men you ever saw. Saunders makes me laugh; he says
he wouldn't take as much from Wrigley now as he would from a common darkey.

Everybody is down on him [Wrigley] and Absolom [Smith]. As a
matter of course they heard of the latter—his remarks as regards your
associating with rowdies and blackguards. Excuse!

The Captain Sterling's mode is very polite. So you say he'd like now
to smooth if he could. Uncle Charles [O'Bryan] heard him say at the
Provost Marshall's office after the last election was held that the people
of Liberty thought a Hardin couldn't be beaten, but he had shown
them differently so you see the gent acknowledged he was
instrumental.

[Zeke] Thompson was here last night the first time in a month.
Mimmie and I had congratulated ourselves that he had discontinued
his visits as we went walking one evening and left him at the house.

Ma has made one cheese and has another in press—she spoke of
sending you one until she found you expected to leave soon.

Leana Johnston has heard from her brother Blair once in a while—
She got Hale [Johnston]'s daguerreotype not long since. Coz King
praises Hale a great deal for his bravery and coolness in their fight on
their retreat from Yorktown [Virginia]. Coz Amanda rec'd a letter
from Coz King dated some time, well, I believe, since the battle of
Chickahomini, but her anxiety is still great as she hasn't heard since
the last fight.

Christy is at the farm. Pa came home yesterday; brought some calves. . . . Uncle Charles' nephew, Camille Salles, came a few trains since. Don't know whether he will take his [refugee] children or not.

I hear that Eugenie got in yesterday. Haven't seen her yet. . . .

I'll send this letter by Mr. Henry [Steusoff]. Also send you a package of envelopes such as they are [tiny advertising ones]—as John Skinner said you were out. . . . All send love.

Shattee *

Shattee was beginning to feel the war. Right after she wrote this letter, she and Mimmie were called to the Army Hospital in Liberty by Dr. Stanwood to help tend twenty sick soldiers who "but for the kind and prompt attention of the ladies, would have languished for want of delicacies that can only be prepared by a woman."[6]

The letter Amanda had received from her husband, Kindallis "King" Bryan, was written after the Battle of Chickahominy, also called Gaines' Mill. It was the bloodiest of the Seven Days' Campaign that had just taken place in Virginia. The first battle had been fought at Yorktown after Union General G. B. McClellan had moved up the peninsula toward Richmond and laid siege for a month. Confederate General Joseph B. Johnston had lost his nerve and had had the Confederate troops withdraw toward Richmond. The Seven Days' Campaign began on June 25 near the Confederate capital. On the twenty-seventh, the battle of the Chickahominy again demonstrated poor coordination by the Southern commanders. The Federals exacted a great toll, but John Bell Hood's Texas Brigade, including King Bryan's company, broke through the Union line. It was one of the most gallant cavalry charges of the war. This campaign came to an end with the Battle of Malvern Hill. McClellan had failed to take Richmond despite his greatly superior numbers. On studying these events, some Southerners realized that they might not win the war, even though Chickahominy had been a Confederate victory. Bee's next letter reflected his concern about how the war would end.

Brenham, July 28th, 1862

Dear Pa,

I set out this morning from Camp about 3 o'clock and walked in to town for breakfast. I am getting as I can take a walk of seven miles before breakfast without feeling the least fatigue. . . .

I suppose the Legion will be moved as soon as sufficient preparations are made. Capt. Wrigley started several days ago for Little Rock to survey the route. Trowell (who I believe by his own and Wrigley's efforts has got some appointment in the Quarter Master's Department) accompanied him for the purpose I suppose of procuring provisions. . . .

As for riding, I believe I had as soon walk as ride.

What do you think of the state of our affairs since the recent operations near Richmond? I should like to have your opinion in regard to the termination of the war. . . .

Bee *

Home, Aug. 13th 1862

My Dear Bee,

"The last among ten thousand"! I do believe, reports about the starting time of the Legion is that you are off today—Wednesday. . . . Gus Wynne, you know him, was wounded, in the mouth, by a ball which passed through his head in the late battle [Chickahominy]. Don't see why he was not killed. The idea of a ball passing through the head only producing a wound! It occurs to me I would feel something like a dead man. We have heard nothing from Powel's Company in the 5th Texas [from Walker and Montgomery Counties]. Most of our acquaintances were with him. Cousin Pryor [Bryan, Jr.] has rec'd a very long letter from Cousin King—giving a full account of the fighting of the Texans on the 27th particularly [at Gaines' Mill]. Poor George Woods was killed on that day. I think died immediately—ball passed through his left breast. . . . Hezekiah Prewitt, B. Crow, Brashear and Frank Whittington from Chambers County all in King Bryan's Company, 5th Regiment [Hood's Brigade].

Hale and Blair [Johnston] were with him in every fight, also Lt. J. E. Cobb. Dahl [O'Bryan] had his canteen shattered and a ball through his haversack. Close work! He says some of the men were on sick list who were more able to do duty than some who were in the battles. Mentioned no names—so we don't know who to accuse of cowardice. Poor fellows, how frightened they have been! even at camp!

We have not heard from Pryor, but intend sending very soon to the place where he was left—the enemy having left the place.

. . . George Davis—I suppose is elected for Dis't. Atty—strut! strut!! strut!!!—Persecuting Atty in this case. Alas! for judge and jury—many a tiresome harangue are in store for them.

Mrs. Geo. Loving [Martha Orr] has sold two of her Negroes to Saunders [Hardin]. The last to get money for John [Loving] to go

West on. He persuaded her that he had committed a penitentiary offense while in Houston a few weeks ago—drew a pistol. And she was
for getting him out of harm's way. Johnny left—and it has leaked out
that it was only a hoax—to get money. Delightful youth! He is "fond
of traveling." She gave him two hundred and he is in Houston now.

Old man Thompson was so rash as to promise Kaleta a bottle
of wine. His heart fails him, and he is too high-minded to come without it.

Next Saturday and Sunday our Quarterly [Methodist meeting]
comes off. Women will take little interest in dresses for the "occasion."
That disagrees with your doctrine that they only go to church to see
and be seen. I hear Gus [Preacher] is unpopular as Orderly Sargt in
Picketts Co. Jeff [Chambers] will have the office when they hold an
election—Gus being appointed. He has forgotten his religion and is
very profane—but I suppose like all the rumors, it will be contradicted
very soon. I did not see Capt. Wrigley while he graced our Town. He
departed as he came, without eclat—on a hand car. Preferred to go
that way I suppose—fine opportunity to patronize his brother, Dutch.

Why can't you write us a little gossip? For instance—the doings and
sayings (how complicated and elegant they are) of Lieut 1st—our polished, polite, and refined cousin [Sterling]. How I want to hear from
you! And a little news about that exquisitely formed fool—the Commissary Clerk [Trowell]. Think it would be good employment for half
an hour to show them up in a proper light. I wish you could have
heard William [Skinner]'s comments on the former. . . .

Did you see the *Houston Telegraph*? Ma and Pa are just reading the
short and nervous correspondence of Sect'ry Seward on the recruiting
subject. Pa says he thinks the termination of the war is very uncertain—as regards time. May last several more years. Letters from the
folks at Richmond [Virginia] say the opinion there is that the war will
end in the winter. That's all fudge—I think.

What think you of the grand Emancipation & Confiscation Act?
Afraid ain't you that the Yankees will take Jim Miller [Bee's horse]?
Tah says he is fat—he attends closely to him and will resist all efforts
to remove him from Texas soil. Regards to Bill [Dugat]. . . .

Mimmie *

Having been a colonel in the militia, Frank had a better concept than
the hot-headed Southern boys of how long the war would last. The
Emancipation and Confiscation Act, which had been proclaimed by

Major General John Charles Frémont, confiscated all property of "those who shall take up arms against the United States" and added that "their slaves, if any they have, are hereby declared free men." If the Yankees came up from Galveston to Liberty, one of the first things they would take would be Bee's fine horse, Jim Miller. When Lincoln announced that all black people joining the Union troops were confiscated from their masters and free, this gave slaves a great incentive to run off. The "nervous correspondence" between Secretary of State for the Union, William H. Seward, and New York Congressman Charles Cook was about whether the North could raise enough men without conscription.

CHAPTER TEN

The Battle of Galveston

BEE'S NEXT LETTER FROM SHAT-tee underscored how dreadful their cousin King Bryan felt about the death of each of his men. John Bell Hood's over-worked Texas Brigade made Texas bravado a byword, "So mad and brain-reeling that to recall it is like fixing the memory of a horrible, blood-curdling dream."[1] General R. E. Lee said of them, "I need them much and I rely upon those we have in all tight places. I fear I have to call upon them too often."[2] King Bryan called his company in the Brigade the "Liberty Invincibles."

August 16th, 1862

Dear Bee:
. . . Coz Amanda rec'd a letter from Coz King. . . . It brought sad news—viz—the death of young Pryor [Bryan] and Gus Merriman. Pryor was left sick on the retreat from Yorktown. Soon after the en-emy got possession of the place where he was left and it was only after the battle before Richmond that the place was clear. Coz King sent immediately an ambulance in, but poor Pryor was dead. Had died the 28th of April. Coz King said although he had prepared himself to hear it, the shock fell heavy. He said he had written the particulars of his death in a letter to Coz Pryor [Sr.] which they have not rec'd yet. In

Coz A.'s letter he only mentioned that Pryor relapsed. Gus [Merriman] died the 16th of June of disease. Coz King has had two other deaths. . . .

Suppose you have seen the list of casualties in the Texas Brigade. The 4th suffered more than the rest. Capt. P. P. Porter died of his wounds. Powell was not on the field, Lieut. Hill was in command. Gen'l [W. H. C.] Whiting in his report mentions the 4th Texas particularly.

I received a letter from Aunt Virginia not long since. Uncle [William] Collins is on a boat running between New Iberia and Franklin—they speak somewhat of coming out in the fall—doubtful tho. All well and send love. . . .

Shattee *

In Robinson Co., Aug. 21, '62

Dear Mimmie,

We are camped nearing a mile from the town of Wheelock [Texas] having marched about eighty miles in six days march. The command day was last Saturday on the Brazos. We found there a barbecue prepared for us on our arrival. Our direction has been very suddenly changed. Orders having been issued to march to Shrevesport. Up to now supposed our destination was across the Mississippi. . . . I had much rather be on the other side of the river. Would there get better arms, and probably better equipped in every way. We will pass through Crockett. Will be a week or ten days getting there. . . .

I am getting along splendidly; stand the march even better than I expected. We have had light showers of rain for several evenings past but by means of our little tents we manage to keep comfortably dry.

I heard of one of your Independence schoolmates at Caldwell, Miss Mollie Johnson, a cousin of George Johnson's; [B. F.] Sterling took supplies at George's father's and saw her there. She sent her love to me, she said, for your sake. If I could have seen her it would not, I possibly believe, have been on that account altogether. . . .

Tell Ma to send me fifty dollars by Sugar Williams. I would like to have notes of as small denominations as is convenient to send. . . .

Kiss all—

Goodbye,
Bee *

Liberty, August 30th, 1862

Dear Bee:

. . . If you go to Shrevesport you'll see all your Liberty friends, as Pickett's, LaCour's and Dark's [now Spear's] Companies are there. . . . I believe we all had rather see you across the Mississippi. Mr. [Gibson] Tracy and Mr. Dunnam staid three days with us. Mr. Tracy was so thin I wouldn't have known him scarcely. Bill [Dugat] was here last night. He came from West Liberty [now Dayton] on the train yesterday. He looks thin too—but just as lively as ever. He gave us an account of yours and his entrance into the box and of all your tricks generally. Says that you and him are compadres. Am glad to hear that you and Bill are such cronys.

Coz K. [Bryan] writes in good spirits. Says all the boys, himself included, think they will spend Christmas home. Oh! I do wish I could think so! We got quite a number of rumors by the train yester-day—but, nothing that could be relied on.

Camilla [Mimmie] is very busy studying French lately. She is now at the Convent reciting her lesson. Christie went up the country Tues-day; hasn't returned yet. . . . Christie has got Jim Miller up [in cor-ral]. When George [black] first rode him they say he tried to jump. I don't believe it. Christie put George up to it to provoke me as he knew I wanted to ride him.

Ma is fattening up and looks better than I have seen her for a long time. I tell her she don't take your leaving so hard or she wouldn't be so fat. . . . Have you had any peaches? Ours have been very good, considering the dry weather. Ma is busy planting a fall garden. She is planting plenty of radishes. You must hurry and fight your battles and get home by the time they are grown. So may it be!

We staid two nights with Leanna [Johnston]—[Aquilla] Beard is [Johnston plantation] manager. [I] tell you he'd be willing for the war to last always could he but keep the control of the plantation.[†]

. . .Bill Dugat received a letter from "Capting" [Wrigley] yesterday stating that he wished him to meet him at Crockett, but Bill says t'would be impossible for him to get the men together and meet him there. So he thinks of going enrail to Shrevesport. Ma will send your money by William [Dugat]. Will $50 be enough? You must recollect you'll be a long way from home. . . .

[†] Beard got permanent control of the plantation by marrying Leanna.

Abb McMurtry has hired a substitute—has gone up with him. Don't know whether he [the substitute] will be accepted. Mr. Nixon was conscripted. He is now clear. Gave a negro girl and several children for a man to go as his substitute. I hear that Bill Cade gave Henry, his negro, to Old [J. G.] Minter if he'd get him one. The substitute mania is running high here. John & Free Green have got them one. . . . Ma says tell you to take as good care of yourself as you can under the circumstances. There is nothing like prudence in the army. It is useless to say how much we all think and talk about you daily.

Have you got your money from Wrigley? Ma wants to know. . . . Ma is standing by me. She says she is in hopes you will get plenty of apples soon, as she expects you have had but little fruit this year. . . .

Shattee *

Sept. 1st, 1862
In Camp, 5 miles from Crockett

Dear Father—

. . .We crossed the Trinity last Friday at the Alabama Crossing and camped there that night. . . . Our last two marches were quite short, only eight miles each. We have marched about a hundred and fifty miles since we left Camp Waul. . . . It is about the same distance from here to Shrevesport. Our longest march we made last Wednesday. . . a distance of twenty-six miles. . . . The division lay over the next day and we were as fresh as ever Friday morning. I believe I had rather walk than ride. . . .

I have not seen a newspaper since leaving Caldwell and am consequently almost entirely ignorant of how the war is progressing. . . . But when we get to Shrevesport we will hear the news sooner than when at home. The health of the Company is tolerably good but three or four not able to walk.

I believe we are waiting for some flour to come up that is being hauled from the terminals of the Central Railroad. If it comes it will be quite acceptable as we have had none but cornbread since we went into Camp. . . . We lost one member of the Company, David Isaacks. He had the measles a short time before. He was left at Wheelock and died the next day. . . .

Bee *

My dear Bee—

We all hate to see William [Dugat] go tomorrow—it is like break-ing the last link. Old [Zeke] Thompson just stepped up on the gal-lery—that is to my displeasure, you know. Ma attacks him about the marriage: This morning Mr. Bigelow and [2nd] Mrs. Wright linked lives at Joe Smith's—third husband and only 27 years old! T goes on to say that they had champagne purchased of him, and it "roiled the stomach" of the groom and he has been throwing up—"cascading" (your expression) all evening, the bride fanning him—how entertaining!

Mr. Bigelow and Mrs. Wright came as fugitives from yellow jack. They hadn't been at Jon Smith's many days before Squire Palmer [doctor and preacher] was summoned and Mr. Bigelow and Mrs. Wright were one!! So you see she didn't cherish the memory of the old Professor long. I was surprised—thought Bigelow wouldn't think of marrying anyone.

Clara [O'Bryan] is here and the girls from the convent, spending the night, and such a racket you never heard! Be sure if the fever ap-pears here we will decamp to the farm.

While walking with Miss Emma H. and Mother this evening, we met Free Green [of Pickett's Company] just in from Shrevesport—has a substitute—and a baby. . . . George Davis was here last night, on way to Chambers County court, and will be here next week. He says there is little to do now. Ma is getting [Zeke] Thompson to change your money—getting as small bills as is possible in Confederate money. We will make exertions to get you some winter clothing. . . .

Uncle Collins was here last week—ran the blockade at Sabine Pass on the *Hind* with sugar. . . . He will run out maybe this week—only piloting—not Captain.

Two schooners ran out last week with cotton. Ma asks Mr. Thompson what hands it falls into. He replys—"I suppose the Yankees get it." Don't you think that stuck in the old man's throat? Particularly the Yankee part.

I like French very much. . . . Be sure you tease Bill about Bettie Day. He is very much in love, so I hear. Bettie blushes and he looks conscious. Very strange symptoms! What else can they mean?

Ma wants to know if it is possible for her to send you some clothing and your boots. . . . We just heard that Clint Hartman is very low—a Shrevesport report which I hope is a mistake. His wife is boarding at [R. E.] Boothes'.

All send love—Ma particularly—

Yours
Mimmie *

In Camp, near Shrevesport, 14th Sept., 1862

Dear Mother,

. . . Yesterday we set out at eight o'clock without making any preparation for dinner, but coming to the intended camping place it was found that the water was bad and we had ten miles further to march without anything to eat but some peaches that we had procured the evening before. We made the march by five in the evening with but little inconvenience. . . . We will remain here tomorrow, and probably go the next day to where the 2nd division of the Legion is camped about 15 miles from Shrevesport. . . . We go from here to Monroe, something over a hundred miles, where I suppose they will give us arms as we will then be in almost striking distance of the enemy. Saw Jeff Chambers yesterday evening. He remained here to see [his brother] Clay, the Regt having started about a week ago for Arkansas. He will start immediately to join his command. We have heard reports of numerous Confederate successes recently but not having been able to get a paper containing the news I cannot tell how much to believe. If all we hear is true (which of course is very doubtful) it would seem that our prospects were bright for speedily conquering "a peace". . . .

There has been a great deal of sickness among the troops that have been long in this vicinity. Twelve men have died of [J. N.] Dark's Company alone. . . . I have not got any money from Capt. Wrigley yet. Have said nothing to him about it. I may ask him for it sometime during the war. I think I will have enough to do me as there is some probability of being paid off in the course of a few months. . . . They say we will get uniforms soon, which I suppose is reliable(?). I do not think we will suffer this winter as we will not probably go far north. Kiss Pep and all the rest for me and good-bye for the present.

Bee *

My dear brother,

Mr. Newton Sweeney is going to Shrevesport with substitutes for some of Capt. Pickett's Company tomorrow, so I write this evening so that I may send it by him. . . . Mrs. Jim Wrigley came back last Saturday night. [Uncle] Milton called and gave us the "items."

Louise [Orr, cousin] came in this morning, intends staying several days. They are on the bed now discussing George Davis. He was here last eve and stayed rather late. Excited Miss Mimmie's disgust. She's been giving him Jessie all day. Tonsie [O'Bryan] has been helping tho' she is not acquainted. Tis Court week. That accounts for the gent's presence in Liberty, as he is District Attorney now. I fear it has rather heightened his conceit. Pet says he offered her a ring last night. Don't know how they "fixed" it—She says she told him she'd wear it on her big toe, but I rather doubt the truth of that. . . . You see that the war hasn't entirely killed off the idea of matrimony. I think [George] Davis will fall an easy prey to some of the women in these scarce times. . . .

Mimmie and Tonsie are kicking up such a row that my ideas are all scattered. . . . Yesterday was Helen [Pep]'s first day at school. She told Pa that, "I was embarrassed when I first began to read"—She went off this evening with her bottle of ink and copy book, also her embroidery. The Nuns are teaching her how. She is very much pleased.

Suppose you have heard of our late battles in Virginia. Hope we will have gained as great a victory as at Manassas a year ago.

Mr. Petty preaches next Saturday and Sunday. We don't have church often. . . . Coz Pryor [Bryan, now a refugee from Galveston] comes over right often to talk about the war. He is uneasy since the last battles. . . .

Tonsie says, "My love! and I am still kicking." The latter is virtually true for she is lying on the bed. Mimmie says, "Tell Bee I am about to receive a ring!" Also, "Her love to the company, 'cept Capting Commissary Clerk." She says ask Mr. Tracy if his "moral persuader" is still safe in his carpet-sack. . . .

Shattee *

Gibson Tracy, of course, was the muleteer for Bee's Company. His moral persuader was probably a club with a piece of metal in the end of it with which he clobbered mules to get their attention. Shattee was a sly one, saying that George Davis would fall an easy prey to some woman in these "scarce times." She had turned him down and now he had proposed to her sister. This made her really scorn him. Since she turned him down, she did not want her sister to have him either, and she had manipulated Cousin Hortense ("Tonsie") O'Bryan to speak ill of George even though Tonsie didn't know him. Mimmie told George that she was not ready to get married, but if he would wait, she would tell him when she was.

Meanwhile, news reached Liberty about the second battle of Manassas, which took place the last two days of August on Bull Run Creek just south of Washington. Again the Southern troops stood just a few short miles from the Union capital. The Union General Pope's army was beaten but not routed. The Federals had over 16,000 casualties and the Confederates 9,197.

Liberty Sept. 29th 1862

Well, Bee, my Boy,

. . . Tah is most of the time up at the farm. Happy enough hunting; he sends meat down quite often. . . . We were however stirred up a little the other day: about 1,000 troops passed on the cars in two days for Sabine Pass. The Yankees came in there and took the little battery, burned what little there was to be found and left before the troops got over there. We had but about ten or a dozen men there. The yellow fever had run all the rest away. The troops all returned yesterday on the cars.

Our arms appear to be in the ascendant now, victorious everywhere. Old Abe may have to leave Washington as he entered, in disguise. Stonewall [Jackson] is no doubt in Maryland and must have possession of all the avenues of communication with Washington across the Potomac. We have heard of but few of the casualties of the Texas troops in the last great battle at Manassas. King Bryan we hear was wounded † and is Maj. of the Regt.

Bee, we have a number of relatives in Tennessee, Mississippi and some about New Madrid, Missouri. I thought I would mention it to you as they might in case of sickness take you in charge if you make yourself known to them. You may be thrown among them, no telling. Your relatives in Missouri are named O'Bryan and Toney. In Hardin

† In General J. B. Hood's famous charge.

Co., Tenn. you have quite a number of relatives of your own name—and also in other portions of the State. In Miss. your relatives are named Shaw and Hardin. If you find any of them you must let them know who you are as they might be of great advantage to you in case of sickness.

Your Uncle Charley [O'Bryan] was here this morning. He calls in very often, is a great deal of company for me. . . . Your Ma is uneasy for fear you will not be able to get shoes. She sent you by [Newton] Sweeney a coat—pants and pr. socks. . . . Bee, I think you had better get your money from Dog Wrigley, if you can. Without you are willing to take it out of his hide with a cow skin, if you ever get back. I feel like I will never want to see him again. He never can live here in peace while I live. I wish I could not think of the villain. . . .

The cars are here from Houston. Just rec'd the news—Blair Johnston and Albert Dugat were killed in the Battle of Manassas. Goodbye, my dear boy!

F. Hardin

[P.S.]
. . . Mr. Daniels from the [Bayou] Boeuf was here not long since, hunting a place to put his negroes in case the Yankees should come to the Bay [Berwick]. All think of you all the time. . . .

Shattee *

Mr. Daniels' premonition was correct. The Yanks were soon back in force at Berwick, burning homes and taking off slaves. Frank's premonition that Bee would need his relatives was correct also because he did fall ill in Mississippi. Frank seemed to have taken up his son's quarrel with Jim Wrigley they way he had taken up his brother's feud twenty-six years earlier. The cow skin whip was traditionally reserved for whipping a thief.

The port of Galveston had been blockaded for the past ten months. Suddenly the Yankees decided to take over the town. Sabine Pass was also high on the Yankee list of objectives. On October 6 the *Tri-Weekly Telegraph* of Houston carried the following article:

The Federals have not yet landed. They have allowed four days time to remove the people before they take possession providing that no batteries are erected in the meantime. They are inside the bay, about a mile from the wharves—It is now understood that landing will be resisted and every step of the progress of the enemy will be disputed—Five of the enemies' vessels lie in the Harbor of Galveston. . . . the [Confederate] position at the Point being rendered useless. Col. Cook, who was on the spot, ordered its evacuation, especially as in a short time it would be exposed to an enfilading fire. . . . The place is still in our hands. No concessions are made to the enemy and none will be. We will make a vigorous stand at Virginia Pointe and try to hold the bridge. Col. Xavier Debray is here in command and the troops hot for fight.

Wednesday Morning, 8th Oct. '62

Dear Bee,

. . . Poor Bill Dugat! What a stroke the loss of his brother Albert will be! They drop off one by one, our friends and relatives, sometimes I think there will not be one left when Father Abraham condescends to stop this war.

I have not seen any of Mrs. Johnston's family since they heard of Blair's death. They are no doubt grieved to death. Poor Leanna! These are sad times. Little did William [Dugat] think when he spent the evening of the 19th with us that next day his brother would be killed! So it is—we can't see the future, and maybe for the better. Although I would like to peer through the misty veil and see the termination of this war! Eugenie was over the river at her Uncle [Dugat]'s last Sunday. . . . Some of the family seemed to have some hope that it was a mistake, but cousin Pryor has received a letter from [Beasley] Dugat, from Maryland—giving the particulars of Albert's death. He was separated from his Reg. and got with the 18th Va., so he said, during the fight. I think it must have been the 18th Ga. as that is in the Texas Brigade. He was killed on the 30th but not found til the next day. He must have died immediately—as he was shot through the breast. It was better that he did not suffer. . . . It is possible that Albert had no acquaintance with him. . . .

What do you think of our prospect of a call from the Yanks? They have Galveston by this time—or will tomorrow—as they had given four days to remove the women and children. The *Telegraph* speaks of "contesting every inch of ground," etc. How silly! When there is nothing to defend the Island with! All the troops are removed to Virginia Point. The only large gun they had was upset by the first fire or two from the Yankee boats that were coming to demand the surrender.

<hr/>

They are also at the Pass [Sabine], fighting about. Have burned the Depot. Col [A. W.] Spaight makes no efforts to distinguish himself. Perhaps he despises glory, fame, etc. and loves his own life better. Anyway he is very inactive. They will be up here soon I think to plant the "Gridiron" on our Liberty pole.

I can scarcely write intelligibly as Miss Josephine is loudly sweeping the room. A very "reliable contraband" she is. Wonder if she knows that she is now free—she is to all intents and purposes since the late proclamation reported here yes'dy that Lincoln has issued. . . .

So you all cook for yourselves! Much better I think. You are pastry cook, I suppose? I never thought to see you attain to such high station as that! Truly a noble mission to correct the many errors in dried peach pie and pancake making that have been committed among the male cooks of this war.

Night: No news by the cars today! The Feds have not taken Galveston yet. Everyone is leaving. I hear that companies will be sent here to guard the Bridge. . . .

Report says that Dr. [Thos. A.] Stanwood will marry soon. The Dr. tells everybody and he ought to know. Shows her letters and says they were to be married the first of this month but he would not leave his patients. She's only 19 and a widow (name Higgs).

Mr. [Newton] Sweeney has returned. We have not seen him, and do not know what he has done with your pants and overcoat which we sent by him. It appears he did not reach the Legion but heard from his son and turned back. How is John Swinney? Has he been sick? We were so glad to hear from Richard [Hardin] that he was well enough to join you. . . .

I heard the other day that Mrs. Grady had really turned Spiritualist and had been excommunicated, in other words turned out of the Church. Of course Olley withdrew—strange work! Must not the fuss attending the transaction been a feast for old Lady M! . . . [Zeke] Thompson was here last night, still "does his business on the track" and is the agent for the town at Houston. Old Thompson purchased a boat and was preparing to run the blockade with cotton, but the appearance of Lincoln [Union ships] at the Pass knocked his schemes in the head and ran his boat up some bayou for safekeeping. The $2200 expended for the boat will not break him unless it breaks his heart. He is now, I wager, devising some plan to evade the Second Conscript Act. Ought'nt to say it of the old man, for I am expecting every visit a bottle of rasberry cordial promised some time since. He has already presented K. with a bottle of "Perfect Love." Very suggestive! (of what?). . . .

For tonight good night
Mimmie

[P.S.]

Pep and Nannie are home as tis Thursday.[†] Christy attends to the farm mostly, is seeing to the building of Pa's pasture. He killed a calf yesterday. Pa is now giving Ma a description of the way he got it. I have no more paper, so goodbye.

Shattie *

The "reliable contraband" named Josephine that Mimmie mentioned was a slave who had come over from Louisiana with the Collins family to care for their children and to be placed out of the reach of the Yankees. This girl was called "Miss Josephine" because she had such highfalutin manners.

The Yankees moved into Galveston Bay right on schedule. They went so far as landing on one of the wharves and taking up quarters in the warehouses where they barricaded themselves, but they never ventured into the city proper. It wasn't long, however, before General John B. Magruder was planning to recapture Galveston.

The power of the enemy was becoming apparent at first hand to the two sisters as well as to Bee on the march. When he first enlisted as an officer in Nichol's Ninth Texas Infantry Regiment, Bee was a warmly idealistic youth eager for adventure. By the time he reported to Colonel Waul, his frustration with army inertia was expressing itself in drinking bouts and high jinks with his buddies. By October of 1862, on his way to Vicksburg, still without guns and with a northern winter in prospect, Bee realized the seriousness of his situation. His illusions were being replaced with a fierce tenacity based on his love of family and the Texas land.

[†] Ursuline observed the French custom of the Thursday holiday instead of Saturday.

CHAPTER ELEVEN

Stuart and Beauregard hats

WHICHEVER SIDE GOT CONTROL of the Mississippi River could win the war. To hold off as many Union troops as possible, Confederate General Braxton Bragg was maneuvering across Kentucky, with Federal troops in hot pursuit under General Don Carlos Buell. Further south, generals Earl Van Dorn and Sterling Price confronted Union troops under General William Rosecrans at Corinth, Mississippi. On October 5, after two days of hard fighting, the Confederates were repulsed and Colonel T. N. Waul's Texas Legion was rushed north to help them at Holly Springs. Bee's company had just arrived in Vicksburg when they were told to board the cars heading for battle, but the track had been sabotaged and they arrived too late to fight. Bee saw many Texas casualties.

Six months earlier a fort on the upper Mississippi River called Fort Donelson had fallen and all the personnel had been taken prisoner. Now these men had been released and exchanged for Yankee prisoners, leaving those same Confederate soldiers free to fight again. Both sides were aware of the importance of Vicksburg in controlling the river.

Camp at Holly Springs
[Sunday] Oct. 12th, 1862

Dear Father,

We left Vicksburg on the cars last Wednesday and arrived here about midnight. The cars were not running more than half the time and although we came a distance of 250 miles,[†] we considered it very slow tracking and upon the whole a very tedious trip. It began to rain Friday morning and . . . in the evening a regular northwester sprung up and it began to feel considerably like winter. I happened to be in a box car and kept dry and comfortable. Others who were in open cars had full benefit of wind and rain. We have at last got almost in sight of the enemy.

This place is about forty miles from Corinth, where a most terrible battle was fought last friday, saturday, and sunday between Van Dorn, Price and [General Mansfield] Lovell on our side, and Rosecrans on the side of the Yankees. Van Dorn made an attempt to take the place, and during the first day took many of the positions of the enemy, but R. being reinforced on the second day, our forces were driven back with considerable loss. Price's troops suffered most. All that I have seen of his army say that it was terribly cut to pieces. I have not been able to learn the number of troops engaged on either side. Although we are so near, it is impossible to hear anything reliable. The 2nd Texas, [General John C.] Moore's old regt., was in the fight, and from all accounts suffered terribly, also [General Elkanah] Green's Regt. and [John W.] Whitfield's Texas Legion.

I have just been looking at Gen. Lovell's division pass here. It is moving north, but I think twill stop near this place. . . . A large number of the Ft. Donelson prisoners that have recently been exchanged have arrived here and are being armed and equipped. I do not know how far off the Yankees are or whether they have advanced at all from Corinth. They no doubt will be very cautious in their movements. If Bragg should whip Buell in Ky., their situation would be somewhat critical. I have been told that we would be in Lovell's division. Our arms were given to us today. They are muskets, rather old, but good guns with bayonets and all the necessary accouterments.

We are in fine spirits, get plenty to eat and the health of the command is excellent. Our cavalry has not yet come up from Vicksburg. The fighting qualities of the Texians are held in high esteem by every one in this country. I have little idea which way we will move from

[†] The letter says "25" but a zero must have disappeared.

here, if at all soon. It depends on the movements of the Yankees. Gen. Van Dorn's headquarters are at this place. He is here now.

Wm. F. Hardin *

Bee sounded confused about what division he would be in. This was not surprising as the whole campaign was one of confusion because General Grant feinted in first one direction, then another. The Confederates were unable to discern where the main attack would come. Retreating south from Holly Springs, Waul's Legion participated in fighting at Greenwood on the Yazoo, where they protected their batteries with cotton bales and knocked out two ironclads that had been sent up the river. There Major B. Timmons was commended for bravery. Bee would serve under him in the last year of the war.

In the next letter, Mimmie reports that Jim Wrigley had asked for a transfer to the army in Virginia. The transfer did not actually occur until just before Vicksburg fell.

About the time the Libertians had become accustomed to the idea of the Yankees being in Galveston, the Union Navy overcame the shore installations at Sabine Pass, and from then on kept several ships at the pass to close the river port. The Twenty-Sixth Texas Cavalry and six companies of men under the command of the French-born Colonel Xavier DeBray were all moved into Liberty to thwart any further Yankee advance and to retake Sabine Pass.

October 16, 1862

Dear Bee,

We condole with Lieut. Wrigley that he should be compelled to leave the sweet companionship of the officers of "his own selecting". . . . Well, peace be with him and with them!

Ma says she is in hopes you are as comfortably situated as is possible for a soldier. She thinks there is an opportunity of sending clothing by [William] Meyer.

Paper is getting scarce, which will readily account for the varieties in color in my letter.

Abe [Trowell] as Commissary Clerk, has been here for a week past. Haven't learned his business as he has kept his distance and seems likely in continuing in so doing. Probably I will not find out at all.

Suppose you know the Yankees have Galveston. [Xavier] DeBray's [CSA] regiment, at least six companies under Maj. Menard, are sta-

tioned from Wallisville up. Capt. [G. H.] Black of Leon County is at
Liberty. Willie [Bledsoe] Hardin[1] and Alec Jackson are in Menard's
old [militia] company, now Armstrong's, which is at Wallisville. Liberty is the same old place [but] the soldiers being here makes it somewhat livelier in looks.

The yellow fever is in Houston, but physicians seem to think it is
too late to spread. Dr. Stanwood reports three cases here. No one
seems to credit the report. You recollect several years ago, he endeav-
ored to raise the dust as to yellow jack. Now many think he is trying
to get revenge because he wasn't believed then and make every
one run.

The Yankees have Sabine Pass. We all feel at last that the war is upon
us. Ma says she don't see no end to it.

Mimmie *

Home, Nov. 3rd, 1862

Dear Bee,

Your letter from Holly Springs was rec'd last week and here I be this
night about eight o'clock, in "our" room to prepare an answer, to
either mail it on to the other side of the Father of Waters, or mayhaps
root up somebody going directly to the Legion. . . . [Zeke]
Thompson says [Dr.] Ashbel Smith goes soon.

Dr. Stanwood returned from Washington (not Yankee) with his
youthful bride, some years Eugenie's junior. Such an incident! Eugenie was here this evening. She went with her father when he married. Says it is far better for her that he took unto himself a wife in
some respects, but in others very disagreeable. I was at the cars when
they came. His buggy was in waiting and he handed her in with grace,
which reminded me that perhaps in some months, very few, seeing
them together would not think them man and wife, for all the attention he would pay her. Don't know how many calls she has rec'd. Mrs.
Branch has spent the day allready. Her tongue, no doubt a very fair
imitation of perpetual motion on the occasion. Let me here note the
fact that she has taken her children, Betsy and William [Branch],
under the "sheltering wing." They are now sojourning at her house.
Blessed time! A wonder the bolt that Betsy prayed for didn't strike her
when she entered.

The Lone Star Cadets stationed here gave a party last friday. We
didn't feel like dancing of course, but Pa and Ma seemed to wish us to

go. It was right pleasant in the hall over Levi [White]'s store. A good many ladies were present.

I see in today's paper that Gen. [John B.] Magruder has been appointed to commander in this state over [Paul Octave] Hebert. Out of the frying pan into the fire: Hebert is incompetent, as you know, and Magruder in disgrace.[†]

Trowell is here now, but goes tomorrow. What can keep him from the Legion so much? How did the election go? Did Captain Bammerou [Sterling] contest it as we heard he did? Who is third Lieut? Have you ever become acquainted with the chaplain?

We wrote you by cousin Luke, who has gone to Virginia. Cousin King [Bryan], I suppose, has joined his regiment by this time. Pa received a newspaper addressed from Mr. Henry Shea from Mobile. He may be there on furlough as he was wounded at Manassas.

So much news emanates from the J. D. Skinner sisterhood over the way that the town is constantly filled with vague and terrible rumors from his writing and, I suppose, invention. Confederate Congress should tender him a patent, for he is certainly a genius. You would think so too were I to pen some of his preposterous yarns. I can see Jim [Skinner] with neutered vision, with his nose rooted to a sheet of paper, writing all the camp gossip, if it sustains such an institution, which would be impossible not to with Jim along.

Uncle Charles [O'Bryan] has gone to the Brazos to make sugar.[††] Did you notice that Capt. Ike [Turner] commanded the 5th Regt. at Sharpsburg, and [was] decorated for bravery at Manassas?

Kaleta has her nose pinned down to Dickens' *Great Expectations* which a gent has loaned her. Of course perfectly delighted!

I hear that they have killed some Yankees at Sabine Pass—pray heaven it is true. About 15—only a report tho'. The telegraph wire is being put up. There will be an office at the "Cheapest Store in Town" [Pickett's].

I wish you could have seen Dr. Robert [White] at the party. His mad endeavor to shuffle his feet in dancing afforded Tah some amusement. How much I will let you guess. You know he has a keen sense of the ridiculous. The Dr. had to perform the arduous duties as "floor manager." Some of the small fry . . . were quite light and pinned a

[†] Magruder lost his reputation in action east of the Mississippi. He would repair it by retaking Galveston.

[††] Planters were then experimenting growing cane along the Brazos River bottom.

handkerchief to his alpaca coat. Christie enacts the scene to our infinite amusement. Mrs. Levi White attended and danced, she is quite
beyond her usual self of late. The Capt. of the Co. here she claims as
"Cousin Black." They have spent the day at Uncle Charles [O'Bryan]'s
together Mrs. W. having borrowed Nene Smith's Beauregard cap[†] and
riding habit for the occasion. . . .

Do I direct your letters right? is the Co. still "B"? I dislike to use
Sterling's name and prefer the letter B.

Mimmie

[P.S.]
Monday Morn
Pa and Christy went to the farm this morning to see to ginning Clint
[Hartman]'s cotton. *

The Dr. White that Mimmie mentioned had been put in charge of the
Liberty Military Hospital. He was married to Florine, Nathaniel Berwick's daughter. Ike Turner took command of the Fifth Regiment at the
Battle of Sharpsburg (Antietam) because his superior officers were
killed. The battle took place in Maryland and has been called the most
hotly contested battle of the whole war. There were over 12,000 casualties on either side.

Liberty Nov. 22, 1862

Dear Bee,
The ladies are getting up Tableaux for Monday evening for benefit
of Mr. Pickett's Co. They are at Post Arkansas, Ark. And I assure you
that we are in excitement about costumes, 'attitudes' and scenery. Oh,
yes! A peck of trouble! We will have simple pictures as cannot prepare
now for any other kind: such as 'Ruth and Naomi,' 'Dressing Moses
for the Fair!'—You have read *The Vicar of Wakefield* and could appreciate: Dahl [Bryan] will be Moses, a novice taking the black veil. School
scene and the closing scene will be Dr. Robert [White] persuading
Old Abe [Lincoln].

Uncle Charles says the Modern Demons[††] have completely taken
them up at Brashear—have taken some eight thousand negroes from
St. Mary's Parish. We have not heard particularly from our relatives—
we seldom hear from Aunt Virginia [Collins]—she spoke of coming

---

[†] See sketch at beginning of chapter.

[††] Organization to move blacks away from the coast and Yankee raiders.

down, but the presence of Abraham [Lincoln] in Galveston has frightened the old Man [William Collins] off.

Mrs. Sidney Turner has been down. I reminded her of my claims on the Capt. [Ike Turner] and she didn't object, and also remarked to Kaleta that Lieut. Herbert was a widower. We are elated—being thus provided for!

Pa encloses a note to his friend Mr. [John] Munson, I believe on Col. Waul's staff, and wants you to hand it to him. They are old acquaintances. . . .[2]

. . . We have not written you about the last party the girls, Amanda, Julia, Bettie, etc. gave to Dahl [Bryan], the returned hero. There was a crowd. Everybody, wife and child there. Lieut, now Capt. [Dugat] Williams arrived from Va. that evening and made his appearance . . . the Capt. on furlough—and will return in about a month.

Dahl [Bryan] has been remarked to be the most modest hero ever seen—the best policy these times, when there are so many.

We are getting some Yankees too. A squad from Capt. Armstrong's Co. took five and killed two at Bolivar.[†] The prisoners passed through here. Most everybody was wild to get a squint at them—Shattee was at the station. I did not go out—so have my first live Yankee yet to see.

They have begun again to block up the Trinity—a foolish business. A good many hands at work down there. The Co.'s still here.

Mimmie *

Home, Liberty, Tx.
Dec. 8th 1862

My Dear Bee,

When I received your letter [now lost] it was a general rejoicing. All hands felt, no doubt, some years younger. Ma did, I know. Mr. [Newton] Sweeney was in town today and is quite uneasy about his son. He may start to Miss. to see about him. . . . Ma is delighted to hear that you stand marching so well. By the way, what a delightful time you all must have had booing about in the dark with the huge voice of your huge "Capting": This or that "column to the left" or right, as the Lord permitted. Tah will go to school to Chappell Hill

---

[†] Corpus Christi, Galveston, and Sabine Pass were all in Union hands after October 15. Three weeks later Leon Smith, in command of the *General Rusk*, charged the blockading ship at Sabine, the *Morning Light*, and she surrendered. Armstrong then attacked shore installations and captured a few Yankees. The Confederates figured this sort of skirmishing would continue and blockaded the Trinity to keep Yankees out. The Union successes kept the timid William Collins from attempting to run blockade any more.

[Male and Female Institute] 1st Jan. . . . Ma and K are busy sewing for the scamp.

A couple of gents, soldiers, have just called, and Kaleta is entertaining. You have not received, you say, our letter by Cousin Luke. Maybe he sent it by Absolom [Smith] and he might have violated the seal, who knows!

Dear Lunny, last night of course, I was called to see those gents, Messrs. Womack and Cox: the latter rather on the Jim Skinner order of beings excessively prim with a flowered jacket of green and red—Jim's favorite colors before he rose to his present high estate—which is, you know, being led around by the snout (so short!) by gentleman Absolom and Jimmie Wrigley. Jim Skinner writes to his wife that he is "now P.M. [postmaster] at Holly Springs with ever so many clerks under him" "Blessed are the meek for they shall be exalted"!

Kaleta has turned millina-maker. Really! She trims and builds all the Shakos and Beauregards for the Village Misses. Is now very busy with one for Lucy Beal. Do you not see some of the fair daughters of Miss. sporting those monkey caps called after the Gen. [Stuart] Commanding at Charlesburg?

Kaleta has purchased a buggy with the funds proceeding from her horse, Jourdan's, sale and whose [buggy]? Verily! Verily! Absolom's! She did not make the trade directly with him or wife. [Zeke] Thompson was the medium. He purchased first and now is running wild over the country in search of harness. A. B. is being detained in Galveston by the Yankees. He reminds me of the entertaining story: Japhet in search of a father. Ma sent him [Zeke] to Mr. McKimm's this morning to purchase his [harness]. If he fails we will send to Alleyton [near Houston]. Fillibuster will be the buggy horse. Jim Miller, your cavalry horse, is enjoying first rate health—tho rather poverty-stricken. Looks as if his corn tasted of shinplasters. . . .

Sterling revealed his promotion in a letter to Moll [his wife Mary Ann Bryan] in the following words: "You are now, my dear, the wife of a Capt." Remember, I did not see it and am not accountable for the orthography which of course was correct! Such a silly! It sometimes bothers me to think that you have to serve Jeff Davis under such an ignorant upstart.

Pa thinks of farming next year, and raising a little cotton. Such a price as it bears now justifies it. It has been selling in Houston at 25 cts. and farther west, 50 cts. Pa sold Clint's cotton some time ago, when it was not so high.

Van [Deventer] has been trying to hire a substitute. Borrowed money of Pa, failed, and bought cotton which he sold in Houston at considerable speculation. He has also bought two negro women and one child—with money for Cornelia's land.

Mimmie *

Jeremiah Van Deventer was married to Cornelia Hardin, Blackburn's daughter. He came from New Jersey and was a Unionist. It was perfectly legal to hire a substitute and Frank agreed that in his case he should get one. Frank lent him $1500, but he was unable to find any man willing to go in his place. He and Cornelia had sold part of her land for $3000. It seems foolish that he would buy slaves at a time when people felt Lincoln had already emancipated them.

A. B. Trowell had been home on leave ever since the first of October, when he shot himself in the foot. It took him six weeks to get over the injury. Because of his ailing foot, he tried to go east via Galveston, but he was arrested by the Yankees. His being made Commissary Clerk added more to Mimmie's scorn because it was said that commissary personnel stole one-third of all the supplies they gathered for the army. Mimmie did not want to be explicit for fear her letter would be opened on its way, but she felt A. B. had gone over to the enemy, so she compared him to Japhet who refused to abide by the ethical tenets of his father Noah. Shortly after the war, to get into the legislature, A. B. swore that he was coerced into joining the CSA, which proved Mimmie correct in her opinion that he was venal.

The reference to Beauregard caps reflected the popularity of the style of hat worn by General P. G. T. Beauregard, who had won the ladies' hearts at First Manassas. He wore an unusual Renaissance style cap with a long, thin feather. The other Confederate general who had the biggest fashion club was the one who commanded at what Mimmie called Charlesburg, meaning Charles City, Va. This was the gallant J. E. B. Stuart, who wore a dashing beaver hat with a plume. Mimmie wanted to know whether the girls in elegant Mississippi thought such hats stylish. Style was still vitally important to her. Many Southern girls had only scorn for a youth not in uniform. Mimmie wore her cap as a badge.

Mimmie's November 3 letter told about Frank having the cotton crop picked and ginned for poor Clint Hartman, the young man who had died of pneumonia on the march to Shreveport. Frank regretted selling it right away as the price of cotton skyrocketed. The year before Frank had sold a wagonload of potatoes to a German colony to the west and accepted payment in the colony's scrip, supposedly redeemable at a New Orleans bank. When the bank refused to redeem it Frank said it wasn't good for anything except to stick in his boot to keep the stirrup from rubbing his shin—a "shinplaster." When a horse looked thin, he would ask whether the horse was being fed shinplasters instead of oats. The story about Bee and Sterling "booing around in the dark" was a ruse they used to frighten the Negroes into staying put, moaning words like, "Dis is your young Marse who can't rest on the bloody field. He's warning you to stay with the Mistis if you don't want the h'ants to get you."

In the next letter Bee tried to convince himself that the Union faced the "most ignoble fate that ever befell a country wrecked by imbecility." This prediction was made after the defeat of the Yankee General A. B. Burnside at Fredericksburg, which was "a great slaughter pen." Lee's troops were well entrenched there and the Yanks were unsuccessful in trying to dig them out.

Grenada, Miss.
Dec. 27th 1862

Dear Mother,

. . . Not a Yankee has dared to show himself here. There is no danger of an attack here soon, if at all, this winter. A portion of the Federal army is reported to be falling back to Memphis. General Van Dorn with his Cavalry force retook Holly Springs a few days since, capturing fifteen hundred prisoners and destroying a million and a half's worth of [Yankee] stores. He has been assigned to the command of the Cavalry and from the start he has made it likely to do considerable service. It is the position he should have held all the time. I think we have better prospects for a speedy close of the war than ever since its commencement. The defeat of [A. B.] Burnside at Fredericksburg seems to have created complete confusion in the Cabinet of Lincoln, and judging from the tone of the Northern press, filled the people almost with despair. The [New York] *World* says, "Alas, for our Country; given over it would seem to be the most ignoble fate that ever befell a country wrecked by imbecility." The [New York] *Herald*: that this is the darkest period in the history of the nation. It is certain that Seward and other members of the Cabinet have resigned. It is the general impression here that if we can hold Vicksburg through the winter and spring the North will be forced to give it up as a "bad job." I have no idea Vicksburg will be taken though there will no doubt be powerful efforts made to capture it. It is the all important point now. Troops are going there from here daily. I hope we will be sent there. . . .

It has been reported all day that Van Dorn has taken Memphis and I have just heard that Memphis papers had arrived this evening confirming the report. It may be so, as he had a large force and probably was joined by [J. H.] Morgan or [N. B.] Forrest. Morgan captured two thousand Yankees at Hartsville, Tenn., a short time since, and Forrest about four hundred at Lexington. I think they will be able to keep the Yankees busy this winter. We are all doing well. On duty quite often, but we don't mind that. . . .

Goodbye for the present
Bee *

The Yankees attacked and retook Holly Springs. Waul's Legion had to retreat. Winter had come and Bee's regiment lost its baggage in the retreat somewhere on the road to Grenada. After they got to the little town of Abbeville, there were no more rations and they were on their own. Bee struggled on to College Hill where he found his Shaw relatives. They gave him news of various cousins he had only heard of but never met. He heard that Marcus Toney, Mrs. Cade's nephew, had been in several important engagements. Calloway Hardin had just managed to lead his mother's slaves through the Yankee lines to a safe place further south. They also told him about a cousin who lived near Vicksburg. The legion was soon under the command of General Pemberton, and it seemed Bee would get his wish to go to Vicksburg.

Liberty, Dec. 27th 1862

Dear Bee,

It is Christmas but the dullest I ever saw! We hear that your army is at Grenada, Mississippi. . . . Ma is very uneasy for fear that you lost all your baggage in forced marches. Dugat Williams expects to start for Virginia in a few days. We will send a long letter to you by him. . . .

Aunt Virginia and Uncle Collins came out about a week ago. They are out at Uncle Charles'. Haven't concluded what they will do. We had an egg-nog Christmas eve. Liquor of every kind is very scarce. The weather is very bad—real Christmas! . . .

Christie is going off to school next week, to Chappell Hill. Old man Stewart engaged him a boarding house. Dr. Morley is the name.

We have heard dreadful accounts of your retreat from Abbeville—

snow, starvation, etc. We are in hopes the report is exaggerated since Jim Skinner and Dog Wrigley have written the principal accounts of which we have heard. All send Love.

Shattee *

The big excitement in Liberty was Magruder's preparations to attack the Yankees in Galveston. The ruse of covering his frail boats, the *Venture* and *Bayou City,* with cotton bales to make them look like ironclads was very successful and deceived the Yankees completely. The Union's *Harriet Lane* had four heavy guns and two 24-pound howitzers, but Captain Leon Smith had so many men hidden in the cotton bales firing rifles at the *Harriet Lane* that she surrendered. Their *Westfield* rammed into the ground and burned down while trying to get out of the harbor.

The Yankees retook the *Harriet Lane* three weeks later and moved her up to Vicksburg. During the brief period that the Confederates held the port of Galveston, Mimmie and her family were ecstatic.

New Years Morn 1863

A Happy New Year, Lunny!

The whole family have been rushing round since daylight. Various reports of cannon heard at Galveston last night. The negroes all heard the fuss, and we still hear reports now and then. Pa has just gone to the telegraph office to ascertain if the attack was really made. It was certainly quite a bombardment and must mean something. Wait and see!

We will miss [Tah] so much—but we all feel that to have him go is nothing, only a small matter, when compared with you being so far and on such an errand. We can only hope that it will end, all for the best. We dance and frolic but I don't enjoy it and wouldn't think of such a thing but for the soldiers who have such a dull time here.

Uncle [William] Collins, Pamela [Charles O'Bryan's daughter] and I expect to start to the Big Creek tomorrow morning. He wants to see the country; will stay a few days. Pa has not rented to him for this year. I expect he will farm himself. Charlie and Mary Cleveland have had their hearts saddened with a girl, really a gal, no farce. They call it Sary Ann.

Pa has just come! Hurrah! Hurrah! they have taken the *Harriet Lane,* the blockading vessel! A dispatch comes that the fight is still going on. We hear the cannon continually don't know if they have taken the Island. Capt. Leon Smith it appears commands the Expedition, a seafaring man. The last dispatch says he has immortalized himself. Hurrah for Gen. Magruder, Jeff Davis and the Southern Confederacy! a nice New Year's trick!

Jan. 2nd: I tell you, Lunny, I can scarcely hold my eyes open this morning. We all, Eugenie, Dugat, Laura [Bryan], Julia [O'Brien], Bettie, Mrs. and Miss Stone, Mr. [Theophilus] Fitzgerald and several of the Military chartered a flat boat and went two miles down the river to a party at Mr. [John] Cole's last night. We all walked to the river and started down about sundown, and had the pleasure of walking up at 3 o'clock this morning. It was tolerably pleasant. I wish you and Bill had been here.

They really were successful! Yes! Took six boats and five hundred prisoners. We know nothing of the particulars, but will know when the cars come in this morning. I just heard that Mr. Sargeant has returned from Ark. One from every Co. was detailed or elected to bring money home to the families of the soldiers that they might want to send to them.

Maj. Dark has returned, on furlough, from Ark.

I do hope and trust, Dear Lunny, that you are not sick. We will be uneasy till we hear from you. May not write more for the present, goodbye.

Mimmie *

Indeed, Bee had been ill and the Alexander Shaws had looked after him. In the next letter he spoke of Waul's cavalry being on a raid with Van Dorn to Holly Springs where they captured almost two thousand Yankees and destroyed one and one-half million dollars of Grant's military supplies. Further north General Bedford Forrest ruptured the railroad tracks and kept Grant from joining forces with William T. Sherman for his attack on December 29 at Chickasaw Bayou north of Vicksburg. The CSA position was too strong to be stormed. Sherman withdrew with heavy losses.

John Hunt Morgan made a very successful Christmas Day raid into Kentucky, but as he was withdrawing the next week he had a big fight at Springfield, Kentucky. Forrest raided Grant's lines near Lexington, Tennessee, and almost did not escape when he was attacked both in front and in back. That same last day of the year was the battle of Murfreesboro, Tennessee, where Bragg and W. J. Hardee met Rosecrans head-on and beat him. President Davis said the army must maintain Vicksburg and Fort Hudson to prevent the Federals from dismembering the Confederacy.

Grenada Miss.
Jan. 1st 1863

Dear Father,

. . . . The Yankees have all left this vicinity but they are having exciting time at every other point we hear from. The Federals made two attempts, on the 29th and 30th inst., to storm our works in the vicinity of Vicksburg but in each were repulsed (in the language of the dispatches) with terrible slaughter. Our forces took five hundred prisoners.

Telegraphed dispatches have just been received in town to the effect that Bragg has had a fight with Rosecrans near Murfreesboro [Tennessee] in which the latter was sorely beaten having [lost] 30 cannon, a large number of wagons and 4000 prisoners. Of course we have to allow a great deal for exageration; but I suppose there is no doubt but a battle has been fought and I feel confident as to the result.

I think we have not much cause for alarm in the appearance of things everywhere at the present time though there is no doubt but the Yankees are making extraordinary preparations for the capture of Vicksburg during the winter or spring. But President Davis says it will stand and I believe it.

Gen. Earl Van Dorn's expedition returned several days ago. He paroled during the trip 2300 Northern prisoners and destroyed a large quantity of property. The Cavalry of the Legion was with him. I forgot to mention in my last letter the visit of President Davis to this place. I had the pleasure of seeing him. There was a grand review of the troops on the occasion. Gen. [J. E. "Retreatin Joe"] Johnston was also here but I did not see him. I must close as the drums are beating for dress parade.

Wm. F. Hardin *

On his western inspection tour, Jeff Davis reviewed the troops at Grenada and went on to Vicksburg, the vital defense point on the Mississippi. Grant thought a canal through the swamps on the north side would facilitate troop movement. A lot of effort was expended on the canal, but it was a complete failure.

The next letter was written by Captain Black, the same man who in Mimmie's November 3 letter took the Widow White on an all-day outing to Magnolia Grove. He was a very dashing fellow from Leon County. By the time he wrote this letter, he was stationed on Galveston Island. Shattee had fallen madly in love with him even though he spelled her name wrong. Shattee corresponded with him for the next two years but they were never officially engaged. She took the following letter out of its envelope so many times that the bottom part fell off and she sewed it back on. In the same envelope was a lay written in her hand about how lonely it was waiting for the beloved who would never return.

Virginia Point Tex.
Jan. 21st '63

Miss Colleto Harden,

The detail, that I was to make to send back after you, is made: and I have given you as good a man as my company affords according to my way at estimating mankind. In all probability when I give you the name you may differ with me considerably; but I hope you will coincide with me as I am rather partial towards my selection. And being fully satisfied that you are the very identical Lady that fills his eye and heart I shall insist on you giving the man of my choice an impartial decision; and let me hear from you as soon as practicable. His name is
G. H. Black (Capt. Comd Co. D) *

Shattee and Mimmie put Hortense ("Tonsie") up to writing Bee on Valentine's Day so he would get a valentine and also some hush-hush news. Cynthia had forbidden them to write their brother about the seventeen-year-old Woods boy killing a slave girl because she revealed their liaison to his father. The Woodses were a well-known family who lived right in back of Seven Pines. Cynthia thought the news would upset Bee, not only because of young Woods' violence, but also because he had stolen Mimmie's horse, Duroc, aboard which he left town for Virginia where he joined the Liberty Invincibles to replace his fallen brother, George. That night, after the shooting, Mimmie had tiptoed over to the girl's cabin to ask her whether she still loved young Woods, but when she heard the girl's stertorous breathing, she knew it was too late for questions.[3]

Liberty, Feb. 14th 1863

Dear Cousin [Bee],

. . . You are much wished for in these happy times, away from the invading foe, but let things be as they are and may content be your lot wherever you roam.

It has been rumored that the Confederates captured at Arkansas Post, 2,500 in number, becoming exasperated by cruel treatment and absence of absolute necessaries, four having died from the effects of hunger and cold, [they] overcame their guards, burned the boats and escaped. This is thought reliable by some not yet being confirmed.

One of old man [J. B.] Woods' sons shot a negro girl of his father's the other day and made his escape.

Aunt Virginia and family are now remaining with us until they purchase a place. Uncle William [Collins] is off steamboating with Capt. [Tom] Peacock up the river.

We received letters from Berwick's Bay stating that the Yankees were there, 5,000 in number, committing great depredations. I suppose you have heard of them having a fight on the Teche after having repulsed the enemy for four hours. General [Alfred] Mouton had our distinguished gunboat *Cotton* [*Plant*] destroyed by fire. Our loss from best authorities amounted to 47 and it is believed that the Federal loss exceeds 250. While they are skedaddling they lost a considerable amount of their stores. . . . I wish you all the success imaginable. Write me soon, adieu.

Your cousin,
Hortense A. O'Brien *

Hortense, Charles's daughter, stayed in close touch with Berwick, where the Yankees had been destroying homes and property. General Mouton had to burn the gunboat *Cotton Plant* when it got stuck, to keep it from falling into enemy hands.

The benefit the Liberty ladies had given the previous November for the men stationed at Arkansas Post was for Captain Pickett's Company. Six weeks before Tonsie's letter was written, the Yankees had captured the post and imprisoned the garrison. There were no quarters to keep the prisoners in and many of them were crowded into boats. They suffered severely. Some of the starving men decided to break out and indeed escaped.

The next letter came from Shattee. Typically she made all manner of fun of Captain G. H. Black and his poor penmanship and grammar, which she felt should relegate him to the rank of private. Any man who gave her his love was subject to her criticism. She could not accept a man's offer of love.

Feb. 16th, 1863

Dear Bee,

We didn't write to you last week—knowing that you had been moved from Grenada to Vicksburg. We are at a loss where to direct your letters. . . . It has been raining here for several days; the roads are as bad as they ever get to be. The river is rising. Capt. [Thomas] Peacock has brought over from Louisiana boatloads of corn from up the river for Government use. Corn here is selling at $4 per bushel.

Judge McCreary was here this evening. He was detained, so the old gent is terribly outdone by the railroading in this country. He says corn is a'plenty up there and only $1.20.

We have been receiving letters from some of the members of Capt. Black's Co. They are prodigies as regards caligraphy, cathography, and grammar. Pet threatens to send yourself and Bill some specimens. They would tickle you somewhat at least. I fear they'd be the death of Bill S. D[ugat]. Pet rec'd one from the first Lieut. that would equal Capting Sterling's best. Oh! the ignoramuses! They should be put in ranks where they belong.

The bridge over the Trinity is about being washed away by the drift. The river is rising very rapidly. The cars can't pass the bridge. . . .

Pa has been up the country for several days. He has been shoe making. Made Mimmie a nice pair. Made Ma one, hasn't finished the mate. Christie started to school to [the] Priest yesterday [having quit Chappell Hill Institute]—is studying Algebra and Arithmetic.

Eugenie is boarding in the Convent. She is here quite often. She has heard from Dugat [Williams] once since he got to Richmond. Dugat hasn't done himself much credit so rumor goes. Old man Pryor Bryan has been terribly exercised about it. Ma and I all busy making Pa shirts. The sewing materials are very scarce. I am not sorry. . . . Good bye—

Kaleta *

Inflation was rampant. There were scarcities of all manufactured items. Since there were no shoes to be bought, Frank Hardin had turned cobbler. The shoes may have looked like Indian moccasins but were no doubt sturdy and serviceable. The competitiveness between Kaleta and Mimmie was now quite obvious. Shattee persuaded Mimmie that they were too sad about not hearing from Bee to attend a party; then sly Kaleta sent Christy to reconnoiter the party and when she was apprised, she went and had all the soldiers to herself.

Liberty, Feb. 26th, 1863

Dear Bee:

It has been nearly two months since we have received a letter from you. The bridge is very nearly gone—will be washed away in a few days. The river is within a foot of being as high as in '43. I can plainly see the water all over the flat prairie. We are in hopes to have some news soon as they are expecting a boat from Houston. . . .

It is the established opinion here that the war will end in the spring—some say sooner. Write to me what you think of it. Everything looks favorable, particularly the growing dissatisfaction in the North with the Administration and the grounds on which the war is carried on. It was reported here, that two [Yankee] regt's in La. refused to fight under Lincoln's [Emancipation] Proclamation. Hope they will rebel everywhere.

Pa has been up the country all this week as Jim [Paine, slave] has been sick with pneumonia. He is better now. Pa and Uncle Blackburn were his physicians. . . . Cornelia Van says she intends writing to you. Mr. Van [Deventer], in fact all the men that escaped from Ark. Post, are ordered to report to Capt. Stovall at Rusk, Cherokee Co.

Maj. Dark was home on sick furlough at the time the Post was taken, also Mr. Sargent on detail. They started the other day to report to Gen'l [T. H.] Holmes. I saw Maj. Dark frequently while he was here . . . says he is very sorry you did not go with him. Told me to tell you so; passed many high encomiums on your character, abilities, etc. Says had you went with him you could have been Capt. of his former Co. He is somewhat elevated over his position—thinks it is a great affair to have an office. He don't love Col. Jim [Wrigley] nor Capting Sterling. He was telling one of the difficulties they had in Galveston (he and S.).

Christy is going to the Priest [Father Berthet], in arithmetic, seems to be getting on finely, a good deal interested too. . . . Camilla goes to school every day in the week. She is learning French rapidly. Eugenie is studying it with her.

Uncle Collins has got a situation on a boat that runs up the river for corn. He seems to be satisfied now since he can get on a steamboat once more. . . . 17th Inst.: Today is Christy's birthday. He is spending it with the Priest. Capt. Whitehead's Co. gave a party last night. Mimmie and I didn't think of such a thing as going. You know we can't enjoy anything of the kind and you absent and at such a time. We sent Chris up after dark—found there was no ladies—so I went rather than have them disappointed, as they had went to the expense of a supper. All send love. . . .

Kaleta *

Bee wrote his next letter in ink made from berries. The last part of it is faded so badly that it is illegible. His company was stationed first along the river, then at Yazoo City. The company was assigned to shoot Yankee gunboats trying to steam down the Mississippi. On the envelope was a note that he had been moved to Vicksburg.

Camp on Yazoo River
Feb. 13th '63

Dear Shattee,
     . . . I was just starting out on a foraging expedition when I got your letter. Bill Dugat and I volunteered to go. . . . We retired day before yesterday. Would have had a very pleasant time had not Bill taken a very severe toothache which is not well yet, his face being very much swollen. Notwithstanding the close proximity of the Yankees we find it very dull in camp. They have camp above and below Vicksburg on the river. It is thought the high water is forcing them to leave the bend opposite the city to find higher ground further up the river. I believe it is the general opinion that their canal has proved a failure.
     One of their gunboats, *Queen of the West*, passed the batteries and went on down the river a short time since. We were taken completely by surprise and were unable to do her any serious damage. She has captured several steamboats, some of them loaded with provisions. It is hard to tell what move they will make next. But they will make every effort in their power to attain that most desired end, the capture of Vicksburg. I believe they are doomed to disappointment. . . .

[Bee]

[On the envelope:]
As you will discover I have made a change of place since the above. *

187

Bee had arrived back in Vicksburg just in time to see the *Queen of the West* safely run back past Confederate batteries. She was originally a Union ram, then was taken over by the Confederates, but recaptured soon after. Vicksburg was now surrounded and isolated, and one-half of Waul's Legion was busy building fortifications on the high bluff and the other half digging trenches on the opposite side of town getting ready for the attack they knew would come. Grant continued to confuse the Confederates, first by running gunboats past the batteries just for sport, and secondly, by using diversionary tactics such as sending General Ben Grierson's cavalry to raid all the way down to Opelousas, Louisiana. Sometimes, as the siege wore on, Billy Yank and Johnny Reb would meet along the shore and swap coffee and tobacco for sugar and meat, and the tension would ease momentarily. Bee learned to brew beer out of the sugar. He once met a local cousin and gave her his stack of family letters so she could become acquainted with his sisters through them.

There were no more letters from Bee during this period because there was no stationery and less and less opportunity to get mail out. In mid-May, Waul's Legion was used to repulse three major attacks. The siege had begun in earnest. In particularly heavy fighting, Jim Wrigley led an assault to recapture two redoubts which had just been lost. He succeeded and himself presented the enemy colors to General Waul on May 22. The siege continued for six weeks.

Grant concluded that the town could only be taken by starvation. The hour of darkness began. Residents moved into caves in bluffs and under their houses. Food was meager: moldy bacon and a few ounces of pea flour were soldiers' and civilians' rations. The corn was already used up. Mule meat, frogs, and rats were delicacies. The soldiers were "wan, hollow-eyed, footsore, bloody."[4]

"Without a change of clothes and one blanket to a man, they fought uncomplainingly under constant fire; the Second Texas Regt. held the fort until the end."[5]

"The fiery shower of shells goes on day and night" but "the shells had lost their terrors for [the soldiers'] dumb and famished misery."[6] General Lee commended Bee's Company for "coolness and gallantry."[7]

The shelling was stepped up:

> Twenty-four hours a day . . . a deadly hail of iron dropped through the roofs and the denuded streets. . . . All you can hear is the rattle of the enemy's guns with the sharp crack of the rifles of

their sharpshooters. . . . at night the roaring of their terrible mortars.[8]

. . . When it rained, they slept in the mud, when the sun burned them, they endured. They drank water from shallow wells. . . . yet when they surrendered, they wept."[9]

The legion's casualties were 48 officers and 245 men killed at Vicksburg. On July 4, J. C. Pemberton surrendered 30,000 men, the largest number ever surrendered in history of warfare until then.[10] When they marched by there were no jibes from the enemy, only a respectful silence. Somewhere during the fighting, Bee and Jim Wrigley had resolved their quarrel about Bee's money. They were friends again before Wrigley left for Virginia. No physical restraint was put on the paroled prisoners, and soon they began to straggle home.

Kaleta "Shattee" Hardin photo made c. 1873 in Galveston. Educated at Ursuline in Galveston and at Andrew Institute. Lived at Seven Pines until her death in 1884.

Louis Schneider (1836– 1876) left Strasbourg for New Orleans at age seven. Shown here in 1873 as president of Germania Bank, with wife Maria and two sons.

CHAPTER TWELVE

LIFE HAD BECOME ALMOST UN-bearable around Berwick and Bayou Sale because of the continual fighting and skirmishing. Both the Ellerslie and Wyandotte homes were Union headquarters at one time or another. As things got worse in Louisiana, more residents left. Aunt America and Captain Stevens moved in with the Bagarleys, and Aunt Virginia Collins could not decide whether to join her children already in Liberty with Frank and Cynthia. Uncle William Collins had no difficulty in finding a job as a carter, and Uncle Alfred Stevens, who had had enough blockade running for awhile, thought he would try hauling.

Although there was no real fighting, there were scarcities throughout Texas. As early as January 1863, the Liberty ladies had petitioned that Sol Andrews be relieved of his military duties so that he could manufacture looms and spinning wheels for them. The cotton and wool they grew had to be carded with a pair of curry combs before it could be spun. Spinning thread and weaving cloth became a full-time occupation for many women.

George wrote to his sister Sallie that he was trying to fill her husband's request that he buy a girl to spin thread for her and the children's clothes.

Dear sister,

Your account, if not a 'reason' for failing to reply to Mr. Somer, is of course altogether satisfactory. Housewives and mothers have an abundance of work to do in these 'squally times.'

Be assured that I regret equally with yourself failure to meet you and 'Bro. Wooldridge' at the nest. What a pity!—reached there just a few hours after yr departure. Well, as experience has ever taught me: in this life every 'sweet has its bitter.' I was prepared anyway to spend a pleasant time with the old folks at home. Mother soon gave me a full rehearsal of yr history from the last chapter up to the present date; and [I] discovered in large the fine health and flourishing specimen of Infantry. No doubt she is the smartest of her age and calibre anywhere in the Southland!

To tell me of the Christmas dinner you and yr household enjoyed only tantalizes me: for it reminds me of the fact that I have not had anything <u>good</u> to eat but once since I left the Mt.—Choice viands, like silks and ribbons, are becoming few and far between with us. "Corn, coffee, hog and hominy" complete our bill of fare now. However this is not the subject of least complaint.

As to Wooldridge's plan for the year—I have ever confidence in his wisdom. I have been trying to buy a girl, but so far no prospect of success. The country has been full of negro-buyers for months. No sales of that description of girl at all. Mr. Hanny and myself have utterly failed to make such a purchase for him. You are a little behind Caroline [sister in Keatchie, Louisiana]. She writes that she, "Wove 5 yards the day before the loom was in full operation." etc. . . . Mr. Hanny is up home on detail for conscripts of Polk—will leave in a day or two and I may go with him to Galveston. If so will try to come up and see you as I return—don't look for me tho'. . . .

Bright is in the army in place of the Johnson draftee. I was drafted but not disturbed. . . . A letter from Mother states that father had sold some cotton at 20¢ and gone to pay for his new land [in Grimes Co.].

Your affectionate brother,
George *

The Hardin family lost contact with Bee after his letter of February 1863. They knew his company was at Vicksburg and assumed after the surrender of July 4 that Bee would be making his way home. But since there was no organized transport, it might take a long time.

With so many men gone to war it was hard for Frank to find someone to manage the plantation. When a young Tennessee relative named Philip Burford suddenly showed up, he hired him. Burford was good while he lasted, but fear that the Military Police were after him caused him to disappear into the Big Thicket. He was replaced by a refugee Creole couple by the name of Gasqué.

Frank was up above the landing one summer day in 1863 when he saw a strangely familiar looking little scarecrow getting off the boat. Frank's heart gave a mighty surge when he recognized Bee. He rejoiced that his delicate son was home, in good health, and apparently psychologically undamaged. As soon as Bee had cleaned up, he put on fresh clothes, threw a leg over Jim Miller and trotted into town to see Cynthia and the girls. Bee was hugged, feted, and fattened up. Helping his mother at the spinning wheel was good therapy for his jangled nerves. Cynthia had just received a book in a contraband shipment from England. It was George Eliot's *Adam Bede*, and she gave it to Bee, thinking that this rational and logical novel with its praise of Christian virtues would be good for him after the horrors of the siege.

Bee belied Grant's prediction that those who endured Vicksburg would never fight again. By the end of October he was ready to go back to the legion, but this time he and Bill Dugat and Sterling and Skinner joined Colonel B. Timmons' company. Another man in that company was Captain J. Hogue, a hero of Vicksburg, who, when a redoubt there had been about to fall to the Yankees, asked to be allowed to take fifteen men to reinforce it. He was already back in charge of a company. Bee's group of veteran soldiers went to Houston and from there took the railroad to Hempstead, where they joined their command. Two days later Shattee wrote to him:

Friday Nov. 13, 1863

Dear Bee:

. . . Wednesday after you left, Pa, Mimmie, and Chris went to the farm. Had it not been that Uncle Collins and the children came the evening you left our family would have been somewhat lessened. We haven't had time to grieve at your departure so you see. We congratulated ourselves on having something to draw our minds off. I did feel awful a while after you left.

Uncle Collins and Uncle Stevens went to Houston yesterday—The cars came very early—they were served pretty much as you were—had to go dinnerless.

Ma has taken all of Aunt Virginia's children until spring anyhow. Nellie [Collins] will go to school at the [Ursuline] Convent with our children. Nellie, Nannie and myself were at Uncle Charles' yesterday evening. Tonsie came in yesterday morning and took Bettie Day out [to Magnolia Grove]. On the way out Morgan White was running a buggy race with them. They came in collision—upset M's buggy and broke the top and hurt his ankle. Tonsie and Bettie came out safely. Uncle Charles was lecturing when we got there. The girls started to make popcorn candy yesterday evening but, unfortunately, we had to leave before it was finished.

Ed Jones is still here. I must tell you—he's in trouble. "J. Fella, Tailor from Paris" made him a [uniform] suit of grey. He complains that the coat is too short—shorter than the present one. And he has decided not to wear it. Am glad his taste is changing from short to long.

By the way, you forgot to take *Adam Bede* with you. Do you want it sent? I can send it by someone going over. Did you find Capt. [J.] Hogue at Hempstead? I guess they [the family] will be all down from the farm Saturday. R. Philip Burford has departed! Give my regards to the boys.

Kaleta *

Mimmie thought it was a great idea to make a nutcake and send it to Bee. She had done this once before with disastrous results because the cake was full of dirt when he received it. Mimmie was determined to try to send another one. Whenever Mimmie got a chance she made a crack about her brother's drinking. She still thought that the cavalry was the only proper place for gentlemen, but she had gotten used to the idea of her brother being proud of not being an officer. Mimmie was in a prickly mood when she wrote the next letter because she was jealous of the parties that she heard her brother and Bill Dugat were attending in Houston.

Liberty Tex. Nov. 30, 1863

Dear Sir,

Yours of no date at all has been received, and I write to inform you that I would like to be the recipient of a letter from your august hand.

Pep snuffles today, whispers and nods at play. Owen [Collins] assisting Mademoiselle Josephine to pick wool. Ma is spinning and says you may expect a box of Christmas goodies. I also have an eye to that said box. I sent word to Chris to save up all the eggs that the farm affords, and have engaged all the butter from Mme. Gasky, wife of Pa's overseer. We picked a lot of pecans. "Angels and ministers of Grace defend you," do you say? Why, the dirt won't show, and eggs and sugar will counteract it and make a fine combination. Get a little La. [Louisiana rum] to worry it down with.

Ma says get Jimmy [Burgess] to go to Houston and select for her the best pair of cotton cards therein. You may advance the cash of which Ma will send you the repayment by first chance. Ma wants Jimmy Burgess to select as she thinks he is a good judge of cards, his wife having been accustomed to spin for a long time. Suppose he will not object to accommodating a body.

By the way Uncle S[tevens] failed in his trip up the country. His wagon was so heavy, and the roads were getting bad, and his team proved insufficient. He returned, selling his sugar to Uncle Bagarly for little more than he gave. He had two hogsheads. Won't the old man have a heavenly time speculating on it?

Uncle Charles [O'Bryan] still entertaining half of La. All his visitors remain, with the addition of two of Dr. Watkins' brothers. I will remain a night when I go for K. She, Mrs. Boon and I are to have a duck hunt at Jose [Coronado]'s Bayou—fine sport for women!

How comes it that your Mars Sterling is in town, as I hear is the case? Have not feasted my eyes on his goodly proportions.

Ma says have you enough covering? Surely you [need] re-cover to fortify you against this whizzing Yankee wind that has been blowing three days.

Old Zeke [Thompson] is safely ensconced at the widow's. He presented me with a bottle of "Eau de Rose" the other day, of which I have, with some lard and wax been concocting all sorts of hair oils. If you and Bill find yourself in need of any, say the word. Expect you could use any amount since you are so frequently found in the parlors of aged gentlemen, fathers of the fair daughters of Houston. Have a care for thyself! Say, are you sure you and Bill behave properly on those occasions? Don't forget to pull off your hats, and don't say, "Yes Mam," and "No Sir," to the servants.

Mr. Cooke of Sabine Pass, the one to whom I loaned *Shirley*, returned me the book and a box of oranges. I wish you could have had some of them. I have written him a most killing note in return to his requesting a correspondence. Couldn't refuse after his kindness but it went deuced hard to write to such an incorrigible old "bach" as he is.

Any talk of your being mounted—not you but the Legion? He had heard something to that effect. How long will you remain where you are?

I have some wool to knit you a comforter. Ma intends having you a pair of gloves knit. They will be warm if not ornamental. All send a power of love.

Most respectfully my dr. sir
C. G. Hardin *

At the beginning of 1864 General N. P. Banks's forces in southern Louisiana started a big push to crush the two Confederate armies in northern Louisiana. General Richard Taylor ordered some of the thin-spread Texas troops over to the Red River to support his men, Bee's company among them.

Shattee wanted to be sure her brother had heard of John Morgan's escape from a Union prison. General Morgan tunneled out of the prison and then climbed over the outer wall. He brashly took a train to Cincinnati, seating himself right next to a Union officer.

In her usual devious way, Shattee would not admit that Lieutenant ("L.") Black was her beau. She pretended that he was Mimmie's. Bee had encountered Lieutenant Black over in Louisiana. Apparently Black had told Shattee that he had beat up Jim Wrigley and that that was why Wrigley had asked for a transfer across the Mississippi.

Feb. 7th 1864

Dear Bee:

Pa is up the country; Christy is here—for the first time in three weeks. He's going to join the army—hasn't decided when. You know where I <u>don't</u> want him to go! He and Ma are playing 'Seven Up.' Pa and Ma have quit chess and have taken up with cribbage. Sat up till twelve nearly every night last week playing.

Adrian Salles has got back. He's clerking in some of the departments. He's quite as mysterious as ever—knows all the news from the Potomac to the Rio Grande. He called a few evenings since with Mr. Spangler [from Missouri]—of Gen. John S. Bowen's Division. He was not at Vicksburg at the time of its surrender—off on business for Gen. Sterling Price.

Have you seen a *Telegraph* [Houston newspaper] with a detailed account of [John] Morgan's escape? If not I'll send it. It seems a miracle.

Mr. Zeke Thompson has "gone out" as he terms it—at least has started for Calcasieu [Parish].

Laura intends leaving school and going to spinning—so Nannie will be alone in her class.

Pet's not here to congratulate you on having your eyes gladdened by a sight of Lieut. "Lafayette" Black. Do you admire his "style"? a favourite expression of his. Tell Bill to look at his [Black's] fist. Then he can account for a certain dog forwarded across the Miss. Do seek his acquaintance, you'll find him workably pleasant.

Mr. Van will be compelled to return to the army. The law is not a bad one.

Peppie has a home-spun dress. Ma spun it. . . . Chris has just come to the door with, "Tell Bee I'll be over there soon."

Shattee *

Christy was a first-class cowboy. Ever since his sixteenth birthday he had been gathering beeves for the army, working under a Major Merrick. Few men were available to ship beef either up or down the river, so the Coushatta Indians has been enlisted to build flatboats to pole them up the river. The cattle were wild as buffaloes; the young ones never having been rounded up for branding due to the shortage of ranch hands. Christy enjoyed the work. They had a bed wagon that carried blankets and tarps and there was a horse wrangler and six or eight cowpunchers. The greatest danger was an electric storm at night. "When a stampede started, the cowboys guarding the herd would pull their six-shooters and begin shooting as they swung with the herd and tried to throw the fear-crazed cattle into a mill."[1] If a horse stumbled and fell the whole herd trampled the pony and rider into the earth. After Christy had his eighteenth birthday he arranged to enlist in the regular army.

In her next letter Shattee mentions having seen Sam Houston, the son of the general. She and Bee played with him when they were children together in Liberty.

Liberty, Apr. 1, 1864

Dear Bee—

Stephen Brashear is going over tomorrow [to Louisiana]. We will send a bundle by him to you—also this letter. I am afraid you have not been receiving our letters as we have had to guess where to send them. You must write your P.O.

Christy got down from the farm yesterday. He hasn't decided what he'll do yet as regards going in the army. He would like, I think, to go with you, but I tell him I would live a deserter before I would swell the lists of Carpenter Captings [Sterling]. He is swelling in these parts so I hear by the way. We received your letter viz the thing.

Pa's corn was killed by the freeze. He has to replant some of it and he is up the country now. The peaches are all killed too. I fear we are in the coming season to have a dry time in the way of fruits—and of eating too. Every price has risen rapidly in last weeks. Uncle Collins is up the country now. Owen [Collins] is such a sweet child. We all love him. He is very much attached to Pa. Calls them Pa and Mama.

Ma says she is having more clothes spun for you. Just write when you need them. The pants are some of her spinning. She will dye some thread to make Christy and yourself some warm shirts tomorrow. She says tell you she misses you very much at the [spinning] wheel.

Mimmie and I do all the sewing. Ma spins when she feels like it. [Aunt] Harriet and Emma spin all the time. I have just finished knitting me a pair of stockings. Am going to knit Pep a pair. Aren't I smart? . . .

Chris is in here laughing and giggling so I can't do anything. . . . He has an engagement with Maj. Merrick in the beef dept. and now has a furlough from him but he will go in the service soon. Chris says be sure to tell him in your next letter what he better do. . . .

Christy is spinning such yarns to Mimmie that I have to stop every once in a while to listen. We had a visit from Florine Shea today. She has grown less supercilious of you. She asked Nellie . . . to come "whisper kisses to Bee from me."

How do you think the war is going now? Should this week be the bloodiest and last of the war?

McMahon's artillery battery was here a few days last week.[†] Your Sam Houston belongs to it. I saw him at a distance. He has grown very much since we knew him. We heard from Houston. . . . they had given a large party at Mr. Cabiness' in honor of his arrival from the army. Twas a very large affair from what I could hear. I would like to have been there. . . .

† This battery distinguished itself the following week in the Battle of Mansfield.

Chris is telling Mimmie about teasing Ez Green [Blackburn Hardin's grandson, age sixteen] about a pistol and Bowie knife he has—by riding off from him and telling him he's afraid. I haven't any more paper so goodbye. All send love.

Shattee *

Shattee wondered if the next week would be the bloodiest and last of the war because she knew the Battle of Mansfield was shaping up. It occurred on April 8 and 9. The water level of the Red River was very low that spring and caused tremendous difficulties to General Banks, who was unable to get his troops upriver. One of the Yankees called this battle "our skedaddle from the Rebs." It broke the back of Banks' campaign.

There is no record of whether Bee was directly engaged in the Battle of Pleasant Hill the next day when the troops were "hotly engaged in fine style."[2] In May he was at Jenkins Ferry in the rain and the mud, the troops displaying great coolness, "firing as though hunting squirrels."[3] Using guerilla tactics, General Thomas Green with 900 men slowed down Banks's 38,000 and, finally, on May 19, gave the Yankees such a drubbing that the Red River campaign failed and Banks gave up any idea of reaching the heart of Texas. In June the legion returned to Galveston's Mud Island to keep watch on the Union forces there and to protect the Gulf Coast from invasion.

Sometime in spring 1864, Bee was injured when a horse kicked him. He had been trying to hitch a partly broken horse to a wagon. Bee, who had become a sergeant, felt that he should show the other soldiers how to do things, but Mimmie thought he was reckless. Mimmie was a real soldier at heart. She referred to the men who stayed behind as "feather beds." Like her brother, she had a great deal of sympathy for the half-starved, underpaid soldiers who deserted to come home and put in a crop to feed their families.

Tuesday, June 1st, 1864

Bee,

Henry Steusoff goes today. We received your letter by Clay Stone.

Clay is scratching mad at the way your animal treated you. I didn't expect any better. Keep on driving—maybe you'll get a thorough!!!

Ma sends you by John Swinney a cheese she had been keeping for you.

Some excitement in town: The Feather Beds have added new laurels to their brows. [They] took out seven deserters and shot them in cold blood.[4]

Goodbye,
Mimmie *

Soon after this Bee came home on a long furlough. The war had started out for Bee and his sisters as a romantic adventure, but had now become an overwhelming killer, ruining their way of life. Bee had seen the value of a gold dollar worth three Confederate paper ones by the end of 1862; by January of '64 worth twenty, and by the end of that year worth forty paper Confederate dollars. By May of 1865 it would be worth seventy.

Things were much worse in Louisiana. In St. Mary's Parish there was an enormous amount of robbing, burning, and even murder of plantation owners. Besides the atrocities, the Louisiana people were learning the truth of what historian Bruce Catton later wrote: "The men who die for patriotism die also for the enrichment of cold-eyed schemers who risk nothing, and every battlefield is made uglier by the greed of men who never fight."[5] Such were the men who had buttered up to "Beast" Butler and traded cotton to the Yankees for Union money. Treasury agents sent to investigate New Orleans said, "It is the general impression here that money will accomplish anything with the authorities."[6]

Ann O'Brien's daughters in Texas were very worried about their mother because she refused to leave her home. Since Alfred Stevens had gone on a long sea voyage, they decided that America was the one who should go back and look after their mother. There was much skirmishing along the Teche. The partisan rangers, who were intrepid raiders, patroled the by-ways and ambushed Banks's marauders. Colonel Ashley W. Spaight's Texas Battalion was pressing the Yankees hard. Shortly before America arrived, her mother's home had been burned and she had moved into a cabin. Losing everything she owned, having her slaves taken by Yankee soldiers, and being so hungry that she ate contaminated food—all added up to kill Ann. Because Louisiana was conquered territory, there was no regular mail delivery, and it had taken six weeks for a letter from Berwick to reach America's sister, Elvira McMahon, in New Orleans. As soon as Elvira received it, she wrote to Texas.

Nov. 8th, '64

Dear sister,

I have just received a letter from America dated Sept. 26th in which she stated that Mother Brien died on the 4th of the same month. She was sick nine days of severe fever and dysentery. Her suffering was intense. She bore it with great fortitude. She was insensible fourteen hours before death. Several hours before she became unconscious she took leave of all, leaving goodbye for all of her children, hoping that they would meet her in heaven. "Where she was sure of going herself," were her words. She did not express any desire to live, only to see the end of the war. Ann and America were alone, Vic [slave] being sick at the time. She says it is a great trial to stand over the bed of Death, especially of a dying mother [and] alone. She sent for one of her neighbors, a Mrs. Adrien. There is but few citizens in the place and most of them were sick at the time.

She was buried under a large oak tree below the graveyard in that place that is near old Mme. Elouisine, a spot selected by Nathaniel Berwick.

[Elvira] *

About this time another family in New Orleans received a very different letter. It was written by Louis Schneider to his sister, Clementine. Louis and Clementine were Mimmie's grocery store friends that she had first met in Ocean Springs in 1858. Louis had moved to Cincinnati shortly after the war started. The purpose of the move was to make connections with a Yankee bank. Louis continued to receive and deposit in the bank money from the family grocery business and also money from Southern friends who wished to get it out and into Union currency. Louis and his wife, Maria, lived a luxurious life in Cincinnati, because, as General Grant complained, "Cincinnati furnished more contraband goods than Charleston and has done more to prolong the war than the state of South Carolina."[7] Louis had a short and skinny younger brother, Jules. Jules enlisted with the Confederate forces, was captured and imprisoned in Louisville, Kentucky.[8] He got his release by swearing that he had been made to enlist under duress. From Louisville he would travel to Cincinnati, but Louis feared that Jules still had Southern leanings. Auguste Blaffer, whom we last met as a bookkeeper in the Schneider grocery, had also served in the CSA. After the battle of Perryville on October 8, 1862, he sent a substitute and came home to his job in the conquered city of New Orleans. On January 4, 1864, he married his boss's daughter, Clementine (Ap. 25).

Louis wrote to Clementine:

Dec. 5th, '64, Cincinnati

. . . Jules will be with us. He has intimated as much and his company is no more agreeable to Maria than it is to me—. We will in that event try and get along with him as cheerfully as possible.

You write of my having neglected to send you my picture and that you placed the one that Ma had into your album. I really was under the impression that I had sent you one of my *cartes de visite* but as you say, I may not have done so, anyhow I enclose a copy for you and when you put it into your album, keep it at a distance from any of your rebel faces that adorn your book and if anyone asks whose picture it is, say it is my brother's, who is a loyal man.

If the art of photographing on *cartes de visite* is introduced in N.O. I wish you would have your pictures taken and send us one, and we would be delighted if Pa and Ma's could be added to our album. Induce them to have them taken as well as Tina and Nellie [Schneider].

Louisa Germann will write to Ma in a few days and also send her her photograph. Maria has one of them but it is not a true likeness, it is very much flattered and such will be the one that Ma will receive.

I cannot close without commenting on the poetical effusion of "Miranda" authoress of the choice morsel, the "Battle of the Fair" which you sent me undoubtedly as being something grand. Now, I have to say that when I heard of the outrage that the women of N.O. committed on that occasion, I but wished that Gen. [Benjamin] Butler was in command in N.O. instead of the good and kind Mr. [Nathanial] Banks, for then the she snakes would not have dared to creep from their holes to spout their venomous treason and commit an outrage upon "loyalty." They took full advantage of their sex to produce a violent outburst of foul villainy and treason and I hope that a recurrence of such a scene may be met with more vigorous consequences and of such a nature as to leave it a life long remembrance to the participants.

Give my kind regards to Mr. Blaffer and our united love to all
at home.

With affection
Louis *

Such were the sentiments of this opportunistic young banker who
had been born in Strasbourg. In spite of "Beast" Butler's orders that his
soldiers should treat any disrespectful woman like a street walker, some
New Orleans women continued to manifest their disdain and hatred of
the conqueror by acid comments. "She-snakes" were female "copper-
heads," the name given to people who professed Southern sentiments.
The "loyalty" Louis spoke of was, of course, loyalty to the Union.
Shakespearean names such as "Miranda" from *The Tempest* were popular
pen names with the rebels. Wealthy New Orleans citizens were often
friendly to the Yankees, as an Illinois Sergeant noted, "I find these
southern nabobs and nabobesses who were going to die in the last ditch
are quite willing . . . to taste the sweets of Uncle Sam's pantry." [9] As to
what happened subsequently to the nouveau riche parents of Louis
Schneider and of Auguste Blaffer, they were well advised to leave the
city for their native Germany and never return. In 1925 Clem's daughter
proudly wrote of her grandparents during the war: "Many were the in-
terviews they had with General Butler. . . . In 1866 our grandparents
left New Orleans for a well-earned pleasure trip in Europe." [10] In truth,
the grandmothers were excoriated so severely by the she-snakes for
being collaborators and war-profiteers that the effects lasted a lifetime.
They never set foot in the South again and their husbands only returned
on occasional business trips. The she-snakes also hissed that New Orleans would never have fallen had it not been for the German boys
posted in the river forts who mutinied when the first of Farragut's ships
came past. [11] No one who had associated with the corrupt Butler was
socially accepted.

Louisiana had had a provisional government under Federal Governor
Michael Hahn following the capture of New Orleans. The only places
the Union controlled in Texas were the ports. Patrol ships guarded the
mouth of Galveston Bay. Union soldiers had a foothold at Galveston,
but never ventured into the town. Bee's company was stationed right
near Galveston on Mud Island. Many other companies were stationed

in the surrounding area, the strategic presence of so many soldiers preventing the Yankees from planning any shore attack.

The next letter was from Bee, who, to keep the sun off while fishing, was trying to braid a straw hat:

Mud Island Sept. 4th '64
Dear Mother,

. . . . I have come to the conclusion that Mud Island is a much more pleasant place than Galveston to be stationed at . . . the fish and oysters are without number and the latter are getting very good. Bill [Dugat], [B. F.] Sterling and I camped out on the beach several nights ago and fished a few hours in the morning. We caught fifteen splendid redfish. We have made arrangements at a house about a mile from the fort to get buttermilk and clabber in exchange for our extra meal. . . .

I have plaited about twenty yards. Tell the girls to write me how much it will take to make a hat, the palmetto is not good. I am afraid it will not make a very nice hat. . . .

Bee *

Mud Island Sept. 30th '64
Dear Shattee,

. . . There was a man died a few days ago who some thought had yellow fever. . . . The boat comes with rations about once a fortnight and the men are not permitted to go aboard except a fatigue party to unload which takes but a short time. . . . You must all be ready to run if it should come to Liberty. . . .

My love to all
Bee *

Mud Island, October 27, '64
Dear Christy,

. . . And so the Waco girls are attracting your attention! You must do more than look at them or you will never be able to captivate any of them. Do you ever call on them? . . . Are you gathering beeves now in McLelland County? Write to me whether you have much to do. I do not know when I will be able to get a furlough. I hope we will get home at the same time. You must write often. Give my regards to Swan [Blackie Hardin's son].

Bee *

Mud Island   Nov. 9th 1864

Dear Nannie,

As Shattee and Mimmie are probably gone [to college] it will therefore fall to your lot to do the writing. . . . We are expecting to be ordered away from this place as soon as the yellow fever is froze out as it will be almost impossible to furnish supplies for so many men during the winter. The boats cannot run here when a Norther is blowing. We have been out of wood once already and during the worst weather we have had. . . . Give my love to Nelly [Collins] and kiss all the little ones.

Bee *

[Andrew College, Huntsville]
Thursday, Nov. 10, 1864

Ma,

We [Kaleta and Mimmie] arrived today. Made two days trip of it. Stayed all night at Dr. Kittriles—he wasn't at home. Tell Pa that we stopped at Mr. [W. D.] Cleveland's and saw him. He seemed to be very glad to see us—delivered Pa's message.

Contrary to expectations we had a very pleasant trip, particularly from Aunt [Catherine]'s house. . . .

Huntsville looks quite natural. You mustn't be lonesome.

Kaleta *

Andrew College had opened up again in spite of the war shortages, and Kaleta had gone back, taking with her her younger sister. The Mr. W. D. Cleveland whom they stayed with was the man for whom the town of Cleveland, Texas, was named.

During the winter of 1864–65, entertainments were conducted at a seemingly feverish pace to ease the tension of impending doom. Christy had finally enlisted with a group of teenagers, some of them younger than he, all of them dressed in homespun clothes, carrying their deer rifles. They had set off for camp with an older officer, the middle-aged Mr. Simmons.

Mimmie sat down in January to write the first letter to her newly enlisted young brother:

Home, Jan. 19th, 1865

Dear Chris:

. . . I had laid off to write last night when here comes a note from the Rev. Cummings saying that he and Bro. Carlyle would take tea with us—during the domestic commotion I took violent offense—wrote them a note that I regretted and that it would be "impossible for me to be home during tea time or otherwise," etc. and took flight to Uncle C's—a lie every bit. During my absence, Bee [home on furlough all month] and Kaleta patched up the affair and sent for them. When I arrive, to my utter affright and astonishment, Cummings is first to greet me. Carlyle had gone visiting elsewhere after my note. Eugenie was here so we had a very pleasant time. Of course Dr. Carlyle would have graced the occasion with his pigeon-tail [morning coat]. Cummings knows infinitely more about how to sober drunk men, how far it is possible to kill one with a pistol, and the various merits of hound dogs and bear dogs, than he does about scriptural texts.

The [program] ticket I send will not explain itself—it deserves a few words. Instead of "Soirée Musical" at the mast-head—should have been "Exhibition of the Branches." Kaleta and I went up thinking it was a dancing party—when lo! and behold! a curtain/stage! etc. The curtain I think is one which divides one of Mrs. Branch's suites of rooms from her dining parlor. It displayed numerous grease spots. Finally it arose displaying Master Gayle Wharton [Branch] in attitude of an orator. He made his bow, delivered himself of his subject: "The Dignity of the Human Mind," and then came forth one of the most learned, lengthy, highflown, metaphysical, foolish, confounded affairs that a Branch brain could conceive. Whereupon followed some simple nothings between Whart and Giles Miers. Whereupon Miss Olive Grady and Gus Raily appear, try to gladden the hearts of the Confederate people with a candle lecture! Then the curtain raises several times and descends on complete failures. Cousin Sarah [McMurtry], Mrs. Thompson and our crowd have incurred the old Lady's displeasure by laughing right out and making all manner of remarks. So much for the public amusements!!

The Miss Scott mentioned (in enclosed program), we discovered to be a pug-nosed English gal, friend of the Raileys—one of their old bar-room associates maybe. There were a good many ladies present. They danced till 3 o'clock. We came home at one. . . . I forgot to mention that "a song" was announced, but they were compelled to abandon it, not being able to get the curtain high enough for Gus Railey's head. Cousin Luke proposed to turn him bottom upwards—stand him on his head.

Bee is enjoying himself very well—he went with me yesterday. We did not have the pleasure of seeing your dear cousin Tonsie [O'Brien]—she and Aunt Felide were visiting.

Pa is at the farm. Peppie went with him on Duroc [sidesaddle]. What a figure!

Tell Mr. Simmons Capt. White announced to the people through the mediums of Morgan [White] and the Dr. [R. C. White] that if Galveston falls, he is a ruined man. Why, no one knows—unless the money for the 3 bales is deposited there.[†] —Give all our love to Mr. Simmons—write often. I have strung this out amazin'.

Yours with love
Mimmie *

Bee had gotten another long furlough perhaps because there was nothing for him to do on Mud Island and there was plenty of work at home. In any case, the soldiers' morale was disintegrating. Knowledge of the devastation in Louisiana and knowledge that they were ruined financially was not as bad as the loss of hope and the fear of the oppressor's heel. The number of deserters from the Confederate ranks was approaching 100,000 men. The commanders were resorting to more and more severe punishments.

Next month Bee was back with his company, now stationed on the outskirts of Galveston. He got off a letter to Christy, who was on the Louisiana border. Bee had told earlier of riots in which he participated, riots caused by lack of tobacco, poor food, and scarcity of furloughs. The sympathetic Bee was on the side of the protestors. How horrible it must have been for him and others—knowing that the war was lost—to see a fellow soldier executed for leaving when there was no longer anything for him to do.

Galveston, March 5th, 1865

Dear Christy,

. . .We have had some considerable excitement of late. But the information you have received about a mutiny in our Reg't is entirely incorrect. Since the famous "tobacco raid" last summer, which I think is the best thing that ever happened, there is never any mischief done that is not at once laid to us. There was a considerable disturbance in town last Sunday night. A number of unarmed soldiers gathered

---

† Of course White would lose what he received for the cotton, as Confederate money would be worthless, but as long as he had self-respect he would not be "ruined."

around General [J. M.] Hawes' Headquarters for the purpose of making some demands of him. I have not been able to learn precisely what. We had roll-call soon after it commenced and there were not a dozen men absent from muster.

Two companies of the 2nd Reg't were ordered out under the command of Major [G. W. L.] Fly of that Reg't to suppress the mutiny. He ordered them to fire into the crowd which they did, killing a young man belonging to our Reg't who was some distance off and had just left the church. He was but a few steps in advance of a number of ladies who were returning from church.

There was a man shot for desertion here day before yesterday. He belonged to a battery of light artillery. We were compelled to witness the sad spectacle. There was an attempt made to rescue him after he was brought on the ground by about twenty men belonging to the same battery. They came out with two pieces of artillery and demanded the release of the prisoner. I think they expected to get assistance from the rest of the soldiers but in that they were entirely mislead. They were very soon surrounded and were arrested without resistance.

Give my regards to Swan and Mr. Simmons. Nothing more today.

Bee *

Bee felt that it was morally wrong to shoot deserters who were leaving their posts because there was nothing for them to do. He felt the war was lost and he sympathized with the protesters and deserters from this time on. He had anticipated that his outspoken regiment would be blamed for an infection that ran through all the soldiers. The man who gave the order to fire on the protesters had been decorated for bravery at Vicksburg and this major, like the newspapers, could not yet accept the fact that the morale of the army had deteriorated beyond repair. On March 2, Bee had written Shattee as follows:

. . . You will probably see accounts in the papers of a riot that occurred in town last Sunday night. I do not know the exact object of the leaders of the affair. Quite a number of soldiers from different Reg'ts collected around Gen. Hawes' Headquarters for the purpose of making some demands of the Gen. They were almost entirely unarmed. One or two companies of the 2nd Reg't. who are doing Provost duty in town were ordered out under the command of Major Fly of that Reg't. to quell the disturbance. He marched them to Headquarters and commanded them to fire into the crowd and, I have heard, without once ordering them to disperse or intimating that it was his intention to fire. Church had just been dismissed and the streets were full of women and children returning to their homes. A young man belonging to our Reg't. was killed. He had just left the church and was a few steps in advance of a crowd of ladies. There were but few of our Reg't. in town and the most of them were at church, though we will probably have the credit of being leaders in the affair. . . . *

Bee felt the blame on his back for the whole war gone wrong. His father had been a winner; he was a loser. He did not complain to his father, although if he had, the older man would have been understanding and supportive.

Galveston, April 16th, 1865

Dear Pa,
    . . . The *Ruthven* went up the river several days ago. She came down one evening and started up the next day. I was on guard and could not write. I wrote by the Steamer *Mary Hill* the last time she went up the river from here. . . . There was a grand review of all the troops on the Island yesterday by Gen. Magruder. He made us a speech after the review. He says from the information he has received he is in anticipation of an attack soon, and that it is his determination not to let the enemy gain a foot of ground except by the hardest kind of fighting. He is going to dig in in earnest. I think from the way he spoke that it is his intention to fortify Liberty and there will probably be several Reg'ts of troops stationed there. He brought back with him ten thousand Infantry and quite a number of Cavalry. He says there are sixty thousand effective men in this area.
    Old "Pirate" Maffit was around yesterday. He is engaged in blockade running at present, I believe. Tell Ma I'm anxious to get home and also that I need a pair of pants as it may be some time before I will draw a pair. Make some of them write by every chance.

W. F. Hardin *

At night in the rain was the most favorable time to slip out for blockade running. The pirate mentioned was James Newland Maffit, formerly a riverboat captain and then commander of the *C. S. S. Florida*, a Confederate ship seized in Brazil. Secretary Seward said it was unlawful to seize the ship there, but other Yankees called Maffit a pirate and said he was fair game. He escaped and came back to Galveston, where, in 1865, he diverted Union cotton ships to friendly hands. Bee met a lot of such characters in Galveston.

The last letter was written a week after Lee's surrender at Appomattox, but before the news reached Texas. By early May, the surrender at Appomattox had sunk into everyone's consciousness, but Texas had not surrendered yet. Frank Hardin realized that the war was indeed lost, but his young friend, Charley Cleveland, was hopeful that Texas could fight on alone. The railroad had started running to the east again. "Wash" O'Brien was home recuperating from a flesh wound. Camilla and Kaleta were making friends with a lot of French refugees from Louisiana. Petticoat patriots were among the last to admit defeat, and Camilla and Kaleta continued to criticize A. B. Trowell for leaving his post, so of course they were not invited to his welcome home party. Poor old Mrs. Branch seemed to be even more off balance after her son's death. Frank characterized her parties as "confounded affairs that only a Branch brain could conceive." E. B. Pickett was from Virginia and had been a very dutiful and righteous soldier. He was given leave because his wife had died, but when he refused to return to his regiment he was arrested. Kaleta included much of this news and more as she wrote to Christy, who was still in the army.

Liberty, May 8, 1865

My dear Chris—

We received your letter by Mr. Edward LaCour. We were at Brett's to see Sip [Edward LaCour, Jr.] and Wash [O'Brien] gave us the letter. Camilla and I have taken a "thorough" amongst the French lately. Went to see Gus LaCour when he came. He is a nice fellow. He's quite handsome and very much improved indeed. So is Sip.

There was a picnic at the creek Tuesday—a grand affair so they say. The Commissary Clerk [Trowell] gave it. We were not notified, consequently did not attend. Most everybody in town was there.

They intended giving a party at Mrs. Branch's. The old lady was teasing! To think she would think of such a thing and Gail Wharton [her son] just died! So they concluded to have it at the court house. Frank Rachel and Jas. came to invite us. We went over on their account but did not like much to go.

Nannie, Helen [Hardin] and Nellie [Collins] went to Uncle Charles' Saturday. Didn't get back until this morning. We heard old

E. B. Pickett was under arrest. Won't he blubber tho! Camilla and he are sparking. Don't you let her know I told you. He likes her pretty well. How do you like him?

Charley Cleveland is here now. It is very seldom he comes after night so you may know the war news is pressing. Charley is hopeful as ever tho Pa is down in the mouth. I'll make him write to you what he thinks. Are you whipped? I know you will stick it out as long as anybody.

We will be able to write you oftener as cars have commenced running. The town is tolerably lucky now, but you know it's lonesome for us when you and Bee are gone. But we must make the best of it and be proud that we have two such loyal lads to send to the Confederacy. . . .

Caesar DeBlanc is in a peck of trouble: he can't get a furlough to come home and marry Miss Rosa LaCour. Wash Bryan is going soon. We will write by him too. We have heard from your saddle. Zach Boothe is going for it. The [Thomas] Peacocks are going to Galveston. Old Pea [widower] won't let his Mary to our last party at the courthouse. His "nice" fit is wearing off. . . .

Did you see John DeBlanc in Houston? He has joined the army. Everybody here thought he had gone to Mexico. We had been frightened half to death for fear the Yanks would come hang him. He's afraid of Jayhawkers too. Old Jerome [DeBlanc] goes armed for them. . . .

Kaleta *

John DeBlanc had accompanied Captain James Kaiser and his soldiers sent up from Galveston to arrest the Jayhawkers, a fast growing number of deserters who were holed up in the deepest part of what is now called the Big Thicket. The Jayhawkers had started out as a group of citizens, led by Warren Collins, who refused to secede from the Union. They had all they needed to survive in the thicket except salt, and for years had solved that shortage by using the Indian trading system of leaving pots of wild honey on a pine hummock on what is still called Honey Island, so that an outsider could pick up the honey and leave salt, tobacco, and coffee in return.

When Kaiser was unable to penetrate their hideaway, he ordered the soldiers one windy day to set fire to the woods on three sides and station themselves on the fourth. Most of the Jayhawkers escaped with their lives but their 3,000-acre hideaway became a desolation of dead trees and ashes.[12] The Union commander in Galveston swore to hang any man who had participated in the fire setting and of course the Jayhawkers were hot to avenge themselves on the raiders as well as on their fathers and brothers.

At Appomattox General Lee had found himself facing a body of infantry numbering 80,000, while his own force numbered less than 5,000 muskets. He told his men, "It is our duty to live. What will become of the women and children of the South if we are not there to protect them?"[13] Standing near Lee was Captain Dugat Williams, "who, with the eleven men of his company were surrendered by General Lee at Appomattox courthouse."[14] The official surrender in Texas came on June 2. Sergeant Bee Hardin was again a paroled prisoner of war, and this time joined by his brother Christy.

CHAPTER THIRTEEN

Galveston Courthouse

TO SHOW THEIR GRATITUDE for the safe return of their two sons, Cynthia and Frank gave a party honoring all the girls who had helped keep up the boys' morale during the long war. Until the wee hours of that autumn morning, Seven Pines resounded to the sounds of music and young laughter. As one guest put it, "All passed off as merry as a marriage bell, and to the entire satisfaction of all concerned."[1]

Bee's parents and friends may have been expecting marriage bells, but Bee was not so inclined. Any drive he might have had to found a family had perished along with the ante-bellum world he had known. As part of the prewar ruling caste, Bee had the wish, though not the strength, to override the new group of landless whites who had moved in during the war. His response to the chaos following the war was to take up the study of law under the tutelage of a local judge, which resulted merely in his drugging himself with eloquence and alcohol. Bee turned inward, toward family affection. At Seven Pines he found a love so warm and proven that "it tried to shut out the rest of the world."[2] Along with some of his cousins, he felt a sense of submission to his fate. Like William Faulkner's "last of the Sartorises," he felt revolted by the new exploiting classes and, inside, became a "hollow man."

Shattee was stressed by many pressures but especially by the impossibility of finding Prince Charming in the chaotic conditions of moral confusion and social decay that followed surrender. It is impossible to say whether she felt guilty about slavery, but she did become more caustic and ill-at-ease in relations with friends.

With Mimmie it was different. She was not searching for the perfect but for the available. Easily changing her lifestyle, she happily took on chores formerly done by extra slaves. After all, she was the younger sister, not "Miss Hardin," and she noted that George Davis adapted with little bitterness to the new life.

It was not so hard for George, since he had been opposed to both secession and slavery, and had never borne arms for the "glorious cause." As a lawyer he had been trained to see both sides of a situation. For refusing to take the oath that he had never voluntarily helped the Confederacy, he was dismissed by Governor Andrew Hamilton from his job as district attorney.[3] He soon went to work for the unpopular Bureau of Freedmen, Refugees and Abandoned Lands, which was set up in Livingston to make contracts between the freed slaves and the landowners and to provide food and medical care for the indigent, mostly black. Nasty remarks about his job by unreconstructed rebels did not upset him, as he had known ridicule ever since his accident with the axe.

The agents appointed to the bureau changed frequently. Some of them were honest, and some were trying to feather their own nests; and then there were those who wanted to grind the oppressor's heel into proud Southerners. George was a practical man and realized that compromises had to be worked out. He drew up contracts between the former masters and the freedmen, recognizing that this was the only way cotton crops could be planted, harvested, and fairly divided. The former masters and slaves "might easily have effected a social readjustment to their mutual benefit, but this was not the game intended."[4]

On March 1, 1867, Texas forfeited its statehood and became a conquered province. The Reconstruction Period was at its worst. No one could even register to vote who refused to take the "iron clad oath" that he had not willingly participated in the rebellion. Unless they were freedmen, that pretty much meant that only liars or Jayhawkers or carpetbaggers were qualified to vote. The registration of voters was directed to ensure the fullest enrollment of blacks and the most complete exclusion of disenfranchised whites. Blacks and radicals were elected to all the official positions: "There was military dictatorship to enforce participation by the blacks in elections, resulting in constituent assemblies made up of blacks and whites whose ignorance and inexperience in politics was equalled only by their malice and distortion of social justice."[5]

Frank Hardin, like George Davis, was a pragmatist and agreed with the younger man that it was imperative to move forward so open wounds could heal. When his pretty niece Hortense married Edwin Cullen, who had lost his right arm in a battle in Georgia in 1864, Frank worked hard at constructing him a leather prosthesis so that he could become a bricklayer.

Some of the bravest soldiers could not fit back into daily life. The war hero King Bryan died of despair before the year was out. Some veterans were pulled apart by psychological tensions. Jeremiah Van Deventer, who had tried every way to keep out of the war and had finally served so as not to be classified as a deserter, came home to realize he had made all the wrong business decisions as well as incurring the implacable wrath of his Yankee family. He just lay down and died. Some men "ran frantically into danger, seeking their own destruction."[6]

Blond, blue-eyed Christy, who was adored by his family, was killed in a hunting accident that second winter home. He was shot by his teen-aged black companion who thought a movement in the brush was a deer. It was a great blow to everyone in the family. Mimmie gave up her trip to France with Mother St. Ambrose, who was going to raise money for the Ursuline School. Aunt Harriet didn't help matters any when she would say, "I seen Christy's ghost again last night down by the gate. He can't rest."

The paroxysm of grief that gripped Mimmie on losing her adored younger sibling whirled her into the arms of George, who was the one person who understood how she felt: "The sun will never shine as bright as it did before Christy left us, but we must keep on." When George pulled out that five-year-old ring, she let him slip it on her finger, feeling some bond to Christy in the act. Something of him would live on in the communion of two people who had loved him. Mimmie was level-headed also: this was a man who was widely respected, who would look after her and love her, and with whom she would have an interesting life.

They were married at Seven Pines by the Methodist minister S.B.B. Dunnam on April 30, 1867. As wedding gift, Frank gave Mimmie three hundred acres of timberland. So that George could help Bee open his law office in Liberty that summer, the newlyweds lived at Seven Pines, and George commuted to Livingston when his business required.

Long-winded George was frequently late for appointments, giving rise to his father-in-law's dubbing him "Sundown."

George had recurring problems with the bureau, but continued to work for it. A brief note from the bureau offices in Livingston dated June 14, 1867, addressed George curtly: "You are hereby notified that a fine of $100 is assessed against you at this office for contempt of official proceedings yesterday." [7]

To many slaves, to be "free" meant to start traveling, thinking that any river would be the Jordan. When they got to a new place, however, they could not find jobs, so they were often worse off than they had been on the old master's plantation. Because Frank had treated his slaves sympathetically, many stayed with him, even though he had very little money with which to pay them. His unmarried daughters took on more chores, but none onerous enough to prevent them from going to Bolivar Peninsula for a summer vacation. When a yellow fever epidemic hit Galveston, they fled back to the old stamping ground at the plantation.

Stubborn as usual, Mimmie refused to leave her new husband and the crowded town of Liberty, despite her family's entreaties that she come up the river to them. Living near Seven Pines in a fine home they had built just before the war on Grand Avenue were Charley Cleveland and his wife, Mary, a daughter of Watson Hardin. Charley was devoted to Frank and every few days he would pick up Frank's mail and the newspapers to which he subscribed and send the bundle up to the plantation, along with his own notes about local happenings. Seven of Charley's letters, excerpted here, were written during the outbreak of the dreaded fever in Liberty that October and November. All but one of the letters are undated. One reveals that Mimmie did, indeed, come down with the fever.

Uncle Frank:

I cannot hear of a single case of yellow fever or even a rumor of such. I have no idea now that we shall have yellow fever, but as you are away, I would not be in a hurry about returning.

———————

It seems there was a Mr. Brewer kept a warehouse at Moss Bluff. . . . A schooner came up from Galveston and was visited by his family. They took sick. Mr. Brewer and three others in his family died, some of black vomit. . . . Mary has been mighty sick. . . . Her case more resembled yellow fever than any case that I have heard of or seen. I do

———————

not believe she had yellow fever, but she had from beginning to end every symptom I would ordinarily look for. . . . I have said more to you in this letter than I have to anyone. I have put wife through on mustard bath, hot water bottles to the feet, orange leaf tea and injections. I gave quinine next day. . . . I learned from the telegraph operator that on yesterday there were only three deaths in Houston. A great abatement of the fever there.

Theophilus [Garrard, freedman] died this morning as I confidently believe of yellow fever. The case as it developed itself from the time I first saw it to the close was yellow fever out and out. Mrs. John Loving was taken sick yesterday. John [her son] came to me, said he would have no doctor and requested me to go see her. . . . Nearly everybody has left town. . . . We have made up our minds to stay and none of us are alarmed or excited but are all quiet and cheerful.

Mrs. Loving's fever is subdued; it lasted sixty hours. . . . Of the other cases, Little George [Loving] is a very stubborn one. Up to last night his skin had been acting well and I had great hopes of him. This morning I found him worse. He was not watched during the night. The Negro woman whom I had procured to stay with them failed to keep the hot water bottles to his feet and let him get out of cover and hence his condition. If I had him at my house, I could save him yet, I think, but with neglect of his nurse he will die. . . . I have had the whole weight of these [Negro] cases [Sarah Holliman and Jane and Harriet, all freedwomen] on me and a hard time. They were utterly destitute of everything—no clothing, no bedding, nothing. I have provided at my own expense bedding and a nurse, a negro woman, the best I could do, and have done what I could but under the most trying difficulties. If I can save them, I shall feel compensated. No white person except Mr. [W.V.] Angell went to them. . . .

I know you are anxious about us—more so, wife says, than we are. We all feel cheerful and are without alarm. I am obliged to Bee for his offer [but] it would be more hazardous now to send my boys than to keep them with us. . . . I am now strengthened [in my belief], which was not willingly entertained at the time, that the symptoms which I gave you in my wife's case were yellow fever. I treated for it and she is well. I have no fear of her having it now.

We have had a case of yellow fever in the family—Camilla—but she is now convalescent and out of danger. I cooled her fever off in forty-eight hours. I gave her no medicine from beginning to end. I pursued my father's plan of treatment throughout. It will win! To cure yellow fever all I want is a syringe, a sponge, a brickbat [†] and the sedative water—lemonade to drink at pleasure.

Mr. [J.D.] Skinner's store was broken into last night. His safe was broken into and about $3000 was stolen. Of his own money he lost about $1000. The remainder belonged to parties who had deposited it. It so happened that my money and [F.G.] Ricca's money was at the bottom, and they could not get well at it. Your land papers were not taken; they are, I suppose, all right. We suspect some parties from Houston, two men, but there must have been a pretty considerable gang, from the sign of tracks, etc. Upon further examination we find that between $500 and $1000 of Ricca's [liquor merchant] money is gone.

Mrs. Paul [Servat] died Friday morning at 1 o'clock with yellow fever. She was [O.J.] Shelby's patient. He seems to be a dead shot in all such cases, physic and science killed her doubtless. . . . We had sent to us from Galveston three yellow fever nurses, two gentlemen and one lady, by the Howard Association. The lady visited Mrs. Loving yesterday and pronounced her case y.f. . . . It is not safe to come until we have a cold spell. A few of the Jews are returning but nobody else.

———

Mr. [B.W.] Durdin was taken sick yesterday. Has had fever straight along. I call it yellow fever. He has no doctor, and don't want any with him. Just as good as any, for he has the constitution of an alligator. . . . I send you a *Civilian* received today. I saw no frost here this morning. We must have a good one to be of any avail.

———

Since I last wrote you there have occurred three new cases of yellow fever. Mrs. Denek [wife of bootmaker], Mrs. Woodsworth [wife of telegraph operator] and a little negro boy [Jeanetot] at Jim Skinner's. They are all doing well so far.

[†] "Injections" and "syringe" in these letters refer to giving a patient an enema. The brick-bat was the equivalent of a hot water bottle; a brick was heated and wrapped in newspaper and put at patient's feet.

———

Quite a number of refugees have returned to town this morning. Jeff Chambers and family, Sterling and family. I send you a *Picayune* to read. Nothing later to send you. The official majority for the Democracy in the State of New York is 49,000, and the Legislature went Democratic on joint ballot of Congress in session. . . . Telegrams represent that body as quite tame, no demonstrations for impeachment [of President Andrew Johnson] or other wild schemes.

Truly yours,
Charley *

The Howard Association nurses were paid for by wealthy Galvestonians like Charley's father. Charley had the good sense to give his patients plenty of fluids. Many of the doctors would not give theirs anything to drink and purged and bled them. Mr. Angell, the English carpenter and preacher who had been in Liberty fifteen years, was now living with the Christie O'Briens.

George was terrified that the fever would take Camilla from him. Indeed her fever was so high that it made her hair fall out. A few days before she had fallen ill, George had written the following business letter to Catherine Bagarley.

Liberty, October 3, 1867

Mrs. Bagarley,

At the request of Mr. Turner who bears this I write for Bee and myself. Mr. Turner calls on you to buy the houses on your place here and he wishes us to address you as to the propriety of sale inasmuch as we do not feel at liberty to deal with him without consulting you. Do you wish to sell the houses at all? Have you any price that you are satisfied with for the houses or would you prefer referring that to us?

We believe that it will be to your interest to sell at a fair price unless you expect to occupy the place soon. What is a fair price depends upon the state of preservation of the lumber and the demand in the market.

After seeing Mr. Turner, if we can succor you please command us. I shall be at home in 10 days.

All send love, etc.

In haste,
Geo. W. Davis[8]

Earlier that summer the Reverend Thomas Wooldridge, husband of

George's sister Sallie, had succumbed to yellow fever in Montgomery, Texas, while ministering to victims of an epidemic there. His body had been thrown into a common pit with theirs. Shortly before his death he had made a will appointing George guardian of his two minor children by his first marriage, Lucinda Hinds and John McKay Wooldridge: ". . . having implicit confidence in his integrity and liberality, I hereby endow the said Davis with full powers . . . to manage their persons and estates . . ." (Ap. 30).

At age thirty-two, George felt it was his responsibility to look after people who could not manage for themselves. His legal training had taught him how to go about it, and his kind heart made him care. He was aware of how much worse economic conditions were in other parts of the South.

There was no regular postal service to many towns due to the Southern states being under military rule, so George asked a man who was traveling to the Barnwell District to carry a letter to his South Carolina cousin, Frank Green, from whom he had heard nothing since they had broken off their correspondence due to George's liberalism. George's parting shot had been that John Isaac's family had been "right" to move to Texas where slavery did not control the economy. In early winter, a reply came:

> Hammond P. O.
> Barnwell Dist S.C.
> Dec 13, 1867

Dear George,

At Barnwell a few days ago, Mr. J.T. Alorich placed in my hand a letter of inquiry as to myself and others of your relations. I shall answer it and beg of you a continuance of the correspondence which has been interrupted since '61. Since that time a war has been waged which has destroyed a system of civilization and ruined a country, but I shall have nothing to say of it only so far as I have been affected by it.

Like everybody I went in—soon tired—quit in November '61— came home not to Barnwell Village but on the Runs [River]—looked on quietly till the spring of '62 when I married Miss [Laura] Turner, who at all times had my heart. After this, I went about farming on a small scale till something should turn up. Nothing has turned up as yet and I am still farming! At the termination of the war I should have resumed the practice of Law, but that event found me with two children and no means to go upon, and the war had so impoverished the

country and unsettled business that I thought it more prudent to remain upon my farm where I was sure of a living. From then till now I
have not regretted the choice. I have now 3 children, two boys and a
girl, respectively of 4 and 2 years old—the baby is 4 months. . . . I am
now doing what all farmers are doing in this section, barely living.
How does the world use you?

If you are doing well and can promise me anything, I shall come out
and live in your land. From your card, one would infer that you were
"right" and I hope you are. Are you a married man?

George, take pains to write me carefully whatever may be an inducement to make one move, who longs to do so. Is there not in some of
those counties in which you practice a good opening? What would
land near the county seat be worth per acre?

I think Father would move—he is now over 60 years old and his
health has been fine up to the last 3 months. . . . My brother, Rhett,
broken down by hard service in the [battle]field, reached home after
the surrender and died in a few weeks. I believe he was about 17 years
old. He was a handsome boy and full of promise.

As to politics, I have to say that S. Ca. (I mean the Negroes) should
have no convention and has again placed herself where she ought to
be. I hope that this whole matter will be settled in my life time. I am
thoroughly disgusted.

Cousinly,
F.M. Green

Frank was wrong about the outcome of the second South Carolina
convention, in which the only voters were freedmen and those who had
taken an oath that they had taken no part in the "rebellion." Frank
thought that the federal government would not accept ratification of the
constitution by this convention, but what with the pending impeachment trial of President Andrew Johnson and the approaching presidential election, South Carolina was readmitted to the Union. Negro
suffrage was made legal and most whites remained disenfranchised until
the repeal of the iron clad oath in 1871.

On the back of the preceding letter, George wrote in pencil:

Jan 5th 1868

Dear Mother,

I received this a day or two ago. Have answered it and told Frank
and all hands to come out here and cast their lot with us in a new

land. I got home that night in pretty good season—found all well here. Mimmie had had quite a time with three niggers [†] who attempted to steal my corn out of the crib. She caught them and with pistol in hand made a man carry a bag of corn into our house instead of his where he had started with it. She is game for sure. I have the bag now here by my side. They are now run off. I met them in 8 miles of Huntsville the morning I left you but did not know what had happened then. I know them well and will catch them yet.

. . . Goodbye. Will write Papa soon.

Your son,
George

In his next letter to George, Frank explained that his town of Silverton was still without a post office because no one in the town could fill postmaster requirements of literacy and willingness to take the iron clad oath. The Barnwell District's only post office was at Hammond.

Hammond P Office
Barnwell, 11 March 1868

Dear George,

Yours of 30 Dec last was handed to me on Saturday by Uncle Billy Green. It is likely the letter had arrived several weeks ago. I am far from the Office. . . . This letter of yours must have afforded much pleasure to Father and Uncle Billy for tears accompanied the reading of it. Uncle Billy told me to say to you that the "old Fellow was still alive." I proposed to him that we should hunt you up; his reply was, "No I shall leave my bones where I have spent my life." He is in his 64th year and a married man for the 2nd time—she was the relict [widow] of one Dr. Bignon and daughter of Old Lewis Bannon of Barnwell. . . .

Uncle George's family have scattered to some extent. James has lived everywhere, except in Texas and now resides somewhere in Alabama—has made several fortunes—but the stone has been rolled till the moss has begun to disappear. Jesse has married a woman who was rich, since the war has been residing in South Georgia. . . . The girls have remained single and are passing into the "sere and yellow leaf." William had been ailing for years—was conscribed in '63. A few months exposure in the service sufficed "to gather him to his fathers." He was the noblest of them all . . . his sons Robert and William have no supe-

[†] George referred to blacks as negroes except when they behaved badly.

riors in this or any other country, for honesty and industry, and the girls combine in their line the good qualities of the boys and are unsurpassed for beauty of form or face. [William's] widow (who is now a Mrs. Pettus and apart from her husband) deprived them of all social position by misconduct. . . .

My sister, Mrs. Prior, lost her husband at Murfreesboro, Tennessee—he was a Capt—she depends upon her needle and Father for the support of her 3 children. She resides in Augusta, Ga. where she owns a home—was well to do before "slavery went up the flue."

My brother John married a daughter of John Forsman and has 2 children and is doing as well as anyone in our section and bad enough at that. He soldiered extensively—was shot in Maryland, the ball penetrating the descending colon and his entire body—fell into the hands of the Yanks and strange to say, lived when death seemed inevitable. He is now "as sound as a dollar and as straight as an arrow." Emily and Jane are still enjoying "single blessedness" and I believe are in "maiden meditation—fancy free."

. . . Father still loves his dram, and one of his greatest satisfactions is to be able to keep it and set it before his friends in these hard times. He could do well if he would take care of his money—owns a fair plantation and it is well improved. Told me to ask you in your next to speak of your country as to its game and fish.

As I stated before in my last, I am only living—have a fine plantation however, containing 600 acres of land said to be the best place on the Runs. . . . I only made 12 bales of cotton last year above a support on a small scale and this year I am not likely to do much better and may do worse.

The Wises are all still alive—the old man holds his own well considering the weight he carries. His sons and daughters have nearly all married and are all upon him. . . . Since freedom, Bill has made of himself a good fisherman and yields in that way more assistance to his father than [he could with any other form of work]. . . .

[F.M. Green]

Hammond S.C.
June 7, 1868

Dear George,

. . . I correspond with no one except yourself and read nothing of the day but an occasional paper. It takes my whole time to provide a scant living for my family and everything connected with the farm is so new to me, of course, [that] I am awkward.

Being of parents poor and living on the farm one would naturally suppose that I should have some experience but it remains for me to turn my first furrow. I am a judge of good work and instinct places me above the hands I can employ in adjusting back bands and setting ploughs. When however I turn out to do a day's work I can't hold out. I have not got the "lick" and a cursed nigger will not work like a white man—he follows in his composition the *Mercury* [monthly magazine]. If you should work with them they would kill you by always being just far enough behind you to throw the whole burden on you and then they work so indifferently you had rather do it all than see it murdered. We have among us whites who are hirelings but they are the tail-end of our race and I have invariably found them to be inferior to the negroes.

The *Mercury* in describing the state convention said that the best element in it was the negro, that it was made up of the best order of the negro and the lowest order of the white. Have you seen a pamphlet by "Ariel" [Ap. 28] in which he demonstrates that a negro has no soul? What do you think of the matter? I have thought much on the subject but as is usual in such cases I have not been able to convince myself. I am musing off from my farm and the labor question, which need not detain one long when "It is as plain as plain can be" that in a short time my farm and your farm and the whole South will be completely ruined. The first year of freedom, work was done better than the second, and the second than the third. That subordination and character of work which the owner had put into the slave had not then left him entirely, but freedom from all white restraint and the radical influence have exhausted them of all that made them of some use. And the generations of negroes that are to succeed these who are with us now, brought up in a degree of laziness and ignorance (I mean of work) not surpassed in Africa. Of them what can the country expect?

I have read of the mess that followed the emancipation of the slaves of Mexico. It is said that no planter in this country, not the richest one in the Mississippi Valley could equal in any respect the splendor which characterized thousands of haciendas in that country, which are now the homes of its birds and beasts. Such must be the condition of this country in a short time without a speedy return to that system of labor which has just been abolished. With us here the country is dying gradually and perceptibly and the pace must accelerate. There was an honest, manly, straightforward effort made in the Dist. to improve [the situation] with free labor—capital was invested judiciously and managed as well as the system admits of, but the prospectors failed. Then the effort has been made to live with it and many have failed at that—now we are trying to stay [alive] and breathe.

Farms are gradually contracted [shrinking]. The fencing is going to decay—The better parts of the lands are growing up rapidly [in weeds] because they are the most difficult to attend and the poorer parts are also growing up because the proprietor can make nothing of them. . . .

I had promised myself to visit you this winter and would do it yet if I could make a crop of cotton. Crop at present tolerably promising if I can clean it. . . .

Josh McCreary I saw at Williston and more recently at Barnwell—health very fine for an old man but is broken all to pieces: "Gave up."

All tolerably well.

Cousinly,
F.M. Green

Frank Green was hanging on desperately, trying not to give up as Josh McCreary had. Year by year as the situation got worse, Frank wished fervently that he had learned how to plow during the years he was "gallivanting" after young ladies.

The Yankees thought it was just retribution for South Carolina to become Africanized; at that time two-thirds of its legislature and four-fifths of its congressmen were black.[9] There was a carpetbagger governor named Scott who ignored the "pathetic appeals of a small body of decent white men who were still striving to maintain their rights against a flood of barbarism."[10] Yet Frank was "still unable to convince himself" that blacks had no soul. "Brutal men, inspired by personal ambition and party motives, assumed the pose of philanthropists and patriots and thus deceived and misguided the well-meaning people [like Frank Green]" in both the North and the South.[11] The terrible result was compounded by the federal government. Pessimistic and discouraged as he was, Frank was never able to pull up roots and move to Texas.

The situation was not so bad in Texas, although Texas did not ratify the new constitution until 1870 and remained under military law until then. Many former slave owners felt humiliated by the Freedmen's Bureau for which George had worked two years. In 1868, George hung out his law shingle in Livingston, and Mimmie moved into his refurbished house there. Her twenty-year-old sister, Nan, accompanied her. Mimmie was expecting her first child and thinking of her little sister, Pep, back on the plantation:

[Spring 1869]

Dear Miss Peppie,

As your fifteenth birthday is just past (and no letter), I suppose your birthday was not celebrated much. Nannie and I remembered the day and would have liked to have had you with us.

I was fortunate enough to get a pitcher of buttermilk from Mrs. Moore this morning. We buy it of her now every other day—a great treat. We are still disappointed in getting up cows. [†] Mr. Epperson [wagon maker] brought us this morning 7 young chickens and Mr. Davis expects to get some venison this evening, as he hears of 2 being killed just out of town this morning. I tell you of the prospect of getting fresh meat because we have had so little lately. We have no beef market like you have [in Liberty].

[Never saw] the like of fruit that there will be in this county. Tell Kaleta I have an invitation out to Mr. Moses even this early. Our strawberries have not ripened much yet; there will be any quantity of dewberries soon. The old Irishman that worked in my garden earlier was here this morning to look at it. He says it is the most forward he has seen. I gave him some lettuce. It is heading now. . . . I made a lot of peach leaf yeast cakes yesterday. They make splendid bread. I will send Ma some by Nan. This [letter] will be sent by our present Bureau Agent—at least he claims to be. . . . Say to Ka that Ep[person] is here at work on the wagon body. I forgot to write of his floral offering to "Miss Nancy"—when he was at work here some weeks ago—brought her a bouquet "from little Hattie"—Little Hattie! Maybe. She cherishes it—freshly baptizing it every day.

Mr. Davis got quite a number of letters this morning per Montgomery mail, on business. . . . Harriet [Paine] is still here. As good as ever—maybe a little better—surely there never was such a servant. . . .

Mr. Davis is quite busy helping Ep. . . . I shall try to make some dewberry wine. If I can get enough berries at one time. Mr. Davis got a business letter from Dr. Brubaker at Navasota this morning.

[†] As soon as a cow had her calf, she was brought to the barn for regular milking.

Nan will not hear of staying all summer, but still clamors for the last of April. I will be so, so lonely when she goes. . . .

Your sister,
Mimmie[12]

Mimmie always referred to her husband as Mr. Davis, and when they sat down to dinner she murmured, "Mr. Davis, will you return thanks?" The baby, a daughter, was born in November, and Mimmie named her Frank Christy for the two men she loved most. In this Victorian day, it was quite acceptable to call the little girl "Frank." George's mother, Sarah, was pleased with her new grandchild, and she must have been impressed with the way in which George's bride had taken over running his house.

Meanwhile, George's taciturn father, John Isaac, was still living at Mount Prospect and had become even more bitter about the economic problems following the war. He allowed three of the freedmen on his land to raise cotton on shares, with him supplying the seed and the land. After the crop had been picked and sent to the gin for baling that year, one of the men, Isham Barker, decided that he was entitled to two-thirds of the cotton that he had raised, rather than the contractual one-third. John Isaac insisted that the larger share was his and had the man at the gin mark it so. Just then all the blacks in the Huntsville Penitentiary had been released by the radical military government on grounds that, since they had been indicted and tried as slaves, they could not have gotten a fair trial. It was the time when morals and ethics reached an all-time low, and it was fair to say that "under the inspiration of an incendiary press," General Philip Sheridan, military governor of Texas and Louisiana, "was permitting Texas Negroes to run amok with guns and knives."[13]

Isham Barker became furious that he could not have his way about the cotton. The next Sunday, he and a friend lay in wait along the road for John Isaac as he returned alone from church in his buggy. The second man grabbed the horse's reins while Isham shot John Isaac, then they sent the horse and buggy on down the road carrying the dead man. On January 10, 1869, there was an article on the back page of the Houston *Tri-Weekly Telegraph* entitled "Glaring Daylight Murder," telling of the cotton planter's death.

It was a horrible shock to all of the family, especially to Sarah, who became too frightened to stay on the plantation, even though a Davis relative from Alabama had come to live with her. Until her nerves calmed down, she went to live with her daughter Caroline in Keatchie, Louisiana.

George asked Mimmie to consider moving into the Mount Prospect house. The widowed Sallie Wooldridge was already living in a smaller house on the north side of the property. Mimmie put on the same black dress she had worn for six months after Christy's death and packed up baby Frank and her nurse, the young black Harriet. Myra's son Dick went along as her driver. Once she settled in, Mimmie spent a lot of time reading John Isaac's books and the magazines and newspapers to which George subscribed. She wrote her sister Pep a long letter that reveals how much pleasure the bride derived from running her own show.

August 29, 1869

Dear Peppie,

. . . Mr. Davis has just gone up to [sister] Sallie's, first offering to harness two mules to the buggy and take me to church to hear Rev. Dunnam [who had married them] where I declined going. Plea: Frank—leaving her! She is cross this morning, is now lying on the floor by me flat of her back playing with the keys and squalling out at intervals. I put her there to look up a book containing "My Life is Like the Summer Rose."

. . . We sent for a specimen copy of the newly gotten-up *Southern Monthly Magazine* at N.O. It is, I find, little better than *The Land We Love*—Will not take it. I don't want it. We get no more *Eclectics*. That is the best magazine I know of and if I had my way I would make it mine from now on. Making it part of the family and keeping them for Frank.

I took Frank and Dick and spent the afternoon with Sallie Wooldridge yesterday. . . . Miss Davis [live-in relative] wants to go over [to Louisiana] this fall and I guess I will have her visit out about then. . . . Sallie has been very unfortunate with her turkeys lately, lost most all with owls, snakes, and freedmen shooting them for wild game.

I have got for Frank a nansook muslin and a Bishop Lawn, the first Sallie insisted on making. She gored the skirt and put on it a ruffle about two inches wide. Above the hem she is braiding it with some stuff like I got you for collar. The lawn I don't think I'll make now. I have tucked all her skirts.

Received a letter from Theresa [O'Brien] last night. . . . She enclosed one from Uncle Stevens of June 28th. If Mr. Davis does not want to keep his letter, I'll enclose it to you. . . .

I am sorry I did not get home before Superior [a favorite horse] left. . . .

May Harper succeeded in arresting the deserters I spoke of in Houston. . . . Tell Pa Mr. Davis knows of John Skinner's business connection with Garey. Worm in cotton everywhere here. Not much damage apprehended tho! Arabian [rose] in bloom.

Ma, I'm glad to hear you have some little distraction in music [like] Bernard [Salles]. Has Eugenie † gone back to Galveston? Where boarding? Where will Superior hold forth down there? . . . Mrs. McCardall and Miss Henry went over the river last week to attend funeral service by Bro. [J.W.I.] Creath of Mrs. Gen. [Jas.] Davis. Neither of the young ladies returned with us. . . .

I'll tell you now what I want. Kaleta must come up and stay this fall and Nan must come up to see us while she (Ka) is here. I have never yet forgiven myself for sending you home, but you'll make up for it in future. . . .

We have lovely morning glories now, five shades of red and blue. I have put up some touch-me-not seed for you. Those in the boxes have been beautiful. The white tea rose is a yard and a half high. I'll transplant it this fall and put out a cutting for Ma if hers is dead and I think she told me it was.

Sept. 2nd: I took Frank and Harriet and spent yesterday afternoon out where Mr. Davis was working at [Sallie's] house. Frank helped to raise it up to put under new blocks—sat on the lever. I'll not wish for you to see her but will only say 'tis a pity you can't. She is well today I think, I intend going out again this evening to the house. Mr. Davis is going to put a room on the north, rough plank and bag a little larger than the log room—with front gallery and a little room on the north end. . . .

I don't think I ever wrote that the negro Isham has been arrested— is now lodged in Huntsville jail. It was done by the Sheriff of Walker County named Stuart, discharged soldier and former Bureau agent. It was done several weeks since, maybe 4. He was found in Louisiana. He awaits trial.[14]

Harriet [Paine] wants excessively to go down [to Liberty] with me

---

† Eugenie had married one of General Alfred Mouton's family, but the young husband had been killed shortly afterwards. Now Eugenie was buying Mimmie's horse and moving to Galveston. Ten years later she would marry Bee.

when I go this time. I would like very much to let her as she has been such a faithful servant. Would not care to humor the most of them. She still is an exception. Dick remains—at times under many difficulties—so he thinks when Marse George gets after him.

We have still some garden beans, peas, okra, cucumbers and tomatoes. I have made no pickles yet—except in the brine. I have a jar that way. Say to Ma and Kaleta that I am fixing my mouth that fashion for their [pickles] and some of those preserves too that they made on Sunday. Pa told on them! Yours respectfully, dear miss,

Mimmie [15]

There was no doubt who was the mistress of this plantation. While George and Mimmie experienced much happiness at home during this period, in the years to come, George would never talk about the Reconstruction, saying only, "I can't. It hurts too much."

Although many ex-soldiers had such a difficult time finding a job, some managed very successfully. One of these was a Jewish immigrant from Russian Poland named Harris Kempner, who had come via New York to Texas before the war. He had served in Parson's Cavalry Brigade out of "gratitude for the unexpected manner of his neighbors in accepting him." [16] He had a fine war record and made friends in the service that would be very helpful to him later.

When Kempner first arrived in Texas in 1857, he was a door-to-door peddler who sold everything from brandy to corset stays to material by the yard. His circuit went as far north as Cold Spring and as far south as Frank Hardin's. Catherine Bagarley was one of his good customers.

Cold Springs, Aug. 2nd 1869

Mrs. Bagarley,
   Madam
   Mr. Jno. Neid started for Lynchburg today. He will be back Friday and will have very fine flour which I ordered for you. Please send word to Dr. Whethersby whether to leave a Bbl. or not. After this week I will be absent, but should you need anything in my line, Mr. Hansbrough will do the same as myself.

Yours very respectfully,
H. Kempner *

Kempner's business was thriving even more since the war, and he found that everybody liked him. In Charley Cleveland's yellow fever letters, it is noticeable that he referred to "the Jews" as a separate group. There was indeed a cohesiveness of these immigrants who were conspicuous by their beaver hats, gold spectacles, black broadcloth suits, and white cravats. Because they were late arrivals, they had less immunity to yellow fever and were wise to run from an epidemic. Most had stores in the little towns, but some called on outlying plantations using a wagon or a cart loaded with dressing and hardware. Their European backgrounds gave them expertise in changing different currencies and keeping ahead of inflation.

During the war, Kempner had made friends with a Mr. Fry of the Bank of New York. Fry was now regularly lending him money.

Cold Spgs.
5th Nov. 1869

Mrs. Bagarley—
I have no Blk alpaca. Plenty delaicie and other Blk worsted goods— Enclosed please find statement as you requested.

Very resply,
H. Kempner

1	Bot. Brandy	1.75
1	Bot. Quinine	2.50
1 oz.	Blue pill	.25
1 pr.	shoes	1.75
4——wool hose 3/		1.50
		7.75 *

One of the first condolence calls Mimmie received after her father-in-law's death was from this Polish peddler who had first sold goods to Sarah Davis at Mount Prospect over ten years earlier. He and George were the same age, and George had found him to be both intelligent and of sound judgment. They both agreed that Galveston had the greatest business future of any place in Texas. Kempner told George that as soon as he had saved up $50,000, he was going to set up a wholesale store there.

Catherine Bagarley bought some things from Kempner for her niece's wedding. This was Nan, who was soon to marry John Skinner, the tall brother of the man with whom Bee had gone all through the war. Nan was a long-stemmed American beauty whose height reminded Cynthia of the first Christopher O'Bryan. This handsome couple planned to move to Lampasas Springs, a tiny spa north of Austin to which a Santa Fe railroad track was now being built. Their wedding was the last social function that Catherine would attend.

A severe loss to Mimmie that summer was her little daughter, who died of the intestinal infection that killed so many babies of that era. A few months later Mimmie produced another daughter, whom she named George Agatha.

Texas had its statehood reconferred in 1871 and was well on its way to recovery. Louisiana, however, was still prostrate, New Orleans being the happy hunting ground of Northern speculators. Between 1872 and 1874 in St. Landry Parish alone, 821 plantations were sold for taxes.[17] So many refugees had flocked into Liberty from Louisiana in the last eight years that they were not so hospitably received any more. Cynthia was upset to hear that the few pieces of her mother's furniture that had been rescued from the fire were sold. The rosewood bed with the roses carved on its gracefully fluted posts and with its blue silk "ciel" was sold for five dollars, the mahogany dining table for seven. This was reported by cousin Mary and Dr. R.C. White when they went back to find what was left of Ellerslie, their home. They could find no trace, not even the chimneys.

Catherine Bagarley died that fall, and because Cynthia was ailing, Frank wrote the sad news to the widowed America Stevens, who had resided in Pattersonville ever since the war. America's pitiful reply came right away.

Pattersonville, Nov. 10, '72

Dear Brother [Frank],

I received your letter yesterday informing me of Sister's [Catherine Bagarley's] death. It was a great shock to us for I had hoped that we should meet again on earth. I would like so much to know how she looked in her old age. Have you a picture of her?

There are but three of us left of a large family—all passing rapidly away. I am so anxious to be in Texas among my relations, and would have gone long ago if our circumstances had allowed, but we are now left homeless and very poor by the war, and have never been able to make anything more than support since. The house we are living in was sold a few days ago. I have to move again, but don't know where as there are no houses to be had in this town.

I feel that I am fully competent to take charge of a boarding house. I can thus have a home rather than move in with some of the family.

Please tell me where is best place for me in your town and what you would advise me to do. I will await an answer from you, as I have a month to remain here. As to our lands in Texas I know that two tracts were sold and there is still a tract remaining, but I don't know which. I expect the agent can inform you.

I will now mention the names of my deceased brothers' and sisters' children. Brother Andrew's: Cambria, Delia, Farley, Percy and Borue are of age, Georgiana a minor. Serena's children: Ann and Vir are of age, Christopher Johnson is also of age but we have never heard from him since the war and suppose he is dead. Virginia's children: Nellie, Virginius, Kalita and Owen are all minors. George's children, Thurlow and Theresa, are both of age.

Any arrangements you and Charles [O'Bryan] make will please me. I am sorry Cynthia is complaining and hope she will not have a spell of sickness. Give my love to your family,

Write soon.

Your affectionate sister,
America S. Stevens *

Luck had run out for Aunt America in Louisiana, and Cynthia and Frank, of course, would find her a place in Liberty. They were spending more and more of their time up the river now, leaving Seven Pines to Shattee and Bee and Pep. Bee had become bored with the legal profession and now ran a store. Shattee, proud and fading, still had beaux. Major Dark had been most attentive, but he could not seem to settle down. He and Van Horten tried to make an oil well at Saratoga when he first got out of the service. They jammed pipe down into a bubbling tar pit, but nothing much came out of the pipe. After Dark became a rancher, cattle thieves kept making off with part of his herd until he began sleeping outdoors with his gun beside him. He became so addicted to having his rifle next to him that he would not go to sleep without it alongside. Shattee disapproved of this, and she was even more disapproving when he told her he wished to be buried with the gun and to have inscribed on his tombstone:

> Remember friends, as you pass by
> As you are now so once was I
> As I am now so you will be
> Prepare for death and follow me.[18]

Shattee said she would put on hers:

> To follow you I'll not consent
> Until I know which way you went.

Nor did she ever consent to marry him. Her tongue became more sarcastic and contentious. Shattee remained unreconstructed and intolerant. Only Bee seemed to understand her and get along smoothly with her. When Nan married and moved to Lampasas, Shattee made fun of her for going out west and said she would be scalped by the Indians. But this was not true; there were no longer any Indian problems in that part of Texas.

Further north, however, in September of 1872, there was a definitive Indian fight on the North Fork of the Red River near Amarillo. Under Colonel Ranald McKenzie, the Fourth Cavalry attacked two hundred lodges of Comanches, killing twenty-three warriors (Ap. 27). The hero of the fight was a man named Major Wirt Davis. He was old John Isaac's cousin, who had left the University of Virginia to join the Union army at the beginning of the war. For that crime, his family had turned his picture to the wall and none of them had anything more to do with him. John Isaac had despised him. Now experts called Wirt Davis the best pistol and carbine shot in the army. George admired this cousin because he was all the things he, George, could never be. He pledged to remember the name whenever he might have a son—a pledge kept in 1873 when his first son was born. Naming his child for a Yankee captain was evidence that, for George at least, the war was indeed over, and that reconstruction was complete.

In the spring of 1872 George tried a case in the beautiful prewar Customs House in Galveston which was now used as the courthouse. He won, and his mercantile banker friend John M. Hutchings took him to dinner at the Tremont House and suggested he open an office with young R.M. Hutchings in a dark-red brick two-story building on the Strand. Young Hutchings would bring with him the legal business of his family's company, Ball and Hutchings, which was soon to be Sealy-Hutchings. George talked to his friend Harris Kempner about some business from his firm, Kempner and Marx. Kempner agreed and wanted to put George on retainer right away and send him to Mexico on a land deal. George also had good connections with the Houston and Central Texas and Santa Fe Railroad.

With its extensive wharves, cotton compresses, and warehouses, Galveston was certainly the premier city of Texas. George knew Mimmie would jump at the opportunity to live there, where she had many old friends like Eugenie. She would be able to attend balls and to drive her old horse, Superior, which Eugenie had bought. George was not keen on the Galveston Mardi Gras because during that week the town was so crowded that you could do no legal business. As he wrote to Sallie:

We have tickets to all the balls and Ka and Mimmie are high up for going but I confess I am not. My past experience on such occasions teaches me how utterly out of place I am at a Mardi Gras Ball. In some moods I might endure them but not now.[19]

So Mimmie had stayed home and the two lawyers sealed their partnership agreement by ordering some fine vellum stationery with their names engraved in a large scroll across the top: Davis and Hutchings.

George leased out Mount Prospect to a cotton planter, and Mimmie went to Seven Pines to await the birth of the next baby. Harriet and Dick were thrilled with the idea of moving to Galveston. During the war they had been "put down" by the city Negroes from Galveston who had come to Liberty as refugees and told exciting stories of Saturdays in Galveston when they were allowed to borrow their masters' buggies and their most exotic clothes and parade up and down the Strand.[20] While awaiting the baby that summer, Harriet shared Mimmie's dream of a high-ceilinged house on one of the avenues, with gaslights along the sidewalk and lovely gaslight chandeliers inside. In her fantasy, the house would become a favorite gathering place for fascinating, worldly people. George would become a celebrated lawyer, and Mimmie would be his indispensable helpmeet, pushing him always to be on time.

AFTERWORD

Mimmie never lived at Seven Pines again, but she often took her children there on visits to her family and Aunt Harriet. Frank took his ease on the plantation up the river, spending more and more time observing and enjoying the wildlife he had always loved. In his quiet, patriotic way he breathed his last on San Jacinto Day, 1878. Shattee "went into a decline" and died at age forty-four. Cynthia lived on at the plantation for some years, addicted to white lawn dresses and her little perique cheroots, her white dress often showing tiny holes burned by the ash she neglected to flip from her cigar.

George Davis was killed in a Santa Fe Railroad train wreck in 1897, after he and Mimmie had moved to Dallas. Mimmie's sister, the stately Nan, became deeply involved in her family's life in central Texas. But Mimmie, in her later years, frequently went to visit her own daughter Geraldine, who had taken over Seven Pines as her second home after marriage to the head of customs in Galveston. Together the two women renovated the old house, adding a grand facade with Corinthian columns and a second story under the new roofline.

During the First World War there was a chimney fire, however, which destroyed the addition, and the columns were removed and the house made into a one-story structure. Aunt Harriet rescued all the letters and papers and stored them in safe cupboards. On some of the long afternoons that Mimmie and Geraldine spent there together they rehashed the old days and wrote notes on the letters. In 1926 Mimmie died in Dallas; Geraldine Humphreys outlived her mother by thirty years, dying at Seven Pines. In her will she left money to build on the site of the hundred-year-old house a library which has become the town's busy cultural commmunity center.

ENDNOTES

An asterisk (*) is used following documents located in the Sam Houston Regional Library and Research Center in Liberty, Texas. At this book's publication, most of the Hardin family letters had been given to the Center.

CHAPTER ONE (pages 1–15)

1. C.R. Wharton, *Republic of Texas* (Houston, 1922), 58.
2. Frank Smith, *History of Maury County* (Columbia, Tenn., private printing), 199.
3. *Letters of an Early American Traveler: Mary Austin Holley, Her Life and Works 1784–1846* (Dallas: Southwest Press, 1933), 82.
4. *The Story of Champ d'Asile* (as told by two of the colonists, Hartmann & Millard), trans. Donald Joseph (Dallas: Book Club of Texas, 1937), 18–19.
5. *Atascosita Census of 1826*, ed. Mary McMillan Osborn (Reprinted from *Texana*, Fall 1963, vol. I, no. 4), Liberty Historical Survey Committee. *
6. *The Austin Papers*, ed. Eugene C. Barker (Washington & Austin: American Historical Association, 1924–28), 2:1034.
7. *Laws of Texas 1822–1897*, ed. H.P.N. Gammel (Austin: The Gammel Book Co., 1898), 42–44.
8. Miriam Partlow, *Liberty, Liberty County and the Atascosito District* (Austin: Pemberton Press, 1974), 67.
9. *Recollections of Harriet Evans, 1900*. Recorded by Helen B. Hardin. Hardin Papers. *
10. Letter from Austin to Musquiz 10-9-1828. *Austin Papers*. U.T. Archives (unprinted).
11. Military Records of the American Revolution, National Archives, Washington, D.C.
12. U.S. Census Records for Fincastle, Greenbrier County, Virginia, 1770. National Archives.
13. Jedediah Morse, *The American Geography* (London: J. Stockdale, 1792), 468.

14. "The Pioneers of Berwick Bay Belt," *The Morgan City Review*, September 5, 1931. Reprinted from New Orleans *Times Picayune* of 1891.

15. U.S. Census Records, Courtesy, Berwick Historical Association.

16. *American State Papers, Public Lands*, 2:434.

17. Harvard admission cards in author's collection.

18. George Cable, *Old Creole Days* (New York: Ltd. Ed. Club, 1943), ix.

19. *Story of Champ d'Asile*, 21–22.

CHAPTER TWO (pages 21–41)

1. Spanish Archives, trans. R.B. Blake, General Land Office of Texas, 75:3.

2. Partlow, *Liberty, Liberty County*, 243.

3. Barker, *Austin Papers*, vol. II, part 2:316.

4. Emanuel Domenesch, *Missionary Adventures in Texas and Mexico* (London: Longman, Brown, Green, 1858), 239.

5. Partlow, *Liberty, Liberty County*, 82.

6. N.D. Labadie, "Narrative of the Anahuac or Opening Campaign of the Texas Revolution," *Texas Almanac*, 1859 (Reprinted Waco, 1967), 128.

7. *Ibid.*, 129.

8. *Ibid.*, 135.

9. *Ibid.*, 135–36.

10. *An Abstract of Original Titles of Record in the General Land Office*, comp. Mary Lewis Ulmer (Austin: Pemberton Press, 1964), entry for April 23, 1831, page 3.

11. J.C. Dey notes in author's collection.

12. *Recollections of Harriet Evans.* *

13. In author's collection.

14. Scrapbook of Camilla G. Davis, author's collection.

15. *Papers of the Texas Revolution, 1835–36*, ed. J.H. Jenkins (Austin: Presidio Press, 1973), 2:212–14.

16. L.W. Kemp, *Signers of the Texas Declaration of Independence* (Houston: A. Jones Press, 1944), xvii.

17. *Papers of the Texas Revolution*, 2:285.

18. Partlow, *Liberty, Liberty County*, 119.

19. Orig. Ms. in Rosenberg Library, Galveston. Copy.*

20. *Manuscripts, Letters and Documents of Early Texians, 1821–1845*, E.W. Winkler, bibliog. (Austin: The Steck Co., 1937).

21. Partlow, *Liberty, Liberty County*, 228.

22. State Archives, Austin.

23. Story told by Wirt Davis, father of the author.

24. "Colonel Delgado's Report," reprinted from pamphlet by Col. W.D. Day of the San Jacinto State Park (Houston: Union National Bank, 1936), 3–19.

CHAPTER THREE (pages 45–64)

1. James M. Day, *Post Office Papers of the Republic of Texas 1836–39* (Waco: Texian Press, 1966), 13.

2. Information gleaned from unpublished family letters.

3. Scrapbook of Camilla G. Davis, author's collection.

CHAPTER FOUR (pages 65–79)

    1. Pencil note by Camilla G. Davis made much later on a letter dated October 25, 1852. *
    2. Burke Davis, *Jeb Stuart, the Last Cavalier* (New York & Toronto: Rinehart & Co., 1957), 29.
    3. Francis E. Abernethy, *Tales From the Big Thicket* (Austin: University of Texas Press, 1972), 178.
    4. Martin Maris, *Souvenirs D'Amerique: Relations d'un Voyage au Texas et en Haiti* (Brussels: M.J. Poot & Co., 1863), 20–21, 89–90.

CHAPTER FIVE (pages 81–90)

    1. Lafcadio Hearn, *Chita* (New York: Harper Bros., 1889), 164–5, 193, 200.
    2. Records of Girod Cemetery, New Orleans.
    3. Mentioned in a Frank Hardin letter (unpublished) of December 23, 1852. *
    4. D.L. Wilkerson, *James Knight, Southeast Texas Pioneer, 1805–46* (Universal City, Tex., private printing, 1984), 19. *
    5. Hearn, *Chita*, 12.
    6. Berwick O'Brien, *The O'Bryan Pedigree* (private printing), 2. *
    7. Hearn, *Chita*, 1–10, 20.
    8. *Ibid.*, 54.
    9. This story was often repeated to the author by her grandmother, Camilla G. Davis (Mimmie). See also James Sothern, *Last Island* (Houma, La.: Cheri Publications, 1980), 46.

CHAPTER SIX (pages 91–102)

    1. R.L. Jams, *Distinguished Men & Women & Families of Alabama* (private printing), Chapter 5.
    2. Josephine Shackford, *History of the Muscle Shoals Baptist Association*, 214–16. Courtesy of the association.
    3. Reuben Davis, *Mississippi & Mississippians*, rev. ed. (University & College Press of Mississippi, 1972), 2–4.
    4. *Ibid.*, 18–20.
    5. In author's collection.
    6. Earl W. Fornell, *The Galveston Era* (Austin: Univ. of Texas Press, 1961), 194.
    7. *The Quitman Free Press* (Wood County, Texas), February 23, 1857.
    8. Davis, *Mississippi & Mississippians*, 258–59.
    9. This letter and the two following are in author's collection.

CHAPTER SEVEN (pages 107–124)

    1. From Camilla G. Davis's scrapbook.
    2. Horace Wyndham, *Victorian Sensations* (London: Jarrolds, 1938), 176.
    3. Also republished in *The Israelite* (Cincinnati, Ohio), July 16, 1858.
    4. Harriet Spiller Daggett, "Legal Aspects of Amalgamation in Louisiana," *Texas Law Review* 11 (December 1932):167.

5. A.I. Menken, *Infelicia* (Philadelphia: J.B. Lippincott & Co., 1890), iv.

6. Constance Rourke, *Troupers of the Gold Coast* (New York: Harcourt Brace, 1928), 180.

7. Paul Lewis, *Queen of the Plaza* (New York: Frank Wagnalls, 1964), 25.

8. George Gordon, Lord Byron, *Works of Lord Byron* (Paris: A.W. Galigniani, 1828) 1 : 378.

9. Marriage records, Polk County Courthouse, Livingston, Texas, recorded April 4, 1856.

10. "Reminiscences of Adah Isaacs Menken," New Orleans *Times Democrat* (n.d.), Harvard University Theatre Collection.

11. Comets had appeared in 1835 and 1846, frightening people and supposedly portending the split between Mexico and Texas and the end of the Texas republic. A comet in 1861 foretold the Civil War, according to some people (Wharton, *Republic of Texas*, 105).

12. Robert Somerlott, "The Medium Had the Message: Mrs. Piper and the Professors," *American Heritage* 22 (February 1971), 35.

13. *Congressional Record*, Feb. 20, 1858, State Archives, Austin.

CHAPTER EIGHT (pages 125–136)

1. John Henry Brown, *Indian Wars and Pioneers of Texas* (Austin: L.E. Daniell, 1896?), 415.

2. O'Brien, *The O'Bryan Pedigree*. *

3. *Famous Trees of Texas* (Galveston: Moody Foundation, 1970), 105. The championship American holly tree (also known as the "Hardin holly") is also photographed and described on page 171.

4. Professor Wright got a divorce, married a young girl briefly, and after that divorce was chased by the widow Stone and Mrs. Branch, whose deceased husband, E.T. Branch, had been a community leader. Mrs. Branch had wild ideas; complained to the judge that Wright was courting her daughter, Betsy, but also making passes at her. When the judge refused to issue an injunction to keep Wright away from her, she had her twelve-year-old son carry a pistol to protect her. She sued Wright for breach of promise in her daughter's name. The son died the following year and the daughter came to a bad end. (Information gleaned from unpublished letters.)

5. Letter in author's collection.

6. Brown, *Indian Wars*, 102.

7. Letter in author's collection.

8. Clementine and Auguste married in January 1864. Their fourth child, R.L. Blaffer, came to Beaumont in 1901. He was one of the founders of the Humble Oil Company, its treasurer for twenty years, and its president 1937–40.

CHAPTER NINE (pages 143–156)

1. James M. Hall, "A Journal of the Civil War Period," unpublished manuscript, entry for March 9, 1862. Photocopy. *

2. In author's collection.

3. Robert Hardin lived in Hempstead, Texas, and died there in 1881. He was not related to the Liberty Hardins. He had five brothers and four sisters. The father, Benjamin Hardin, moved to Texas from Knox County, Tennessee, in 1838. He died in Moscow, Texas, in 1845. One of his children was James B. Hardin, who married in Navarro County and died in Red River County. He was the father of John Wesley Hardin, the famous gunslinger. Another brother of Robert was Joseph, who lived in Limestone County.

4. One of B.F. and Mary Ann Sterling's children, Ross, became the thirty-second governor of Texas and the first president of the Humble Oil Company.

5. The soldiers were from E.B. Pickett's Third Regiment of Texas Mounted Volunteer's called Carter's Brigade. Guise was forty-seven years old; George Ricks was forty-eight. His son, William, who was in the same company, was only fifteen years old. They trained at Camp Carter near Hempstead. Colonel J.W. Carter was the one who made the speech to them about how he was recruiting 19,000 men.

6. Houston *Tri-Weekly Telegraph*, July 25, 1862. *

CHAPTER TEN (pages 157–168)

1. Alexander Hunter, *Johnny Reb and Billy Yank* (New York: Neale Pub. Co., 1905), 244.

2. N.A. Davis, *The Campaign From Texas to Maryland, With the Battle of Fredericksburg* (Austin: The Steck Co., 1961), 114.

CHAPTER ELEVEN (pages 169–189)

1. Willie Bledsoe Hardin received a Davis Guard medal for being at Sabine Pass on Sept. 8, 1863. The medals were Mexican pesos with the mint engraving rubbed out and the inscription "D.G." carved in its place.

2. Frank loved John Munson's free and intrepid spirit. They were old friends and Frank wanted to recommend his son Bee to him. If the letter had arrived a little sooner possibly Bee would have been detached to join the partisans with Munson. These partisans were called Col. Mosby's guerillas. One of their most daring raids was the capture of Gen. Sheridan's paymasters and $170,000 in bills. They used some of the money to buy buff-trimmed grey uniforms, and gold braid and ostrich feathers with which to enrich them. (J. Munson, *Reminiscences of a Mosby Guerilla* [Boston: Moffat, Yard & Co., 1906].)

3. Note of later date written by Camilla G. Davis. *

4. H.S. Commager, *The Blue and the Gray* (Indianapolis: Bobbs Merrill, 1950), 2:665.

5. *Official Records* (of the Civil War), vol. XXIV, part 2, 383–84.

6. Commager, *Blue and Gray*, 2:666.

7. Col. O.M. Roberts, *Confederate Military History* (Atlanta, Confederate Pub. Co., 1899), 11:261.

8. *Ibid.*, 174.

9. *Ibid.*, 173.

10. Commager, *Blue and Gray*, 2:669.

CHAPTER TWELVE (pages 191–212)

1. W.K. Baylor, "The Old Frontier," *Frontier Times*, vol. II, no. 10 (July 1925):13.

2. Roberts, *Confederate Military History*, 11:201.

3. *Ibid.*

4. There was no account of this execution in the *Tri-Weekly Telegraph*; however, it is recorded in a *History of Trinity County* by Flora G. Bowles (Groveton Independent School District, 1966) that so many deserters and thieves and murderers were roaming the neighborhood in the late days of the war that the sheriff got together a vigilante committee who hung seven men on as many trees (page 32).

5. Bruce Catton, *Terrible Swift Sword* (Garden City, N.Y.: Doubleday, 1963), 360–61.

6. *Ibid.*, 358.

7. Bruce Catton, *Grant Moves South*, (Boston: Little, Brown & Co., 1960), 350.

8. National Archives, Washington, D.C. Military records of Jules Schneider: a) in prison at Louisville, Kentucky, Oct. 28, 1864; b) took oath ("Deserted to avail self of amnesty proclamation"), Dec. 1, 1864.

9. B.I. Wiley, *Embattled Confederates or Illustrated History of Southerners at War* (New York & London: Harper & Row, 1964), 177.

10. Alva Blaffer, "Our Grandmother Schneider" (unpublished manuscript, 1925), in author's possession.

11. Commager, *Blue and Gray*, 2:812.

12. Abernethy, *Tales From the Big Thicket*, 75–78.

13. J.E. Cooke, *A Life of Robert E. Lee* (New York: Appleton & Co., 1875), 456.

14. Tombstone of Capt. Dugat Williams, Bryan-Neyland Cemetery, Liberty, Texas.

CHAPTER THIRTEEN (pages 213–235)

1. Hall, "Journal of the Civil War," entry for Sept. 28, 1865. *

2. Joseph Gold, *William Faulkner, A Study in Humanism* (Norman: Univ. of Oklahoma Press, 1966), 39.

3. *The Biographical Encyclopedia of Texas* (New York: Southern Publishing Co., 1880), 95.

4. C.G. Bowers, *The Tragic Era: the Revolution After Lincoln* (Cambridge: Houghton Mifflin Co., 1962), 47.

5. W.A. Dunning, *Reconstruction: Political and Economic, 1865–1877* (New York: Harper Torchbooks, 1962), 182.

6. W.K. Everett, *Faulkner's Art and Characters* (Woodbury, N.Y.: Barron's Educational Series, 1969), 84.

7. Document in Texas State Archives.

8. This letter and the three that follow are in the author's collection.

9. Dunning, *Reconstruction*, 216.

10. J.S. Reynolds, *Reconstruction in South Carolina, 1865–1877* (Columbia, S.C.: The State Co., 1905), 136.

11. Bowers, *Tragic Era*, vi.

12. In author's collection.

13. Bowers, *Tragic Era*, 59.

14. See State of Texas v. Isham Barker, Walker County Courthouse, Huntsville, Texas, Criminal Court Proceedings E:506–7, 530.

15. In author's collection.

16. "Harris Kempner: the First One Hundred Years," an address delivered at the second annual meeting of the Texas Gulf Historical Association. TGHA Publications, vol. II, no. 1 (March 1958).

17. Bowers, *Tragic Era*, 438.

18. Partlow, *Liberty, Liberty County*, 223.

19. Letter in author's collection.

20. Fornell, *Galveston Era*, 116.

APPENDICES

1. Variations in Spelling of Family Names
We are dealing in this book with Indian, Irish, German, etc., names as spelled by English, French, and Spanish authorities.

a. Kalita, the Coushatta Indian chief is also: *Kaleta, Colita, Colleto, Coleto.*

b. Christopher O'Bryan
Wilma Barber Mattingly, *Old Korner Days That Have Come and Gone*, Ms. in Mt. Belvieu, Texas. Installment I: On arriving in America is alleged to have changed name from O'Brien for fear of being apprehended and returned to Ireland.

American Revolutionary Army records: Christopher *O'Brien* and *Bryan.*

On arrival at Bryant's Station, Ky.: Christopher *Bryant.*

On Spanish passport in Louisiana Archives: *Cristoval.*

Berwick O'Brien, *The O'Brien Pedigree*: On arrival in Louisiana he is *Christophe O'Brien.*

c. Katherine Kimberland: also *Kimberlan, Kimberlin, Kimberley, Kamberland, Cumberland* and *Comberlam.* She came via Virginia from Germany according to *Annotated Abstracts of the Successions of St. Mary's Parish, La., 1811–1834*, and also in D. J. Hebert, *St. Martinsville Church Records* (1978).

d. Berwick is spelled *Burwick* and (Bayou) *Barwick*; Thomas *Berviquet* in *Louisiana History*, 1976, Vol. XVII, No. 2; Tomas *Bairvique* in Spanish records.

e. Eleanor Wallace of Ireland:
In Gladys L. deVillier, *Church Records of First Families of Southwest Louisiana*, 1776–1806: Helen *Ouzez.*

In Rev. Don J. Hebert, *Southwest Louisiana Records* (Cecelia, La., n.p., 1978–1985): Elena *Ouzez*, Helene *Wales*, Elenore *Wallis*, Elena *Bois.*

f. Kindallus is *Kindalus* on 1818 birth certificate, and *Kindallis* later. It was the middle name of the first Christopher according to NSDAR.

2. Early Records of People and Places

a. Archie McDonald, "First 150 Years in Texas," *Dallas Times Herald*, March 1982:

Camino Real, running east and west through Nacogdoches, was blazed by Louis Juchereau de St. Denis in 1714. *Casa de Piedras* was the name of a stone fort built on the east side of the Trinity in 1780 by Antonio Y'Barbo after Indians destroyed the settlement on the west side.

b. Mary McMillan Osborn, Ed., *The Atascosita Census of 1826*, Texana (Liberty, Texas: Liberty County Historical Survey Committee, 1963), Vol. I, No. 4:

Atascosita [a settlement started in 1757 to keep French out] is a name seldom uttered in present-day Texas. Those who know can reveal that the town of Liberty is on the site of old Atascosita and that the names were changed in 1831 by J. Francisco Madero, General Land Commissioner for the Department of Texas for the state of Coahuila and Texas. Madero was in this region of the lower Trinity River basin in an attempt to clear up the land titles of some Anglo-American "squatters." Madero was not able to issue the coveted land titles to the Anglo-Americans, a fact which further widened the ideological gap which eventually led to the Texas Revolution. The frontiersmen involved in this effort had long been seeking title to the land they inhabited, and it was no doubt because of this that the document which has come to be known as the "Atascosita Census" was created on July 31, 1826.

Atascosita first appears in the annals of history on a map made in 1757 by Bernardo de Miranda, a Spanish explorer. It was in the latter half of that year and the early part of the following one that events called for the establishment of a Spanish mission at "El Atascosita." The mission at El Orcoquisac was not doing well so the Spaniards desired to move it. . . . Jacinto de Barrios y Jauregi, Governor of the Spanish province of Texas, favored a site on the Trinity River known as "El Atascosita" or "El Atascosita y Los Tranquillos." . . . It was in April, 1758, when [Barrios] first ordered a triangular stockade built and crops planted "within two gunshots of El Atascosita."

c. King Brian Boru

Sheamus McManus, *The Story of the Irish Race* (New York: Devin-Adair Co., orig. pub. 1944, revd ed. 1967), 282:

By 1001 a.d. he became the accepted monarch of all Ireland and had his royal seat at Kincora, near the Shannon River. On April 23, 1014, Brian Boru won a decisive victory over the Danes in his life-long struggle to expel the Vikings from Ireland forever. In the battle of Clontarf, however, he fell mortally wounded and his fifteen-year-old grandson, Thurlow, perished also.

d. Thomas Berwick

Born in Pennsylvania, sailed to Charles Town, South Carolina, where he married; then went to West Florida.

Louisiana Historical Quarterly, Vol. XXIII, No. 1, Jan. 1940, 363:

Apr. 24, 1769, In the West Florida Council Chamber at Pensacola: Rec'd the Petition Thos. Berwick setting forth that he and his wife and one child and expects some more of his family shortly from Charles Town. That he is desirous of obtaining a Tract of Land for himself and them to cultivate. Therefore, praying for 500 acres or whatever quantity to the Council would seem meet, wherever vacant near Natchez. . . .

[Just as Berwick was about to settle near Natchez, the Spanish began a drive to build up their sparse settlements in Louisiana. Gov. Galvez asked Berwick to take on the job of royal surveyor. His layout of the town of Opelousas drew praise and soon Lt. Col. Francisco Bouligny hired him to lay out a second site for the town of New Iberia, the site chosen by Bouligny along the Teche, the first site having sunk beneath seven feet of floodwater. In 1780, Berwick was in charge of constructing roads and buildings as well as moving the settlers from Malaga.]

C.G. Din, "Lt. Col. Francisco Bouligny and the Malagueños Settlement of New Iberia," *Louisiana History* (Louisiana Historical Association, 1976), Vol. XVII, No. 2, 199:

In his second reply to the governor, Bouligny provided new information about what had actually gone on in New Iberia. The families, it seems, had shown little enthusiasm for tilling the soil, knowing that assistance to them would terminate with the harvest. Only when the lieutenant colonel declared to them that anyone who did not tend to the crops planted on his land would receive no help after the harvest did the Malagueños show greater aptitude for farming. As to what the slaves had done with their time, Bouligny prepared a lengthy list of the many projects they had worked on. They transported the families to the new site of New Iberia. They plowed, planted, and cared for seventy-five arpents of corn at the new site and thirty-five at the old, twenty-five of rice, and four or six of potatoes, as well as some tobacco, all of which they distributed to the families. They constructed houses for the blacksmith, the families of the Artache, Prados, Migas y Vida, and Ybañez; two houses for the Germans and two for the soldiers; and houses for Mr. Flammand and Mr. Henderson who also had a warehouse built. They constructed a royal warehouse, a great shed in which to make bricks and lime, and a large enclosure for the oxen. They looked after the livestock. Finally, they made lumber out of the trees they felled and transported to the settlement. All this was done before Bouligny departed New Iberia in August, at which time he left Mr. Henderson and Mr. Berwick in charge of the slaves who continued to work building the settlement.

e. Christopher O'Bryan.
Census Records, National Archives, Washington, D.C.:
1769—He was surveyor in Fincastle, Greenbrier Co., Va.
1777—Private in Capt. Cleon Moore's Company 6 for 3-year hitch.
1794—Mercer Co., Ky., owned 2 horses and 4 cows.

3. Marriage Records of the O'Briens
Rev. Don J. Hebert, *Southwest Louisiana Records* (Cecelia, La., n.p., 1978–1985) [translated from French by Trammell]:
Today, the 24th of June, 1804, appeared before me, Michel Bernard Barriere,

priest of this parish of St. Martin of the Port of Attakapas in the diocese of New Orleans in Louisiana, **Luke Bryan** and **Christopher Bryan**, residents of this parish, and with them John Choate native of Natchez and living in this parish for ten years, legitimate son of John Choate, native of Bedford County, Virginia, and of Sarah Holston, native of South Carolina, living in this parish.

On the other presenting side, **Catherine Bryan**, native of Greenbrier, Virginia, legitimate daughter of **Christopher Bryan**, native of Ireland and of **Catherine Cumberland**, resident of this parish. Proceeding both from the consent of Mr. le Cournand and the consent of their respective parents, all of the parties professing Anglican religion, these parties will be asked to receive and to be witness to the marriage which they agree to contract according to the rite of this Anglican church.

At which time I, priest and appointed vicar, have received the marriage vows of these parties who have declared themselves contracted by this announcement and by this word, from now on promising to live their lives together in a perfect and indissoluble union as long as it will please God to leave them together. All I have administered to them has been in the presence of **Joseph Berwick**, William Lee and Benjamin Ros Russ of this parish who have declared not to know how to sign day, month and year except by sight.

Luke Bryan   John Choate
Christopher Bryan II   Sarah Choate
Michel Bernard Barriere, Priest

[It seems odd that on the groom's "presenting side" there were the bride's two brothers, Luke and Christopher, as well as the groom's mother. On the other side were the bride, her brother-in-law Berwick and the notary, le Cournand, who appears so little acquainted with her family that he swears that her mother also gives her permission and is resident of the parish when in truth she had died eight years previously in the States. So one wonders whether old Christopher was still withholding his consent. Prodded by the influential Joseph Berwick, the sympathetic notary might well have certified the missing consent of the absent parents. The old priest carefully recited that Joseph Berwick and two respected locals witnessed the ceremony. There are some fifty other marriage, birth, and death records of the O'Briens and Berwicks in the parish records.]

Other marriage, baptism, and death certificates of the O'Briens are found in Hebert, *Southwest Louisiana Records*; in deVillier, *Church Records*; D. J. Hebert, *Abstracts of the Successions of St. Mary's Parish, La., 1811–1834*; and Hebert, *St. Martinsville Church Records*.

For information on Berwick and O'Brien lands see:
American State Papers, Public Lands II: 454, 855, 857. III: 121, 148; Wm. H. Perrin, ed., *Southwest Louisiana Biographical and Historical*; Carter, *Territorial Papers of the United States*, IX: 986.

4. J.L. Cathcart and His Journal
William Harlan Hale, "General Eaton and His Improbable Legion," *American Heritage*, Vol. XI, No. 2, 27–28:

Cathcart was a seaman on an American ship at age eighteen when he was taken prisoner in the Mediterranean and spent the next ten years as a slave of the Bayh of Algiers. With the help of the American Ambassador he was finally released and after his return to the States was something of a celebrity. After this he never trusted blacks and in Louisiana had trouble hiring a pilot he could trust. Like most parvenus he took himself very seriously and was scornful of the local rustic people. He stayed at local taverns on his cruise, being seldom invited into private homes.

———, "Journal of Jas. L. Cathcart," *The Louisiana Historical Quarterly*, Vol. XXVIII, No. 3 (July 1945), 14–15:

Between Renthrops and McGows, or Muggahs, there is a ridge of tolerable good live Oak which we had not seen before, the proprietors of which would be glad to permit any individual to take it away gratis, merely to clear their land but if the United States were to order the purchase they would not fail to demand an exhorbitant price for it probably from 3 to 7 dollars per tree, for patriotism is a plant which does not grow in this climate and Uncle Sam is considered fair game! . . .

This evening we were under the disagreeable necessity of confining two of our crew (Steers and Brown) in jail for mutinous behavior during intoxication; one of them threatened to cut the officer's throat, it seems they had procured Tatlia from the negroes on the plantation in the vicinity in barter for some of their clothes. . . .

5. Early Road From Berwick to Liberty

Wilma Barber Mattingly, recorder, *Old Korner Days That Have Come and Gone*, Installment II:

. . . [Old Korner] says this trail ran across Orange and Jefferson Counties. . . . On July 3, 1837 . . . the road reviewers [were] to lay out a road . . . from Ballue's Ferry to Beaumont . . . from the next ferry on the Neches to . . . Thos. D Yoakum's . . . thence to Wolf's Point. . . . A winding trail that increased the distance almost double, that ran through dense woods, crossed wide streams of great depth, and over immense stretches of deep swamps, with their trees festooned with moss and the entire route infested with wild animals of all kinds, deer, bear, panthers, wildcats and innumerable other animals that crashed through the underbrush in the day and the nights were filled with the hoots of owls, squalls of panther and grunts and squeals of other animals. A winding trail filled with chuck-holes, rutty and often blocked with fallen trees. A lonesome trail where one seldom met his fellow man. A trail upon any mile of which hostile Indians were liable to appear to kill, to plunder and drive off the stock or where some wandering band of friendly Indians might show up.

6. George O'Bryan (1789–1856) and
George "Wash" O'Brien (1833–1909)

[George O'Bryan, twice widowed, left his children in Berwick until he could establish himself on Bolivar Peninsula near Galveston. It was a strange place; ever since Lafitte's day, there had been from there two modes of transferring cargo and illegal Negroes to the United States—one by water through Bayou Lafourche, the other by land from Point Bolivar to Bayou Boeuf and Alexandria. There is no record that George was connected with this activity, but he certainly lived near it. He drove cattle and arranged shipments of crops and importation of coffee and manufactured goods to settlers in Texas, and he delivered their mail.]

Cooper K. Ragan, "Diary of Capt. Geo. W. O'Brien," *Southwestern Historical Quarterly* Vol. LXVIII (. . . July 1963), Nos. 1, 2 & 3:

Wash was the son of George O'Bryan by his second wife, Eliza Brien Bryan. He came to Texas in 1848 long after his father had planted the famous big oak tree in Beaumont with Cave Johnson. He carried the mail on horseback from Galveston to Beaumont along the beach and moved to Beaumont permanently in 1852. He strongly opposed secession but after the war started he joined Company F, 5th Texas Regiment under his cousin, Captain "King" Bryan. He was invalided home after the measles in 1862. He organized his own company in Spaight's Texas Regiment and fought in various Louisiana battles until the war's end.

He organized the Gladys City Oil, Gas and Manufacturing Co. in 1892 with Patillo Higgins. They drilled several dry holes at Spindletop and in 1900 leased their land in the Veatch Survey to Anthony Lucas. The following year Lucas brought in his gusher on the adjoining land of Wiess, etc. O'Brien and his family owned half of the Gladys City stock. This land was then leased to Guffy & Galey and formed the basis of the Gulf Oil Co.

7. Earliest Hardin Records

From John Henry Brown, *Indian Wars and Pioneers of Texas*, 415:

1685—Ann Hogue Hardouin arrived in America with five sons. She was the wife of Marc Hardouin of Rouen, France, a French Huguenot who left after the St. Bartholomew Massacre. Marc had five sons, one drowned, two stayed in Virginia, one moved to Pennsylvania, and one went to the Carolinas.

From census records:

1716—Mark Hardin granted land in Prince William (Fauquier Co.), Va.

1723—Mark bought 642 more acres at Elk Run.

1735—Mark's will probated in Prince William's Co., Va.

8. South Carolina Hardins During the Revolution

[Five or more of Mark Hardin's descendants served in the American Revolutionary forces. Three fought under General Francis Marion. At the battle of King's Mountain a young Henry Hardin of Ashe Co., N.C., was cited for bravery as "the one who kept the fires burning." Using an island as his depot and rest base, Gen. F. Marion was known as "the Robin Hood of the cypress swamps." His irregulars went home for planting, harvesting, and family emergencies, their total number ranging from twenty to around three hundred. "A moment in the British camp—a moment—and away back to the pathless forest before the peep of day."

After chasing Marion for months with a vastly superior force, General Tarleton, the best British commander, admitted, "As for that damned old fox, the devil himself could not catch him."]

Some Carolina Hardins spelled their name with an "e". Col. **William Harden** of South Carolina is referred to by Edward McCrady in *The History of South*

Carolina, (N.Y.: McMillan, 1901): "Another leader now took to the field whose deeds were to rival those of [Gen. Thos.] Sumer and [Gen.] Marion."

Wm. D. James, "Letter from Col. Wm. Harden to Gen. Francis Marion," *Sketch of Life of Brig. Gen. Francis Marion* (Marietta, Ga.: Continental Book Co., 1948), Appendix, 31:

Camp on Saltcatcher [River]
April 17, 1781

Dear General,

I marched on, and got within sight of Fort Balfour at Pocotaligo [sic] at twelve o'clock in the day. I placed my men, and sent ten of the best horses [cavalry] to draw them out, but luckily Cols. Fenwick and Letchmere were at Vanherst, and were taken with seven of the dragoons and brought to me. The rest were in the fort. I then sent **Capt. [William] Harden** [Jr.] with a flag to demand the surrender of the fort and the men in it. They sent an answer, they would not give it up. I sent the second time, and told them that if I was obliged to storm the fort, that I would give no quarter. Col. Kelsey then desired half hour to consider. I gave him twenty minutes. They then agreed to give up the fort on the terms which I granted; and in two hours the fort with one militia colonel, one major, two captains, three lieutenants and sixty privates of Col. Fenwick's, one lieutenant and two dragoons with their horses, gave up to me, and they marched out and piled their arms without the abbatis; and I marched in and took possession of it; and during the night and the next day had it destroyed.

Wm. Harden

[This feat was accomplished without the loss of a single man, but the rebels needed more men and one of the colonel's big jobs was to recruit more. Harden further wrote to General Marion]:

The men about Pon Pon are the backwardest, though when I went there I learned they were all to be in arms, only waiting till they could send a man to you for commissions when they were to turn out. I beg you will send some immediately with your orders. It seems they wait for Col. Hayne and he says he cannot act without a commission, and I am sure if he turns out at least two hundred will join him. If so I am very certain that this part of the country may be held.

9. Colonel William Hardin's Will

Recorded 1810, Franklin Co., Ga., Will Book 1786–1815, 109–10:

In the name of God, Amen.

I, William Hardin, of the State of Georgia and County of Franklin being of perfect sound mind and memory, and having some worldly goods to dispose of at my decease, do make and ordain this my last Will and Testament. And first, I order that out of worldly Estate, my executors do cause me to be buried in a decent and Christian like manner, and after my just debts are paid out of my Estate aforesaid, I give and bequeath the remaining part in the following manner . . . To my well beloved wife, Sarah, the land and premises whereon I now live during her natural life, provided she remains my widow, and also the whole of my negroes, as well those which I may have lent to any of my children, and those which I now do or may hereafter possess, to remain in her possession during her life and widowhood as aforesaid, having it fully in her power to aid and assist my said children in a just and equal manner, by the loan of said negroes, as their respective circumstances may in her opinion require; also my stock of every kind, plantation utensils household and kitchen furniture, to remain in her possession, and on the principles last mentioned at her discretion. I also give and bequeath to my two sons, Martin and Richard, the lands and premises whereon I now live to be possessed by them at my wife's decease or when she is no longer my widow, and to be divided in the following manner: Beginning at Major's old house, from thence to be marked on a direct course to where the line of said land crosses the branch which empties just below Hatten's Ford, my said Son Martin to have the upper end of the said land, including the Island, and my said Son Richard to have the lower end of said land.

And lastly at my wife's decease, or when she shall cease to be my widow, I give and bequeath to all my children (to wit) Henry, Mark, Swan, Martin, Richard, Cynthia, Sarah, and Suckey, the whole of my personal property, the negroes to be divided in the following manner (that is to say) each negro is to be valued by respectable and impartial persons to be chosen by my executors hereinafter named and when so valued, the name of each negro with the price of valuation, to be written on a ticket of paper and put into a hat or box, which shall be drawn out by my children above named, each child owning the negro or negroes whose names he draws as aforesaid and should it happen that one or more should draw a negro or negroes to a greater valuation than the others, he she or they drawing the same, shall return to the others the balance in cash, in such manner that each of said children, shall have an equal value in the said negroes. And the balance of my personal property to be equally divided among my said children . . . on the principles above mentioned. And for the due execution of this my last Will and Testament I do constitute and appoint my beloved wife aforesaid Executrix, and my dutiful Sons (to wit) Mark, Swan and Martin my whole and sole executors, to this my last Will and Testament.

In witness whereof I have hereunto set my hand and seal, this seventeenth day of October in the year of our Lord one thousand eight hundred and three.

William Hardin (Seal)

Signed, sealed and declared in the presence of Mary Whitney, Gadwell Ayers, Obadiah Trimmur.

[Codicil, n.d.]

I William Hardin being weak and low in body but of perfect sound mind and memory, do make the following alteration in my within will, it appearing to me that there is not that probability of my Son Richard, making that proper use of the property I designed to give him as I could wish, I therefore give the whole of the property both real and personal which is mentioned within for him (the said Richard) to my wife to be disposed of at or before her decease as she may think proper, but it would still be my desire that if my said Son Richard should conduct himself prudently, that my wife may give him the said property. I have at present made no provision for him, except five shillings which I hereby give him.

10. Documents of the Hardin Murder Trial

[The shooting occurred Oct. 1, 1825. Wm. H. Williamson was twenty-eight years old. His brother-in-law, Isaac Newton Porter, was twenty-two years old and the "handsomest man in the (Maury) County." (Jill K. Garrett, *Soldiers of Maury Co.* [Tenn., n.d.], p. 159.)

The Hardins were at a disadvantage in defending themselves because their code of honor did not permit them to give any motive other than a "private difficulty."]

a. Murfreesboro Courthouse, Rutherford Co., Tennessee:

Indictment Of Swan Hardin, Benjamin W. Hardin, Benjamin F. Hardin, and Augustine B. Hardin For The Murder of William H. Williamson and Isaac N. Porter—December 21, 1825

The Jury also indorsed Joseph B. Porter, prosecutor, John Porter, Peter J. Noorkins, Jepi W. Egino, Nimrod Porter, Peter R. Booker, Abner Prewelk, John Gordon, William Cherry, James Dobbins, and Joshuah Guest, all sworn and charged to the Grand Jury.

. . . [The grand jury] do present and say that . . . on the first day of October [1825], Benjamin F. Hardin of said county yeoman, Swan Hardin of said county yeoman, Benjamin W. Hardin of said county yeoman, William Hardin of said Prinste [*sic*], Augustine B. Hardin of said county yeoman, not having the fear of God before their eyes, but being moved and seduced by the instigation of the Devil, with force and arms at the town of Columbia in the county of Maury aforesaid in and upon one William H. Williamson, then and there being in the peace of God, and of the State aforesaid, feloniously, willfully, and of their malice aforethought, did make and assault. . . . And that the said Benjamin F. Hardin a certain pistol of the value of five dollars, then and there charged with gun powder and eight leaden balls, [with] which pistol, he the said Benjamin F. Hardin, in this right hand . . . did strike . . . Williamson H. Williamson in and upon the back of him . . . between the lowest points of the shoulder blades [and] afflicted the said William H. Williamson one main wound of the depth of seven inches and the breadth of half an inch, of which said mortal wound, he . . . did die. And that said Swan Hardin, Benjamin W. Hardin, William Hardin, and Augustine B. Hardin . . . were present, aiding, helping, abetting, comforting, assisting and maintaining the said Benjamin F. Hardin, the felony . . . to do and commit. And so the Grand Jurors . . . do present and say that the said Benjamin F. Hardin, Swan Hardin, Benjamin W. Hardin, William Hardin, and Augustine B. Hardin . . . did kill and murder the said William H. Williamson against the peace and dignity of the state.

And the Grand Jurors . . . do further present and say that afterwards . . . the said Augustine B. Hardin, Swan Hardin, Benjamin W. Hardin, William Hardin, and Benjamin F. Hardin not having the fear of God before their eyes but being moved and seduced by the instigation of the devil, with force and arms at the town aforesaid in the County of Maury . . . did make an assault in and upon one Isaac N. Porter . . . and that the said Augustine B. Hardin, a certain pistol of the value of six dollars . . . did shoot off and . . . did strike, penetrate, and wound the said Isaac N. Porter in and upon the left side of him . . . giving to him . . . one mortal wound of the depth of eight inches and of the breadth of half an inch, of which . . . N. Porter, then and there, instantly died. And that the said Swan Hardin, Benjamin W. Hardin, William Hardin, and Benjamin F. Hardin . . . were present, aiding, helping, abetting, comforting, assisting, and maintaining said Augustine B. Hardin the felony and murder last aforesaid in manner and form last aforesaid to do and commit, and so the Grand Jurors . . . say that the said Augustine B. Hardin, Swan Hardin, Benjamin W. Hardin, William Hardin, and Benjamin F. Hardin. . . .

Sgd   Thomas B. Craighead
Solicitor General of the
Ninth Solicitorial District
of the State of Tennessee

Affidavit in Case of State of Tenn. vs. Swan Hardin, *et al*

Joseph B. Porter, prosecutor in the case, makes oath that the Defendants have several blood relatives living in Hickman, Lawrence, Wayne, and Hardin Counties, who have shown themselves to have a deep interest about the event of the case, that some of them are men of very extensive influence, and he is informed and verily believes have exerted that influence, so that they have produced a feeling and prejudice in favor of the defendants in the minds and dispositions of the people to such an extent in these counties that the state cannot have a fair and impartial trial in any of them, and he therefore prays that the venue in this case may not be changed to any of these counties.

Sgd   Joseph B. Porter
December 22, 1825

Affidavit of Swan Hardin and Others

The above named defendants make oath that they are charged with the murder (or aiding them in) of Isaac N. Porter and William H. Williamson. That the said Isaac N. Porter was the son of Joseph B. Porter, Clerk of the County Court of Maury, and he the said Isaac N. Porter for several years past has performed the duties of said office, and as these defendants believe the said Isaac N. was much esteemed by his numerous friends, and his death much lamented.

The high sheriff of the County and one of his deputies are also cousins of the said Isaac N. Porter, and in addition to the above, there is a large respectable and influential connection of the said Isaac N. in the county, whose feelings are much engaged in carrying on this [trial]. These defendants also state that they are charged with aiding in the death of William H. Williamson, who was a young in-law of much merit, and highly esteemed, as is believed by all his acquaintances, who are numerous and respectable. These defendants state that altho neither of them are charged with actually taking away the life of either of the deceased persons, or doing any act calculated in itself to produce such event, but same is charged upon the other defendants named in the bill of Indictment, yet great exertions have been made by the friends of the deceased and by the enemies of the defendants to produce an impression on the public mind of their being participants in the death of the said Isaac N. Porter and said Williamson. These defendants also state that immediately after the [shootings] took place, Joseph B. Porter, who is the prosecutor and a man of influence, caused a statement to be made and published the same in two newspapers printed in Columbia, and which circulated extensively in this county, and which statement strongly implicated the whole of the Defendants in the murder of the deceased, which statement and publishing in said newspapers is here produced as part of this affidavit. They both and each of them do verily believe that owing to the prejudice which has been produced and now actually exists in this county against them and each of them, that neither of them can have a fair and impartial trial in the County of Maury.

These defendants also state Isaac N. Porter and Joseph B. Porter the prosecutor, have numerous respectable and influential family connections residing in both Giles and Williamson Counties, who are as believed by these defendants, feel much solicitude in the event of this prosecution.

They also state in Bedford County as they have been informed and believe, a Hand Bill similar to the statement contained in the newspaper above referred to, was reprinted and circulated extensively through this county by persons residing there, who are hostile to the defendants.

These defendants also state that some of their enemies in this county, who are not so far as they know, particularly the friends of the prosecutor or the deceased have much means of influence in the county of Lincoln, and these defendants are apprehensive that the same would be used to their prejudice should the trial take place in that county.

Your petitioners, therefore pray that the venue be changed to some adjoining county, and they believe that none of the counties above named are so.

Sworn to in Open Court

December 22, 1825	Sgd Swan Hardin
(Sgd) George M. Martin,	William Hardin
Clerk	B. W. Hardin

Martin Toney, Thomas Wilson, and Major Wallis make oath that owing to the prejudice which exists against the defendants in Maury County, they do not believe that a fair and impartial trial can be had in said county at this time.

Sworn to in Open Court

December 22, 1825	Sgd Martin Toney
(Sgd) George M. Martin,	Thomas Wilson
Clerk	Major Wallis

b. Swan Hardin's Trial, Rutherford County, State of Tennessee:

And now at February term, 1826, of said Rutherford Circuit Court convened on the 3rd day of March, the said Swan Hardin, Benjamin W. Hardin, and William Hardin were led to the bar in custody of the Sheriff of said county, and thereupon came the State of Tennessee by Samuel A. Laughlin Esquire, Attorney General of the Sixth Solicitorial District of said State, and it being demanded of the prisoners if they were ready for their trial, and the said Swan

Hardin having declared that he was ready to proceed with the trial, and demanded of the court that he should be tried separately and alone from the other prisoners, which was allowed by the court. . . .

[The said jurors] upon their oath aforesaid, do say that the said Swan Hardin is not guilty of the murder in manner and form as charged in the Bill of Indictment, but that the said Swan Hardin is guilty of feloniously slaying of the said William H. Williamson and Isaac N. Porter in manner and form as charged in the Bill of Indictment.

And it being demanded of him if he had anything to say why sentence of the law should not be pronounced upon him, he answered that he had nothing more to say than he had already said, and prayed his benefit of clergy, which was by the court here allowed. It is therefore ordered by the court that the said Swan Hardin be forthwith in the presence of the court here, branded in the brawn of left thumb with the letters M L, that he be imprisoned three months in the jail of Rutherford County, and pay the cost of this prosecution, and that the Sheriff of Rutherford county be forthwith charged with the execution of this sentence.

The said defendant, being dissatisfied with the foregoing sentence and judgment of the court, prays an appeal, in the nature of a writ of error, to the Supreme Court of Errors and Appeals for the Fourth Judicial Circuit at Nashville in the County of Davidson, on the first Monday in January next, which is granted him upon his entering into a recognizance of two thousand dollars, and Allen Brown and William Brady in the sum of one thousand dollars each, for his appearance at the said Supreme Court. Whereupon, the said Swan Hardin, Allen Brown, and William Brady personally appeared in open court and acknowledged their indebtedness to the State of Tennessee, to wit, the said Swan Hardin in the sum of two thousand dollars, and the said Allen Brown and William Brady in the sum of one thousand dollars, each to be respectively of their goods and chattels on condition the said Swan Hardin make his personal appearance at the next Supreme Court of Errors and Appeals for the Fourth Judicial Circuit in the State of Tennessee, to be holden at the courthouse in the town of Nashville, County of Davidson, on the first Monday in January next, to answer a charge of the State against him for Murder, and not depart the court without leave, and to abide by and perform the sentence, judgment, and decree of said court.

I, William Ledbetter, Clerk of the court of said county in the fourth judicial circuit of said state do certify to whom it may concern, that the foregoing contains a just and true transcript of the record and proceedings in the case of the State of Tennessee v. Swan Hardin and others in the said Circuit Court for the murder of William H. Williamson and Isaac N. Porter.

In testimony whereof, I have hereunto set my hand and cause the Seal of said Court to be applied at office in Murfreesboro, Tennessee, 25th. January A.D. 1828.

Wm. Ledbetter

State of Tennessee
Sam Houston, Governor in and of the same:
To all who shall in these presents, greeting:
The affidavit of the official signature of William Ledbetter is the same as at the

time of making, and that it was duly fixed in and for the State of Tennessee. That all faith and Trust are due and might be given to his affidavit as such.

March 22, 1828   Sgd   Sam Houston
                                                  Governor of the State of Tennessee

Frank Smith, "Interview With Colonel N.W. Jones," *History of Maury County, Tennessee* (. . . February 17, 1906), 199:

It has been established that Swan Hardin had no part in the murder of William Williamson and Isaac N. Porter, only his four sons were involved. Swan Hardin did leave the county, however.

c. Letter from James K. Polk, Congressman from Columbia, Tennessee. *American State Papers*: Public Lands, 1789–1837:

Washington City
April 1, 1828

The Honorable Henry Clay,
Secretary of State
Washington City
Sir:

I have the honor to present through you to the President of the United States, accompanying documents forwarded to me for that purpose by Joseph B. Porter Esquire, respected citizen of the State of Tennessee. He solicits the Government of the United States to aid him in having surrendered to justice the murderers named in the enclosed judicial record, who have fled from the United States, and taken refuge in the Province of Texas, within the Mexican Dominion. The names of these murderers as will be seen by an inspection of the record, are Benjamin F. Hardin, Benjamin W. Hardin, William Hardin, and Augustine B. Hardin. Swan Hardin has been taken and is now in confinement in Tennessee.

Mr. Porter whose son was one of the unfortunate persons slain, and at whose instance I make this application, employed an agent during the past year to go to the Province of Texas, for the purpose of taking the offendants into custody to the end that they might be delivered over to the judicial tribunals of the State of Tennessee for trial. That agent determined in what part of the Province they had taken refuge, but was unable to take them into custody for the reasons assigned in the enclosed correspondence between him and the Commandant of the Military division in that part of the Mexican Dominion.

Mr. Porter has abandoned all hopes of bringing them to justice unless he can obtain the favorable interposition of the Government in his behalf.

He therefore, through me, respectfully requests the President of the United States, if in his opinion consistent with the Constitution and the obligations of the Government to its citizens, to cause a demand to be made of the Government of Mexico to surrender the offendants to the authority of the United States that they may be dealt with according to law. Mr. Porter will at any time when advised that it is proper to do so, send an agent to identify these persons. Any communication to him on the subject can be made through me. I will only suggest that the offending have a numerous group of friends in the

United States, and if measures should be taken for this arrest, it will be prudent that it should remain secret, lest they should be informed of it and be thereby enabled to escape.

When the President shall determine on the course properly pursued, be pleased to advise me of it.

> I have the honor to be
> Very respectfully your
> Obedient servant
> James K. Polk

[The shooting happened at the same spot on Seventh Street where a Mr. Hays had fallen dead previously, felled by a bullet from W.H. Polk, a relative of the Columbia Congressman, Wm. K. Polk. Neither Clay nor Polk could be personally self-righteous. Clay's nephew, Nestor, was also a Texas refugee from the law.]

d. Authority for the arrest in Texas

Original and its translation in the Rare Book Room, S.F. Austin State University, Nacogdoches, Texas. The complaint from Joseph Porter's representative was enclosed with this letter from Juan de Beramendi:

> Bexar, October 15, 1828

To the Constitutional Alcalde
of the Town of Nacogdoches

The Most Excellent Governor of the State [of Coahuila] on last June 28th has communicated to me [Juan de Beramendi] the following order:

The Most Excellent Secretary of State and Relations on the 7th of this month told me that his Excellency, the Minister Plenipotentiary of the United States of America [Joel Poinsett] in a note of the 3rd of the current month told him as follows:

"Excellency [Sec. of State of Mexico], I have instructions from United States Government to delivery of four persons that are accused of having committed a most atrocious assassination in the State of Tennessee, and who have escaped and have sought refuge in the State of Texas and Coahuila. These persons, whose names are Benjamin F. Hardin and Augustine B. Hardin, fled from justice after a formal bill of indictment against them had been published by a Grand Jury the 21st of October, 1825. By the enclosed correspondence between the person that was going in his [Porter's] presentation to Nacogdoches and the military commander of that place, Your Excellency will see that he had represented himself to that officer in March, 1827 in order that he shall give the guilty ones up and he exactly informed the General Government of Mexico of it. My government knows very well that it has no right to ask the delivery of these men; but it is an act of courtesy between civilized Nations, to deliver assassins and swindlers at the request of a friendly power. Situated as they are respectively the nations with relation to one another the blackest crimes can be committed on our territories with impunity if the criminal, to free himself from punishment, only has to cross the limits. In one of the articles of the Treaty of Friendship, Navigation and Commerce, the reciprocal delivery of the fugitives that have committed the crime of assassination is agreed upon, and even though they were not ratified in this Treaty, nevertheless the Articles which united here, does not make any exception in respect to the crimes committed before its conveyance, and perhaps none should be made were it to be put into practice immediately. I venture, therefore, to believe with all my trust that this Government, moved by a sentiment of justice and impelled by the dispositions which until now have [been] manifested by the conversation of a good neighbor, would order that these persons be delivered to the Official of United States. I take advantage with great satisfaction of this opportunity to repeat to Your Excellency the confidences. . . . [Poinsett]"

By order of the Most Excellent President, I send your Excellency [the Alcalde of Nacogdoches] a copy of these so that you may command the arrest of these criminals now under discussion, and their delivery in the manner solicited, and having its results. This I communicate to Your Excellency for your information and accomplishment for which purpose you [may] state the proper decision and besides you will observe the views which follow:

1st. As by the note of the Most Excellent Minister Plenipotentiary of the United States [Poinsett] it appears that the criminals are four and only two are named. The antecedents that on this subject exist in the Secretary's Office reveal that they are five, that is: Benjamin F. Hardin, Swan Hardin, Benjamin W. Hardin, William Hardin and Augustine B. Hardin. Your Lordship will explain this incident to the Commandant or Judge who will make the arrest of the criminals with the purpose of preventing any mistake, and also to avoid the escape of those who remain in other places in which it will be difficult to arrest them.

2nd. In order to facilitate the arrest of the culprits according to the security of the act, Your Lordship could come to an understanding with the Commanding General requiring of him the help of the armed troops in case that is considered necessary; and if not, Your Lordship could make use of the National Militia of the Colony of San Felipe of Austin, taking from it sufficient force to assure the result, in consideration that the Government has information that the criminals live on the Trinity River.

3rd. After they have been arrested they shall be taken to Nacogdoches and shall be delivered to the Alcalde of that Town, to whom Your Lordship will explain what is suitable so that he will guard them carefully, putting them in strong prisons, and if necessary will have the help of the military force to prevent any escape; with the understanding that the Alcalde shall be responsible in case the culprits escape, through his negligence or omission.

4th. Immediately the Alcalde of Nacogdoches shall send an official letter to the superior police authority of Nachitoches [La.] giving the information of having the arrested criminals in his possession, designating them by their names so that he will communicate it immediately to the Most Excellent Governor of the State of Tennessee, in order that a legally qualified Commissioner or authority will come to receive them, with the power of satisfying the expenditures which have been occasioned by their arrest, custody and maintenance, unless that for the latter, the culprits, at the time of the arrest, had properties with which to pay for these expenses, since in that case it will be at their cost, and the remainder will be returned to them, or the cost of the trip will be charged to them, taking a justified account of everything for any case.

5th. The Commissioner who comes to receive the criminals must identify their persons before the Civil authority of Nacogdoches by witnesses that either he brought with him or by some others of the Country, before they are delivered to him, to avoid any mistake.

6th. If the [United States] Commissioner can only take over the culprits at the Sabine River, the Judge of Nacogdoches should convey them there, guarding them with sufficient force, the corresponding procedures will be carried out on the [border] line to the account of this same Commissioner.

7th. All the orders and dispositions which your Lordship gives for the investigation of the place in which the criminals are, shall be agreed [upon] and shall be carried out with all the necessary precaution and security in order to prevent the escape of the culprits, who make the most efficacious measures mandatory.

In view of all this and with the punctual compliance with the orders which emanate from the Supreme Government, copies of the Documents cited in the previously inserted order are enclosed.

And I send it to you in order that in its fulfilment you will proceed with the necessary promptness and precaution for the arrest of the criminals Benjamin W. Hardin, Swan Hardin, and Augustine B. Hardin, fugitives from their establishment on the Trinity River, and William Hardin, who having just escaped from the imprisonment from which he was suffering in the dungeon of the quarters of the Company of the Alamo also took part in the same case. I am advising you that in case they are in the boundaries of your command, you will arrest them and put them in a safe prison and will inform me opportunely in order that I may instruct you of the rest that ought to be done in the matter, and to order that Franklin Hardin, who for a same crime is in prison at La Bahia, be placed at your disposition in order that all may have simultaneous delivery to the Commissioner, who for that purpose will [be] nominated by the Most Excellent Governor of the State of Tennessee, according with instructions 4th., 5th., and 6th., taking authority in all cases from the military authority of your garrison.

God and liberty.

Juan Martín de Beramendi
(Rubric)

11. Muster Roll of the Liberty Volunteers *

Of the Liberty Volunteers under my command but three have deserted since we have been in the army, and none within the last few days.

The following are the names and rank of the officers and men under my command Nov. 21st, 1835:

1st Lieut. **Franklin Hardin**	Orderly Serg't **Prior Bryan**
2nd Lieut. Wm. M. Logan	2nd, do. James Drake
	3rd, do. **Milton A. Hardin**
[Privates:]	
Aaron Cherry	Jackson Griffin
Wilbur Cherry	Benj. J. Harper
M. Binsted	Wm. McFaddin
Joab Blachner	Hiram Pace
Josiah Blackman	George Reynolds
Stephen Blount	John Riddle
Kindallas Bryan	James Stephenson

Ferrar Buxton	Washington Tevis
Wm. Collins	Henry White
Thomas Cope	Jesse White
Sam O. Cromwell	Andrew Wiley
Philip Dever	Charles Williams
Thos. Dever	Hezekiel Williams
Joseph Doand	Wm. Williams
John W. Fogg	Wm. R. Williams
	Christofer Yocum

Of these men I think there are six or eight who will refuse to follow me into San Antonio. The rest will go, intending to conquer or to die.

A. Briscoe, Capt.

[Several of the defectors were replaced by other Bryans.]

12. Discharge Papers for Headrights *
[The discharge Frank Hardin wrote for each of his soldiers entitled each one to 320 acres of land as a headright for fighting in San Antonio or the Battle of San Jacinto. The following is an example of these discharges.]

This certifies that Jordan West entered into the service of Texas on the 7th day of July last, for three months and has faithfully performed all the duties of a soldier. His time of service being expired he is this day honorably discharged.

Liberty, Oct. 7, 1836
Franklin Hardin, Capt.

Received
Auditors Office
Houston, Oct. 11, 1837

13. A.B. Hardin's Letter About Fraudulent Land Titles
[The following document is one of the resolutions sent to Mexican authorities by A.B. Hardin, chairman of the Citizens Meeting in Liberty in August 1835, after Santa Anna blamed fraudulent land titles on the Anglos (State Archives in Austin):]

Resolved,

that we have remarked with surprise, a disposition to attribute the late movements of the general government, to recent reported speculations, in the Lands of Texas, and to charge the speculators, as the authors of the present disquietudes,

that we reprobate all nefarious and fraudulent speculators in the public domain, as warmly as any portion of our fellow citizens can do,

that we know nothing of the merits or demerits of the alleged speculations, but the reports of vague rumor, but we can perceive only a short sighted puerility, in attributing radical changes in the government of Mexico, to the intrigues of a few speculators in the Town of Monclova,

that we hope and believe the Laws are adequate to the redress of any wrongs the state may have sustained from the corruption of its functionaries, or the no less culpable frauds of its citizens, in relation to its vacant Territory.

A.B. Hardin, Chairman

14. Founding of Galveston

S.C. Griffin, *History of Galveston* (Galveston: A.H. Cawston, 1931), 23–24:

"The undersigned [Col. M.B. Menard] as agent of John N. Seguin, in the year 1834, located a grant of one league and one labor of land on the east end of Galveston island, and applied to the alcalde [James B. Woods] of the jurisdiction of Liberty for a title to the same, who was legally authorized commissioner for that purpose and from him received a regular title.

The undersigned, at the time, sold said league and labor of land to nine other persons, reserving a tenth interest himself, who are now the legal owners of same. The undersigned and the owners have long since laid off said league and labor of land into town lots and have made arrangements for a profitable disposition of them. The suspicion attaching to all titles in Texas, however, prevents them from consummating their engagements, as capitalists are not willing to purchase and improve town property while the title is doubtful." . . .

After some delay, this proposition was accepted by the government of Texas and one league and one labor of land was deeded to Col. Menard and such associates as he might "hereinafter" include, for the sum of $50,000. The transaction was completed in December, 1836. . . . The original trustees and directors were: Michel B. Menard, president; and Thomas F. McKinney, Samuel M. Williams, Mosely Baker, and John K. Allen. Among the large stockholders were: Levi Jones, Thomas Green, William R. Johnson, **William Hardin** and Gail Borden, Jr.

Under the direction of these men, the city of Galveston was planned. The first meeting of the directors was held on April 17, 1838, and a public sale of lots was ordered for April 20th. Dr. Levi Jones, who had been appointed as agent for the new company, advertised in the Telegraph and Texas Register for bids for the construction of a wharf on the channel. . . .

[William Hardin's Galveston residence site, at the corner of 16th and Market streets, was given after his death to the Catholic Church and became the site of the Ursuline Convent of the Dominican nuns.]

15. Galveston Port of Entry Record

DATE IN 1840	SHIP	MASTER	FROM WHERE	NAME	OCCUPATION
Sept. 20	*Savannah*	Capt. Wade	New Orleans	Mrs. Hardin and	Lady
				Miss Hardin [Jane Jerusha]	Lady
Sept. 20	"	"	"	Mr. M. Hardin [Milton] and servant	Planter

16. Land Holdings of the Hardins

From Gifford White, ed., *The 1840 Census of the Republic of Texas* (Austin: Pemberton Press, 1966), 50, 65, 70, 103:

[The reader must take into account that the declarers "talked poor" at tax time and minimized their holdings except in the case of number of acres.]

NAME	ACRES	SLAVES	WATCHES GOLD	SILVER	CATTLE	HORSES
Frank Hardin	8,000		1	1	35	50
Frank Hardin, agent for deceased Wm. Hardin	112,000 & 11 lots in Galveston	4			75	5
Frank Hardin, agent [for two other men]	20,619					
A.B. Hardin	16,908	1			200	5
A.B. Hardin, agent	4,605					
Gerusha [Hardin]	5,158	6			45	
B.W. Hardin	6,642	3		1	85	1
M.A. Hardin	2,067				55	
Sarah [William's widow]	2,222 21 lots in Galveston	2	1			

Tax on each slave from $1 to $3 a year, depending on age. It was $1 for silver and $3 for gold watches.

The 1840 Census (page 131) lists one man owning more land than the William Hardin Estate: General John T. Mason, an absentee owner involved with Galveston Bay Company, using Thomas J. Rusk of Nacogdoches as agent.

[Six hundred acres of Milton Hardin's land was incorporated into the Alabama-Coushatta Indian Reservation in 1854 (Aline Rothe, *Kalita's People* [Waco: Texian Press, 1963], 121–23.)

Frank Hardin had at least two slaves. Perhaps he considered them "free people." A.B. showed two less slaves than he otherwise would have had, because according to *Southwestern Historical Quarterly*, XVI, 106: In 1839 A.B. Hardin bought from John Taylor two slaves, Sashla and Edward Whittaker; when he found they were actually freed negroes from British Barbados, he turned them over to Commander Joseph Hamilton in January 1840.]

17. Frank Hardin Records
a. Frank Hardin as Sheriff

According to records in Liberty County:

[Frank was sheriff of the Atascosito District for one term, beginning in 1837. He replaced a sheriff who was held in contempt for releasing from jail the County Treasurer, who had been arrested for embezzlement. The sheriff had to provide the prisoners' meals and frequently the jail itself. In the absence of a jail, irons were used. The county was to repay the sheriff for out-of-pocket expenses. Frank wrote one request: that the county empower him to pay a physician to look after indigent and sick prisoners.]

b. Frank Hardin's Surveys
   1834–35 and 1838–43—Surveyor
   1849–52—Co-Surveyor

A League of Land Surveyed For William Hardin: *

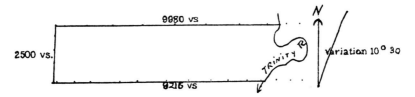

Beginning on the west bank of the Trinity River about a mile below the In-dian fields of the Long King Village at a cottonwood 20 in. dia. marked on two sides thus X . . .

Thence West 2000 varas [1 vara = 33 inches] to [Indian] trace. Thence W. 7980 varas and cornered on a stake in a prairie [is] a red oak 30 in. dia. bears S. 32 E. 96 varas and a Spanish Ash 6 in. dia. bears N. 12 E. 40½ varas, both marked on sides with corner thus X.

Thence South 300 varas to timber thence S. 400 varas to [Tarkington's] prai-rie, thence S. 1900 varas and corner on a sweet gum standing on bank of branch, an ash 8 in. dia. bears S 48 W 6¾ varas, a lynn 8 in. dia. bears S. 32 E. 4 varas, both marked on sides mark corner thus X. . . .

Thence East 9316 varas to the bank of said River Trinity cornered on a spanish oak 42 in. dia. marked on two sides thus X. . . .

Thence up the said river with its meanderings . . . to the place of beginning making an area of 25,000,000 square varas, one fifth arable the balance pas-ture land.

White, red & black oak, walnut, cherry, ash, hickory, magnolia, peach, lynn, hackberry, cedar with extensive cane breaks.

Franklin Hardin, Compass Bearer   Surveyed 26th Aug. 1833
Geo. M. Patrick, Marker   Edward Tanner, Dep. Surveyor
Willburn and Jackson, Chain Carriers

[Among other early surveys worked on by Frank Hardin and his assistant, Napoleon Magruder, were various Hardin lands, land for Judge Holshousen, Henry E. Looney, Mrs. Mary Magruder, Dr. Jas. H. Isbell (over 18,000 acres), the T.J. & D.H. Williams Estate (administered by A.B. Hardin). He also worked on many surveys outside Liberty Co. Unfortunately his map of the planned town of Liberty has been removed from the Texas Archives. More of his survey records are said to be in Mexico City Archives.]

18. Letters From Frank Hardin to J.P. Borden, State Archives, Austin

Surveyor's Office
Town of Liberty
July 21, 1838

Hon. John P. Borden
Gen. Land Office [Houston]
Sir:

I find it wholly impossible to make a connection map of the old work done in this county from any data to be collected here.

This is therefore sent to enquire of you whether you would permit me to visit your office and take charge of the files of notes of surveys which have been made in this county until I could connect or copy them. Please answer this by return mail and oblige. . . .

Yrs Respectfully,
Franklin Hardin

Liberty, June 11, 1839

J.P. Borden
Sir:

In reply to yours of 6th inst. I have to inform you that no part of the western boundary of this county has been run. I have made arrangements to run the line between this and Houston counties. The surveyors were here on the 8th inst for that purpose. I also made arrangements for running the line between this and Jefferson which I fear will not be carried into effect. I am deeply impressed with the importance of having this county line established but it is next to impossible to engage surveyors to do the work.

Very respect'y
Franklin Hardin C.S.C.L.

Liberty, Mar. 21, 1840

J.P. Borden
Com. Gen. L.O.

Herewith enclosed I send you the names of a number of individuals selected from the abstracts of titles in your office, the most of them I think are in this county though some may not be, copies of whose field notes I shall expect to receive as soon as your commission will submit. I shall perhaps in the course of my work have to call on you for others as they come to light.

My map you shall have as soon as possible.

Very resp'y yr. serv.
F. Hardin C.S.C.L.

Liberty
June 9th, 1840

Hon. J.P. Borden
Com. Gen. L.O.

In addition to the field notes already received, I must beg the favor of you to send to me a sketch of the map or notes of a five league survey including the town of Anahuac now owned by Gen. T.J. Chambers, title issued by

Padilla. The title is on record here but no measuring notes given. Besides all in Spanish such that I cannot make anything of it.

Your compliance at an early date will be gratefully received by yours respectfully—

Franklin Hardin
Chief Sur. Co. L.

P.S. Gen. Chambers contends that his survey after leaving the Bay at the mouth of South Bayou follows the South Fork. I am of different opinion. Any information that you have on that point will be thankfully received that you may better understand my meaning I shall include a sketch of the Bayou—
28 / 3 / 30

F.H.   C.S.C.L.

Liberty, Apr. 23, 1841

Hon. J.P. Borden
Com. Gen. L.O.

I enclose you a copy of a connection made by E. Jewell, a deputy surveyor of this county map five of the easternmost surveys, to wit A. Lester through G. Gemworth and J.L. McDuffee's—appear to lie east of the county line but I am informed by Jewell, the surveyor, that the surveys must be in this county which I think myself is altogether probable in as much as the connection that I have to the line between this and Jefferson counties was obtained from old surveys (most of whose distances are not to be relied upon). I see an advertisement requiring county surveyors to send to the Sur. of the State their bonds. I long since filed my bond with the chief justice of the county. He says he has notification through the Sec. of State of the same. I am etc. . . . .

F. Hardin   C.S.C.L.

19. Military Orders, 1842–43 *

[The originals of these orders were in the possession of descendants of Frank Hardin. The first four were preserved in the same envelope.]

Special Order   Headquarters 2nd Regiment
Liberty Mar 13, 1842
To Maj. J.R. Johnson Comdg. 2nd Batn. 2nd Regt. 2nd Brig.
Sir:

Herewith I send you General Order No. 1 from Department of War and Marine and General Order No. 49 from Brigadier Gen. E. Morehouse, as also Regimental Order No. 3.

You will, according to the requisitions of said order with the least possible delay proceed to organize from your command sixty-six men, one half cavalry and the other infantry and have them at this place on the 23rd inst. subject to muster and inspection. Your battalion is composed of Beats. No. 1-2-3-4 and 5 of Trinity and Menard Counties: No. 5 includes all of the Trinity County west of the Trinity River. No. 5 and 6 have been consolidated—according to rolls from the different captains' Beats. The regiment consists of 596 men (privates). Your battalion consists of 301.

[Col. F. Hardin]

General Order   March 9, 1842
                                                 Head Quarter 2nd Brigade
                                                 City of Houston
    Attention—2nd Brigade!!!
    Positive information just received from our western frontier members it is
probable that the whole available, or at least a part of the force of Texas would
be necessary in the field to protect the lives and property of our citizens now
threatened by a fast moving invading army of Mexicans who are in actual possession of some of our frontier towns. Should your country demand your services your conduct will doubtless be regulated by the same principles by which
you have been governed in the previous anguishing struggle through which you
have successfully passed. The long-wished-for crisis has probably arrived when
your chivalrous arms will convince the enemy that the country belongs to free
men. Let the blow be decided.
    In accordance with orders received from the Dept. of Secretary of War and
Navy, the Commandants of Regiments, Battalions, and Companies, will hold
their respective commands in readiness at the field at a moment's notice.
    It is imperative that every individual will have no hesitation responding to
the call.

                                                 E. Morehouse

                                        San Jacinto March 11th 42
Col Hardin,
    Since coming here I find that Maj [illegible] (was Captain) has ordered out
on duty the citizens of this section, which if it is not done forthwith he will
require a draft of the same quota. He will be on the march with the entire company the day after tomorrow. In the meantime volunteers are leaving constantly.
Some left yesterday in the 6 hours after I passed and others leave this morning.
I hope as many volunteers will be sent off as possible without delay from your
regiment. Active and efficient persons should be dispatched through the country to explain the emergency and hasten them on.
    I would further suggest that should a further confirmation arrive of the
news—a draft be made and the men so drafted march immediately onward. If
there are 20,000 men in the country we shall have a hard fight to stop them at
the Brazos. We may be able to check this march with the forces now in the field
but at the sacrifice of much blood. I hope (if you have not done it) you will
dispatch an extra patriot with edict to Nacogdoches and request the people
there to keep it moving on. You shall have the earliest intelligence of further
emergency and our movements. Expect another dispatch.
                                        Very respectfully yours,
                                        H.H. Allen
    The Whigs and the Tories are very frightened and object to turning out. They
chose to follow the procrastination of Austin—the cowards seemed to like it.
                                        Yours H.H.A.

Regimental Order # 3   Headquarters Liberty
                                                 March 13, 1842
    The first Battalion of the Second Regiment, Second Brig. T.M. will with the

utmost possible dispatch raise from their respective commands the proper number of men in accordance with the General Order #1 from Brig. Gen. E. Morehouse, copies of which are herewith enclosed.

F. Hardin, Col. Commanding

Regimental Order No. 5   Headquarters 2nd Regt.
2 Brig. T.M.
Liberty Oct. 9, 1842

The officers commanding the companies composing 2nd Regt. 2nd Brig. T.M. will forthwith upon the receipt of this order parade their companies and call for volunteers to march westward in pursuit of the enemy who is now retreating towards the Rio Grande. The object of the expedition will be to chastise the enemy for the injuries done by marauding parties upon our western frontier. The importance of the measure needs no comments. The troops from the 1st Battalion will rendezvous at Liberty on the 18th Inst. and from the 2nd Batn. at Swarthout on the 20th Inst. mounted equipped and prepared for immediate and active service.

F. Hardin
Col. Comdg.

Near Swarthout,
[Oct.] 20th 1842

Col. Hardin—
Dear Sir:

As will be seen by your return it is necessary I meet with you on next Thursday in the Town of Liberty for muster and inspection.

In my stead I present to you Mr. J.J. Franks whom you will please accept as a volunteer substitute in my place.

In much respect
I am your humble servant
Wm. Keys

13 Feb. 1843, Liberty
Headquarters 2nd Brig. T.M.

To Lieut. Col. E. T. Branch
Comg. 1st Battalion
Sir:

I herewith send you copy of an order from Brig. Gen. E. Morehouse dated Houston 13th Inst. You will comply at once with said order. Have your whole muster at the town of Liberty on the second Monday in May next at 11 o clock prepared for grand muster review and inspection. A strict compliance will be expected from every officer and soldier. Will also be required to make out and to turn in first time a full report of the strength and comp. of your battalion and comply in every particular with the provisions of the laws referred to in its aforesaid Brigade Order. The commander will be personally present at the Meeting.

F. Hardin
Co. Comdg.

5th June 1843, City of Houston
Headquarters 2nd Brig. T.M.

To Col. Franklin Hardin
Com'dg 2d Regt. 2d Brig. T.M.
Liberty County
Sir:
    Accompanied please find General Order No. 63 dated 1st Inst. for your
Guide. The General commanding this Brigade expects from your patriotism,
zeal and devotion to the public cause, that you will bestow your best exertions
to carry the said Order into effect and make a detailed and speedy return.

By order of Brigade General
E. Morehouse, Comdg 2d Brigade T.M.
Geo. Fisher, Brigade Major & Inspector

Swarthout, Oct. 15, 1843

Co. F. Hardin—
Dear Sir,
    I send you by Mr. Hardie, an account of the prospects of raising volunteers
in this Division. There has been considerable exertion making for a short time
past and the people seem to be much in the spirit of turning out. Col. Wood is
now on Wolf Creek, doing what he can. I have not heard of his success. I think
there will be fifty men or more in the Northern and Eastern Divisions ready
to march by the 20th Inst.

Yours respectfully
John B. Johnson

20. Feud Between David Burnet and Sam Houston *

Austin, January 12, 1847

Confidential for the present
A.B. Hardin, Esqr.
Sir:
    You were a member of the Convention at Washington in 1836. I do not
know whether you have seen a recent publication made in New York—a book
styled Sam Houston and his Republic. It is full of misrepresentation and
falsehood; and I am persuaded you are not willing the history of our revolution shall go down to posterity distorted and perverted by a thousand errors.
    I contemplate making an effort to expose some of the prominent errors in
that book and in order to do so am anxious to procure all the veritable information I can from the few living witnesses of the scenes and events of the
revolution—Will you be kind enough to answer the following enquiries as
fully and as soon as your convenience will permit.
    [1] Were not the members of the Convention dissatisfied with Genl.
Houston for remaining too long at Washington, and not going to the army in
March 1836?
    [2] Was not his commission as commander-in-chief given by the previous
Provisional Government considered as valid and sufficient?
    [3] Did he, Houston, resign that commission *before* his re-appointment by
the Convention?

[4] Was not Genl. Houston frequently *intoxicated* during the time he remained at Washington in March 1836?

[5] Was there not at the time the convention adjourned *sine die*, a general panic running through the country? And was not that panic caused by the intelligence of the fall of the Alamo, and of the *flights of Genl. Houston and his troops from Gonzalez?*

[6] Do you believe that the removal of the Government *Ad interim* from Washington to Harrisburg, had any influence in producing or increasing the panic which then prevailed?

Any other facts relating to the history of our revolution, and the operations of the army will be thankfully received.

Yours etc. in haste,
David G. Burnet

21. Frank Hardin's Obituary

Galveston News, April 28, 1878:

An old correspondent of the *News* furnishes some incidents in the long life of Capt. Franklin Hardin, an old pioneer and veteran of the Texas revolution, a hero of San Jacinto and of the Anahuac fight between the colonists and the Mexican garrison under Bradburn, long before the Texans were compelled to declare their independence and choose between resistance and extermination. . . . Franklin Hardin was born in Franklin County, in the state of Georgia, on the 25th day of January, 1803. When quite young he removed with his parents to . . . Tennessee. In 1825, in company with his brother, Blackburn Hardin, he emigrated to Texas, where subsequently the rest of the Hardin family came and settled near the present town of Liberty.

Franklin Hardin followed the profession of land surveyor in the eastern colonies under the commissioner Antonio Nixon, until the land offices were closed by the convention owing to the invasion of the country by the Mexicans, under Gen. Cos, who occupied the city of San Antonio. When volunteers were called up, Franklin Hardin, with many others, responded, and served until Cos surrendered to the Texans under Colonels [Ben] Milam and Johnson. When Santa Ana with an overwhelming force returned to drive the Texans beyond the Sabine, and massacred all who refused to fly, and began his operations by the siege and slaughter of the Alamo, a company was formed in Liberty County to go to the relief of the beleaguered fortress. Wm. M. Logan was elected captain, Franklin Hardin first lieutenant, B.F. Harper second lieutenant, I.N. Moreland acting temporarily as sergeant until E.T. Branch was elected. This company proceeded as far as the [Damon] Mound near the Brazos, where it was met by the intelligence of the fall of the Alamo and that the army under Houston was retreating. The company however, after a number had left it, pushed on and joined the forces under Houston and on the east side of the Colorado, and remained in the service until the army under Santa Anna had been totally destroyed at San Jacinto and the remainder of the Mexican invaders were driven beyond the Nueces. The company was discharged in June 1836.

In July President Burnet made another call for volunteers, and the deceased was chosen captain of the company and marched to the west. The men were afterwards disbanded at Victoria. After the war Capt. Hardin was elected sheriff and held other offices of honor and trust in Liberty County, but he was devoid of ambition politically and preferred the walks of private life. He lived and died respected by all who knew him. He was a brother of Judge William Hardin, one of the ten original proprietors of the city of Galveston.

22. Ophelia Hardin's Tragic Marriage

W.F. Hardin, *Hardin Family Record* (manuscript, 1880): *

Jane Ophelia Hardin (1833–78) and William Joseph Hardin (1831–61) were the children of William Hardin and Sarah Looney. In 1856 at the home of her mother in Waco, Ophelia married her third cousin, Jim Hardin, son of Toney Hardin and nephew of Cynthia Cade. Two years later Ophelia complained to her brother Joe that Jim abused her. [The brother called on Jim and admonished him never to lay hands on Ophelia again. Jim got angry and reached for his gun. The brother killed him in what was judged to be self-defense.] Joe died at his mother's home in 1861.

23. A.B. "Blackie" Hardin, Jr.

[Born in 1819, Maury County, Tennessee, Hardin arrived in Texas in 1838 with his mother, Mary Elizabeth, and two children born to her after her separation from A.B. Hardin Sr. A.B. Sr. recognized his son and did all he could to give him a good start in business. The boy was called "Black" or "Blackie" and was resentful. He married first to Mary Garner, second to Mary Price in Leon County.

It seemed to bother A.B. Sr. that he had committed himself to Catholicism in 1826, but had quit attending church after Texas independence. In 1854 he began to attend mass again. No other Hardins seemed to have made genuine commitments to Father Muldoon.

Through his father's help Black Hardin became captain of two steamboats on the Trinity River. One night while he was ashore, the one called *Black Cloud* sank opposite his father's plantation, with only the smokestack protruding from the water. Black remarked, "That's about the best death she could have died." The father died about this time and the bell was removed and installed on the cupola of the Methodist church in Liberty. Black joined the Catholic church and was a generous supporter. He moved to Lampasas where he died leaving an estate of $55,000.]

24. Domestic Service Contract

Memorandum of Contract Entered into this 18th Day of March, 1867 between W.F. Hardin as Employer and the Freedwoman Louisa Nash: *

The State of Texas
County of Liberty
   Witnesseth—
That the said employer hath this day hired the said Freedwoman as a house servant from this date until the 23rd day of December next. The said employer obligates and binds himself to furnish the said Freedwoman and her child, about three years old, with good quarters and sufficient rations, and medecines,

but in no case to pay physicians' bills. Time lost to sickness to be deducted from wages.

And the said Freedwoman obligates and binds herself to work diligently at all necessary work such as cooking, ironing, and milking and all such work as servants are required to do about a house and yard. Also not to leave the premises without the permission of employer. In consideration for such service the said employer obligates and binds himself to pay to the said Freedwoman for the present month, March, five dollars in money or clothing. For the residue of the time, five dollars per month paid at the end of the year.

W.F. Hardin
Louisa (X) Nash
(her mark)

A.H. Mayer
Sub Asst Cour.

[Thus Bee Hardin hired a cook for Seven Pines as his parents were living upriver on the plantation. Such contracts were required by the Freedmen's Bureau.]

25. J.A. Blaffer's Military Service

John Dimitry, A.M., *Confederate Military History* (Atlanta: Confederate Pub. Co., 1899), Vol. X, 349:

At age twenty-three Blaffer enlisted in 1861 as 2nd Lt., Co. G, 1st Louisiana Volunteers and served for seven months in New Orleans. In 1862 he enlisted as a private in the 5th Co. of the Washington Artillery and left New Orleans just before it fell to the Yankees. He was in the battle at Corinth, Miss., and marched on into Kentucky. Around October 8, 1862, he contracted typhoid fever near Perryville, Ky., and was sent to hospital in Mobile, Ala. When he was well enough to rejoin his company his parents put up money to buy a substitute to serve in his place.

[He came home to the conquered city to take up his old job as bookkeeper at the Schneider and Zuberbier grocery. He was required to swear to the Union commander that he would not leave the city. A year later, on January 4, 1864, he married Clementine Schneider. His younger brothers did not serve.]

26. Deed Reserving Family Cemetery on B.W. Hardin Half-League [Located near juncture of State Highway 146 and FM Rd. 1011].

Recorded in the Liberty Courthouse on July 23, 1891 in Book J, 236:

[The descendants of Swan's eldest son] . . . granted, bargained and sold . . . south ½ of the league of land granted to B.W. Hardin by the State of Coahuila and Texas . . . 11 May, 1831 . . . 2,214 acres more or less . . . saving and reserving the burying ground containing about two acres. . . .

[The deed then recites the earliest conveyance of this land]:

Mr. Commissioner [Madero]:

Benjamin Watson Hardin, a native of the United States of North America, with due respect would represent to you that wishing to establish myself

under a wise and just government that extends to the protection of its benefi-
cient laws to an honorable and industrious citizen I immigrated into this
country in the beginning of the year 1827 in the intention of settling in it
forever. I selected a tract of land on the waters of the Trinity River. I am
married and one of the persons included in the resolution of the Supreme
General Government dated August 27, 1828. Therefore relying upon the phi-
lanthropy of the Government in conformity to the colonization laws and the
instructions under which you are acting as commissioner for distributing vacant lands and issued titles I respectfully request you to grant me as settler the
league of land which I am occupying and cultivating issuing me the corresponding title with the understanding that I will pay the amount specified by
way of acknowledgement in the colonization law subject in all cases to the
general laws of the Federation and particular laws of the State wherein I shall
receive favor and mercy for which I am applying.

Benjamin Watson Hardin

Atascosita January 28, 1831
. . . I, José Francisco Madero commissioned by the Supreme Government of
the State of Coahuila and Texas for giving possession to the inhabitants established within the twenty border leagues to the Sabine River and to those who
live on the banks of the Trinity and San Jacinto Creek . . . I grant and transfer
unto [Hardin] and put him in possession of one league of land . . . [for]
which he shall pay the state the sum of thirty-seven dollars six and a half rials
by way of acknowledgement. . . . [He] must settle and cultivate it in conformity to the law strictly complying with all its mandates and shall never
transfer it in morhenam . . . etc.

J. Francisco Madero

27. Biography of General James K. Davis
Robert D. Armstrong speech at Cold Spring Historical Marker Dedication
October 27, 1967:
. . . James Davis was born July 17, 1790, on a plantation near Richmond, Vir-
ginia, the eldest son of Mr. and Mrs. John Davis. Mrs. Davis was the former
Mary (Polly) Easton of Virginia. His early education was with private tutors
and he later studied law. In 1812, at the outbreak of hostilities with England,
he joined the army. Under General Andrew Jackson, he fought in the battle of
New Orleans in 1815. Later, James Davis met Miss Anne Eliza Hill who was
born in Raleigh, North Carolina, on September 20, 1795. They were married
May 10, 1816.
When the federal government ordered the sale of public lands in Alabama in
1818, John Davis, his father, bought a section of land and moved his family to
[Russellville] Franklin County. James and his wife joined them there. That same
year, 1818, Governor William W. Bibbs of Alabama appointed James Davis sher-
iff of Marion County.
In 1820, he was commissioned Brigadier General of Second Division of the
Militia of Alabama. In 1823, he was made Judge of the County Court of Franklin
County. In 1827, he was appointed Solicitor of the Judicial Court of Alabama.
1830–1831, he was consul of United States to Santa Fe, in the United Mexican

States. The document was signed by President Martin Van Buren and Secretary of State, Andrew Jackson, in 1831. In 1832, James Davis was elected Major General of the Second Division of the Militia of Alabama. . . .

[In Texas] he built a large home which was noted for its comfort, beauty, and hospitality. In 1834, his home was finished and James Davis, his wife, seven children, and a number of slaves, moved to Texas from Alabama. The "Stranger's" room was occupied frequently as there were no taverns near. The home was fortified with a cannon and guns as the Mexicans and Karankaway Indians, who lived along the coast, were dangerous. In fact, the Indians were cannibals. In 1836 . . . he was appointed by Houston to recruit and train the men who had come in from the United States for the Texas army. . . .

In 1842, General Houston ordered James Davis, who was then Adjutant General of the Texas Army, to proceed to Corpus Christi to organize and drill volunteers from Texas and the United States for the Texas Army, and hold them in readiness for an invasion from Mexico. On June 7, 1842, James Davis was in command of 192 trained men on the west bank of the Nueces. He was attacked by Colonel Antonio Canales and his army of 700 men. When the cannon was fired, Canales and all of his officers were killed and the Mexican Army retreated in disorder. The Texans had no casualties.

In 1846, James Davis became Brigadier General of the First Brigade, Third Division of the Texas Militia. In 1848, at a Democratic State Convention in Austin, General Davis was appointed one of the delegates to represent the State of Texas in Baltimore, where the President and Vice President of the United States were nominated.

In 1850, Cold Spring became his home. He was a member of the Masonic Lodge, and of the Laurel Hills Baptist Church, for which he gave the land on which the church stands. He also gave the land for the cemetery, and he and his wife are buried there. His death occurred in 1859, and she died in 1869. . . .

28. Extremist Views of Buckner H. Payne

"Ariel" was the pen name of Buckner H. Payne, who published in Cincinnati in 1867 a booklet which he disseminated widely among Southerners at his own expense. It was entitled *The Negro—What Is His Ethnological Status*:

Payne had heard of Darwin's theory of evolution but he based his extreme views on his own version of the Bible's tenets. He differed with the popular belief of the day that, because "Ham" meant "black" in Hebrew and because Ham was cursed by his father Noah, these two facts proved that Ham was the progenitor of the black race. Payne pointed out that other people were cursed in the Bible and they did not turn black and besides, since Noah and his wife were white, they could not produce black children. He said the true story of the Flood was that when the beasts went aboard the Ark two by two, right after the baboons and the gorillas came a pair of hominids and they were the ancestors of black people, who should be properly classified as beasts.

Payne said that negroes were beasts who could talk, and pointed out that since the Bible said that Adam was God's last creation, they could not have been created after Adam. Payne also explained that the Flood was sent to destroy mulattoes and was God's punishment for the crime of sodomy between the city's inhabitants and black people. He further noted that Africans were similar to beasts because they "built only for the day." He carefully explained that they were not related to black Egyptians because Egyptians have straight instead of kinky hair. The booklet ends with: "The finger of God is in this. Trust Him. The Bible is true."

29. Biography of General Wirt Davis

C.T. Brady, *Indian Fights and Fighters* (Lincoln: U. of Nebraska, 1971), 316:

On September 27, 1876, after Custer's last stand, Col. Ranald McKenzie destroyed a Cheyenne village and its winter supplies on the N Fork of the Powder River near the Big Horn Mountains of the Wyoming-Montana border. This victory ultimately led to the downfall of the Sioux Indians. Brady says that if Capt. Wirt Davis had not brought his men to support Maj. G.A. Gordon and Capt. J.N. Hamilton in the desperate hand-to-hand fighting, the day would have been lost. Davis followed in after the Cheyennes and attacked them in the gullies where they tried to make a stand.

[. . . Born near Richmond, Va., he ran away from the University of Virginia to enlist in the Union Army as a private in the 1st Cavalry May 12, 1860. . . . He became a sergeant in the 4th Cavalry where he was commissioned a second lieutenant April 22, 1863. He won a brevet at Chickamauga, participated in the Mississippi Cavalry expedition of 1864 earning another brevet and a third at Selma, Ala. He took part in many Indian affairs with the 4th Cavalry after the Civil War. "During his fighting days he was a hard drinker, but once on an Indian trail he would sober up."

Davis had a conspicuous role in Forsyth's fight against Loco's Apaches at Horseshoe Canyon, N.M., April 23, 1882. He led at least two extended scouting (trips) into the Sierra Madre of Old Mexico during the Geronimo operations of 1885 and 1886, performing rugged, valuable service.

He was considered by Carter probably "the best pistol and carbine shot in the Army." "Davis was a wonderful pistol shot . . . It has been said that a stagecoach was held up between Silver City [N.M.] and Tombstone [Ariz.] when he was sitting up beside the driver. Instead of coming up with his pocketbook, he came up with his revolver, shooting one of the bandits . . ." said another acquaintance. Davis became a major in the 5th Cavalry in 1890, lieutenant colonel of the 8th Cavalry in 1898, colonel of the 3rd Cavalry in 1900. In the Philippines in 1900–1901 he operated against insurgents. Davis retired in 1901 and was promoted to Brigadier General in 1904.]

See also, Appointment Commission Personnel File 4360–1878–9W3, 19/27/0—National Archives, Washington, D.C.

30. Will of Thomas Wooldridge

Montgomery County, Texas
June 7th, 1867

Item 1

I, Thomas D. Wooldridge . . . desire my just debts be paid . . . in the discretion of my executrix [Sallie Davis Wooldridge] . . . .

Item 5

I hereby appoint . . . Geo. W. Davis, of Livingston, Polk Co., the true and lawful guardian of the persons and estates of my beloved children, Thomas McKay and Lucinda Hinds Wooldridge and enjoin upon them the duty of abiding by his counsel and admonition along the uncertain pathway of youthful life, and having implicit confidence in his integrity and liberality, I hereby endow the said Davis with full powers and discretion to do and perform any and all acts in and about the management of their persons and estates that (he) may deem best for them without requiring him to comply with the usual rules of law touching such appointments. . . .

T. Wooldridge (Seal)

[Will was probated during the September term of the Montgomery Co. Probate Court. The eldest daughter, Rebecca Green, is not mentioned in Item 5 because she had married just before will was written. Attached to original inventory of his estate including community land of 770 acres in Grimes Co. and his separate property, a 640 acre headright in Limestone Co.]

INDEX

Berthet, Father, 185,186
Berwick, Ann Dawson (Mrs. Christie [O']Brien), 11,18. *Also see* O'Brien, Ann D. Berwick.
Berwick, Eleanor (Wallace), 10–11. *Also see* Wallace, Eleanor.
Berwick, Florine, 174
Berwick, Joseph, 11,12,52,53,60,87
Berwick, La., 4,10,47,48,53,89, 165,191,244
Berwick, Nathaniel, 18,104,201
Berwick, Priscilla. *See* Orr, Tilpah.
Berwick, Rebecca. *See* O'Brien, Rebecca Berwick.
Berwick, Thomas (1740–1789), 10–11, 18,245
Berwick, Thomas II, 18,53,54
Berwick Bay, 53,165,184
Berwick family tree, 18–19
Berwick Plantation, 14
Betty Powell, riverboat, 119
Bevil's settlement, 27
Bexar (San Antonio), 8,27–28
Big Thicket, 125,193,211–12
Bigelow, Mr., 161
Bignon, Dr., 222
Black, Capt. G.H., 172,183,184
Black, Lt. L., 196,197
Black, Bayou, 51; sugar mill, 52
Black Cloud, riverboat, 270
Blackburn, Augustus, 16
Blaffer, J. Auguste, 136,201,203,271
Bledsoe, Sarah. *See* Hardin, Sarah B.
Bledsoe, William, 110
Blockade running, 149,161,167,209
Blockades, 149,165,175
Boeuf, Bayou, 50,64
Bolivar Peninsula, 45,175,216
Bolling, Mrs., 150
Booth, R.E., 162
Borden, Gail Jr., 261
Borden, Comm. John, 46,264–65
Boru, King Brian, 87,89,90,245
Bowen, Gen. John Stevens, 196
Boyer, Col., 52
Bradburn, Juan Davis, 22–23,24,25,41
Brady, William, 6
Bragg, Gen. Braxton, 169,181,182

Branch, Betty "Betsy," 129,131,172
Branch, Lt. Col. E.T., 267,269
Branch, Mrs. E.T., 127,129,172,206,210
Branch, William, 172
Brashear, Mrs. C.D., house of, 72,73
Brashear, Dr. Charles, 115
Brashear, La., 174
Brashear, Stephen, 197
Brenham, Tex., 146,147,148,153
Brien. *Also see* Bryan, O'Brien, O'Bryan, Bryant.
Brien, America. *See* Stevens, America.
Brien, Ann D. Berwick. See O'Brien, Ann D. Berwick.
Brien, Christie. *See* O'Brien, Christopher II "Christie."
Brien, George, 51,52
Briscoe, Capt. A., 260
Brown, Dr. Allen, 6,7
Brubaker, Dr., 226
Bryan. *Also see* O'Brien and O'Bryan.
Bryan, Amanda Wynne, 153,157
Bryan, Christopher II. *See* O'Brien, Christopher II "Christie" (1779–1853).
Bryan, Christopher III (1815–1860), 19,33,35,110,128
Bryan, Elizabeth Whitlock, 35
Bryan, John (1803–1842), 19
Bryan, Kindallis "King" (1818–1866), 130,151,152,157 158,173,215,259
Bryan, Kindallis "Dahl," 19,174,175
Bryan, Joseph, 18,28,30,35
Bryan, Laura, 112,148
Bryan, Luke Sr.(1777–1841), 9,11, 15,18,33
Bryan, Luke II (1807–1869), 18,33,35
Bryan, Mary, 61,66,148
Bryan, Pryor (1810–1873), 33,*44*,58, 61,66,79,157,163,185,259
Bryan, Pryor Jr. (1832–1862), 154,157
Bryan, Sarah Whitlock, 35
Bryan, Tom, 33,35
Bryan, Tonsie. *See* O'Bryan, Hortense "Tonsie."
Bryan, William, 52,56
Bryant, Christie. *See* O'Brien, Christopher ("Christie") II.

Bryant's Plantation, 12
Bryant's Station (on Ohio River),
    9,10,244
Buchanan, James, 96
Buell, Gen. Don Carlos, 169,170
Buffalo Bayou, 25,45
Bureau of Freedmen, Refugees, and Aban-
    doned Lands, 214,216,225,226
Burford, R. Philip, 193,194
Burgess, Jim, 195
Burnet, David G., 28–29,30,32,33,35,
    36,37,41,95; feud with Sam Houston,
    268
Burnet and Vehlein's Colony, 25
Burnside, Gen. A.B., 178
Bustamante, Pres. Anastacio, 22,24
Butler, Gen. Benjamin "Beast,"
    149,200,202–3

C

Cabiness, Mr., 198
Cade, Betty Day, 17,71. *Also see* Day,
    Betty.
Cade, Cynthia, 17,74–6,*103*
Cade, Sam, 17,85,86
Cade, Dr. Samuel M., 17,75,*103*
Cade, William (Bill), 17,86
Caldwell, Tex., 158
Calhoon, Joyce, *ix*
Camino Real, 1,245
Canales, Col. Antonio, 273
Carlyle, Dr., 206
Carpetbaggers, 214,225,232
Carrol, Mr., 30
Casa Consistoriale, 30
Casa de Piedras (Old Stone Fort), 1
Cathcart, James Leander, 12,13,247
Cedar Bayou, 72
Chambers, Clay, 162
Chambers, Jeff, 122,129,155,162,219
Champ d'Asile, 5,14
Chance, Mrs., 134
Chappell Hill Institute, 185
Charleston (Charles Town), S.C., 10,201

Chetimachaux tribe, 13
Chickahominy, Battle of (Gaines' Mill),
    153
Chickasaw Bayou, 181
Chinaberry trees, 83
Choate, John, 10,11
Church of the Latter Day Saints, 85
Cincinnati, Ohio, 201
Civil War, inflation, 185. *Also see* Money,
    paper.
Claiborn, Gov. William, 12
Clark, Carrie, 98,99,105,134,135
Clay, Henry, 6,53
Clayton, Bill, 75
Cleveland, Charles, 180,205,210,211,
    230; yellow fever letters of, 216–19
Cleveland, Tex., 205
Cleveland, W.D., 205
Clontarf, Battle of, 87
Clopper, Joseph Chambers, 45
Cobb, J.E., 154
Cold Spring, Tex., 95,116
Cole, John, 181
Coleman, Adelia (Mrs. Benjamin Watson
    Hardin), 9
College Hill, Miss., 2,4
Collins, Martha (Mrs. Andrew O'Brien),
    53
Collins, Nellie, 194,205
Collins, Virginia O'Brien,
    136,149,158,174,191. *Also see* O'Brien,
    Virginia.
Collins, Warren, 211
Collins, William, 51,82,149,150,158,
    161,175,180,184,191
Columbia, schooner, 48
Columbia, Tenn., 3,5
Columbia Reporter, 3
"The Comet," 118
Comstock, Rachel (Mrs. Thomas Berwick
    II), 18,53
Concepcion, Battle of, 29
Conscript Act, Second, 167,192
Cook, Col., 166
Cook, Rep. Charles, 156
Cooper, Eliza, 93

F

Family trees: Berwick-O'Brien, 18–19;
  Davis, 104–05; Hardin, 16–17
Fannin, Col. James, 33
Farish, Oscar, 95,149
Farley, Brien, 14,18,46,52,53,60,61,68
Farley, Catherine (O')Brien, 14,15,18,*44*,
  45,46,48–53,56,59–61,68,77,81,
  84–87,89,90
Farley, Henry, 14,18,46,52,53,58
Farley, Dr. Henry Wise, 14,15,18,28–29,
  35,47,48
Farley, Swazey, 18,46,52–54,60,68–69,
  81–82,84
Fatheree, Dr. and Mrs., 109,111
Fenner, Dr. Charles, 82,84
Fields, Miss, 147
Filkins, I.P., 144
Fillmore, Millard, 96–97
Fischer, Mr. and Mrs. J.E., 135
Fisher, George, 22,55,268
Fitzgerald, Rev. Theophilus, 181
Fly, Maj. G.W.I., 208
Forrest, Gen. N.B., 179,181
Forsman, John, 223
Fort-Davis (Ft. Davis), Ala., 94
Ft. Donelson, 169
Ft. Pointe, 143,166
Franklin County, Ga., 3
Franks, Burril, 33
Fredonian Rebellion, 8
Fremont, Gen. J.C., 156
Fudge, Mrs., 98

G

Gaines' Mill, Battle of, *viii*,153–54
Galveston, 4,36,46,61,71,79,144,165,
  180,234–35; Bee stationed in, 207;
  blockaded, 143,144,165; business future, 231; Mardi Gras, 235; mutiny of
  Confederate soldiers, 208–09; Union
  soldiers and, 157,171,203
Galveston Bay and Texas Land Company,
  25,29
Galvez, Gov. Bernardo de, 10

Gasque (refugee Creole couple), 193
Gayle, Billups, 65,75
Gayle, R.W., 65
Germann, Louisa, 202
Gillard, Numa, 108
Girod Cemetery, New Orleans, 84
Gonzales, Mexican troops at, 27
Grady, Olive, 206
Grant, Gen. Ulysses S., 171,188
Grayson, Capt., 45
Green, Mrs. Absolom. *See* Stallings,
  Sarah.
Green, Amanda, 94–95
Green, Amos, 22
Green, Billy, 222
Green, Gen. Elkanah, 170
Green, Emily, 99
Green, Ez, 199
Green, Frank (F.M.) 96–98,105; family
  of, 220–23; on slavery, 224
Green, Free, 160,161
Green, John, 160
Green, Rhett, 221
Green, Sarah Moody. *See* Davis, Sarah
  Moody Green.
Green, Steven, 76
Green, Gen. Thomas, 199
Grierson, Gen. Ben, 188
Griffin, James, 68
Groce, Leonard W., plantation, 34
Guise, John, 148
Gum Lake, 131

H

Hahn, Gov. Michael, 203
Hamilton, Gov. Andrew J., 214
Hardee, Gen. W.J., 181
Harden, Col. William (1720–1782),
  17,250
Hardin, Augustine Blackburn, 1–9,16,
  20,21,28,29,68,85,86,149,252–60,
  262,268
Hardin, A.B. Jr. "Black", 3,4,16,
  85–86,270
Hardin, Bee. *See* Hardin, William Franklin
  "Bee."

Kitrile, Dr., 205
Knight, Mrs. Eliza Green, 85
Knight, John, 85
Know-Nothings, 96–97

L

Labadie, Dr. N.D., 24
LaCour, Brett, 76
LaCour, Edward, 210
LaCour, Gus, 210
LaCour, Memie, 122
LaCour, Rosa, 211
Lafitte, Jean, 4
LaFourche, Bayou, 12
Lake Verret, 12
Lampasas Springs, 231
LaPlace Academy, 100,101
Last Island, 87,88
Laura, steamship, 45
Laurie, Johnnie, 126
Lee, Gen. R.E., 188,210,212
Liberty, Tex., 9,21,22–24,28,29,32,
    35–38,45–48,52,68–70,75,76,
    87,89,99,108,111,113,116,119,124–
    26,129,131,149,164,171,172,174,180,
    191,194,197,209,215,216,219,226,
    229,232,233,235
Liberty Gazette, 111–13
"Liberty Invincibles," 157
Liberty Methodist Circuit, 62
Livingston, Tex., 101,214,216
Logan, Celia, 115
Logan, Capt. M., 33
Logan, Capt. William M., 23,269
Loganport, La., 101
Lone Star Cadets, 172
Long Island, Tex., 110
Long King, Chief, 2
Looney, Sarah, 9. *Also see* Hardin, Sarah
    Looney.
Louisiana Purchase, 12
Louisville, Ky., 69
Lovell, Gen. Mansfield, 170
Loving, George, 217
Loving, Dr. Gus, 126
Loving, John, 154

Loving, Mrs. John, 217
Loving, Martha, 154
Lynchburg, 45,52,72
Lynch's Ferry, 72
Lynn, Capt., 48

M

Macon County, Ala., 94
Madero, Comm. Jose Francisco,
    21,23,26,271
Maffitt, Capt. J.N., 209,210
Magnolia Grove, 125
Magruder, Gen. John B., 168, 173, 209
Malvern Hill, Battle of, 153
Manassas, First Battle of, 163
Manassas, Second Battle of, 164
Mansfield, Battle of, 198,199
Marion, Gen. Francis "Swamp Fox,"
    3,249
Maris, Martin, 79
Marshall, Tex., 84
Martinez, Consul Francisco Pizarro, 38
Mary Hill, steamer, 209
Maury County, Tenn., 3,5
Maxcy, H., 134
McCardell, Miss, 229
McClellan, Gen. G.B., 153
McCord, Adelaide. *See* Menken, Adah
    Isaacs.
McCreary, Judge John, 185
McCreary, Josh, 225
McGaffee, John, 33
McKenzie, Ranald, 234
McMahon, Elvira O'Brien, 19,63,82,200.
    Also see O'Brien, Elvira McMahon.
McMahon, John, 62
McMahon's artillery battery, 198
McMurtry, Abner, 127,160
McMurtry, Jim, 127,149
McMurtry, Sarah, 206
Menard, Maj., 171
Menard, Michel B., 261
Menard, Peter J., 29–30,47
Menard County, Tex., 55
Menken, Adah Isaacs, *80,*111–15
Mercury, 224

O'Brien, Theresa, 19,84,87–90,228
O'Brien, Thurlow, 19,84,87–90,233
O'Brien, Virginia, 19,49,51,60,61,64,233
  Also see Collins, Virginia O'Brien.
O'Brien family tree, 18–19,233
O'Brien marriage records, 246
O'Brien oak, 126
O'Bryan, Charles, 19,125,126,152,
  173,174,194,210,233
O'Bryan, Christopher I (1745–1811),
  9–11,12,19,45,231,244
O'Bryan, Christopher II. *See* O'Brien,
  Christopher II "Christie."
O'Bryan, Daniel, 9
O'Bryan, George (1789–1856), 9,19,
  45,248
O'Bryan, Hortense "Tonsie," 19,
  163,164,183,184,207,215
O'Bryan, Katherine Kimberland, 45. *Also
  see* Kimberland, Katherine.
O'Bryan, Luke Sr.(1777–1841),
  9,11,12,18,48
O'Bryan, Mary Catherine (Mrs. John
  Choate), 9,11,19
O'Bryan, Pamela, 180
Ohio, schooner, 8
Opelousas, La., 4,11
Orange, Tex., 136
Orr, George, 4,5,8,15,87
Orr, Louise, 163
Orr, Martha, 154
Orr, Tilpah (Priscilla Berwick), 4,15,
  86–87

P

Padilla, Comm. Juan Antonio, 26
Palmer, Squire, 161
Panny, Jno. P., 100
Parson's Cavalry Brigade, 230. *Also see*
  Regiments.
Partlow, Miriam, x
Pattersonville, La., 81,84,232
Payne, Buckner H. ("Ariel"), 224,
  273–274
Peacock, Capt. Thomas, 119,184,185,211
Pemberton, Gen. John Clifford, 179,189

Pensacola, Fla., 10
Perryville, Battle of, 202
Perryville, Ky., 271
Pettus, Mrs., 223
Pickett, E.B., 149,210
Pickett's Company, 161,163,174
Piedras, Jose de las, 1,8,25
Pierce, Pres. Franklin, 76
Pleasant Hill, Battle of, 199
Pleasant Hill, La., 101
Poinsett, Joel, 6,257,258
Polk, James K. 6,256
Pope, Gen., 164
Porter, Isaac N., 3,5,254–56
Porter, Joseph B., 5,8,254
Porter, Nimrod, 5,6
Porter, Capt. P.P., 158
Porter family and Hardin murder trial
  records, 252–259
Powel's Company, 154. *Also see*
  Regiments.
Preacher, Gus, 126,129,131,155
Preacher, Mrs., 68
Prewitt, Hezekiah, 154
Price, Gen. Sterling, 169–70,196
Prior, Mrs., 99,105,223

Q

Queen of the West, gunboat, 183,187,188

R

Rachel, Frank, 210
Rachel, Mrs., 51
Railey, Gus, 206
Reconstruction, 213 *ff,* 230
Regiments and military units: Fifth Regi-
  ment, Hood's Brigade, 154; First Texas
  Cavalry, 144; King Bryan's Company,
  154,157,173,174; Nichol's Ninth Texas
  Infantry, 143,168; Second Texas Regi-
  ment, 188,208; Twenty-fifth Regiment,
  Texas Cavalry, 144,149; Waul's Second
  Battalion, 143,169,196
Regulator-Moderator War, 78

Texas Battalion, 200
Texas Legion, Waul's, 169
Theodore, Adah Bertha, 122. *Also see* Menken, Adah Isaacs.
Theodore, Auguste, 113
Thompson, Ezekiel "Zeke," 152,161, 167,172,176,195,197
Tiger Island, 10,13,53,54,63
Tilton, Mr., 132
Timmons, Maj. B., 171,193
Toney, Marcus, 164,179
Toney, Martin, 6
Tooke, Mrs., 134
Tracy, Gibson, 146,150,163
Travis, Col. William B., 23,24,33,37
Tremont House, 74,234
Tri-Weekly Telegraph, 165,166,227
Trinity River, 4,5,8,9,14,15,72,94, 108,124,160,186
Trinity settlement, 27
Trowell, Abraham B., 66–67,112,126, 128,129,147,150,154,155,171,173, 177,210
Trowell, Tom, 129
The True Evangelist, 119
Truesdale, Miss, 129
Turner, Capt. Ike, 173,174,175
Turner, Laura, 220
Turner, Mrs. Sidney, 175
Turtle Bayou Resolutions, 24
Twenty-sixth Texas Cavalry, 171

U

University of Texas, established, 123
Ursuline Convent/Academy, Galveston, 65,70,108
Ursuline School, Liberty, 122,215

V

Van Deventer, Cornelia Hardin. *See* Hardin, Cornelia.
Van Deventer, Jeremiah, 122,177,215
Van Dorn, Gen. Earl, 169–170,178,179, 181,182

"Vaporings," 113
Vasquez, Gen. Rafael, 55,57
Veramendi, Gov. Juan Martin de. *See* Beramendi.
Verret, Lake, 12
Vicksburg, Miss., 170,171,178,179, 180,182,192; siege of, 188–89

W

Walker, Gen. William, 95
Walker County, Tex., 133
Wallace, Eleanor (Mrs. Thomas Berwick), 10–11,18,244
Wallisville, Tex., 129,172
War of 1812, 2
Waring, Fielder, 76
Washington-on-the-Brazos, Tex., 29
Watkins, Dr. S.S., 68,69
Watkins, Mrs. S.S., 75
Watson, Benjamin, 16
Watson, Elizabeth, 16
Watson, Page, 7,16
Watson, Sarah Ashley, 16
Waul, Col. T.N., 169,171,181
Waverly Institute, 99,102
Wells Fargo, 12
West, Jordan, 260
West Liberty (Dayton), 72
Westfield, ship, *180*
Wheelock, Tex., 158,160
Whethersby, Dr., 230
White, Lenbron, 75
White, Levi, 173
White, Mrs. Levi, 174,183
White, Morgan, 194,207
White, Dr. Robert Catlett, 173,207,232
Whitehead, Capt., 187
Whitfield, John W., 170
Whiting, Gen. W.H.C., 158
Whittington, Frank, 154
Wilcox, Charles, 30
Williams, William Dugat, 123,143, 158,159,175,185,212
Williams, Isaac, 75
Williams, Jack, 120,123,130
Williams, Judge John A., 36,47,122

Williams, Laura, 123
Williams, Margaretta Dugat, 36,122
Williamson, Robert McAlpin "Three Leg-
    ged Willie," 23
Williamson, William H., 3
Winchester, Tenn., 91
Wise, Emma, 99
Wise, John T., 94,136,223
Wise, Sini Ann Davis, 93–94,98,99
Wofford, Mrs., 54
Woll, Adrian, 57
Woods, George, 116,154,183
Woods, James B., 183–84
Woodville, Tex., 76
Wooldridge, John McKay, 220
Wooldridge, Lucinda Hinds, 220
Wooldridge, Sallie. See Davis, Sallie M.
Wooldridge, Rev. Thomas D., 99,133,
    134,145,192,219, 274–75
Wright, Prof., 129,131
Wrigley, Ben, 129
Wrigley, Capt. Jim "Dog," 67,119,143,
151,152,155,162,165,171,180,
    186,196
Wrigley, John, 119,143
Wyandotte plantation, 10,191
Wynne, Gus, 154
Wynne, Amanda, 126,127

Y

Yazoo City, Miss., 187
Yeagher, Mr., 148
Yellow fever (yellow jack), 47,48,217–18;
    in Galveston, 204,216; in Houston,
    172; in Liberty, 216; in Montgomery,
    Tex., 220.

Z

Zacatecas, massacre in, 28